MW01277166

A Voice
for Animals

A Voice for Animals

The Social Movement That Provides Dignity and
Compassion for Animals

Suzana Gartner, J.D., LL.M.

ARCHWAY
PUBLISHING

Copyright © 2023 Suzana Gartner, J.D., LL.M.

All rights reserved. No part of this book may be used or reproduced by any means, graphic, electronic, or mechanical, including photocopying, recording, taping or by any information storage retrieval system without the written permission of the author except in the case of brief quotations embodied in critical articles and reviews.

Archway Publishing books may be ordered through booksellers or by contacting:

Archway Publishing
1663 Liberty Drive
Bloomington, IN 47403
www.archwaypublishing.com
844-669-3957

Because of the dynamic nature of the Internet, any web addresses or links contained in this book may have changed since publication and may no longer be valid. The views expressed in this work are solely those of the author and do not necessarily reflect the views of the publisher, and the publisher hereby disclaims any responsibility for them.

Any people depicted in stock imagery provided by Getty Images are models, and such images are being used for illustrative purposes only. Certain stock imagery © Getty Images.

ISBN: 978-1-6657-3290-1 (sc)
ISBN: 978-1-6657-3289-5 (hc)
ISBN: 978-1-6657-3291-8 (e)

Library of Congress Control Number: 2022920669

Print information available on the last page.

Archway Publishing rev. date: 02/16/2023

This book is dedicated to my family, friends and to animal lovers—pet parents, foster families, adopters, volunteers, donors, defenders, supporters, animal advocates, activists, rescuers, rescues, animal shelters, shelter staff, sanctuaries, animal welfare organizations, environmentalists, vegetarians, and vegans. It is also dedicated to *all* animals that share this earth, including companion animals, farm animals, captive animals, wildlife, and animals used in research.

As well, I dedicate this book to animal friends that I have met along the way. Each one of them taught me so much and holds a special place in my heart. Thank you, Charlie, for inspiring me to write this book; Freddie, Gucci, Lily, and dearly departed Jackson and Sasha, for your love and companionship. They didn't ask for much and provided unconditional love, affection, and friendship during good times and difficult times, whenever needed. There is no doubt they are individuals with their own distinct personalities, and each one is special, and touches our lives. When they are gone, they are missed and remain forever etched in our hearts and in memories. I chose a photo of my departed dog Charlie and cat Jackson for the back cover of the book.

I dream of the day when a proper respect for our fellow creatures will prevail, and each animal life (big or small and regardless of species) is treated with dignity and compassion.

CONTENTS

ACKNOWLEDGEMENTS

I am grateful to my husband, Peter, for his support and patience while I wrote the book, and to our boys, Andrew and Brad, to come along for the ride on adventures and help animals in need. Visiting animal rescues and sanctuaries and caring for our family pets.

I want to thank my mother, who believed in my dreams and shares my love for companion animals; my stepfather, who inspired me to go to law school. Thanks to my mother-in-law, brother-in-law, and dearly departed father-in-law for their support. Also, thanks to my good friend, Sarah Shaw, for encouraging me to finish the book and to my friends that chose to adopt an animal in need and provide a loving family home.

I give thanks to the Etobicoke Humane Society (EHS), to join this amazing organization.

Thanks to law students, in particular to Daniel Fin, animal law lawyers, volunteers, staff, research assistants, and my esteemed colleagues, for their contribution, and to those clients who believed that I could bring justice for their beloved pets.

Thanks to my copy editors Leena Paul and Carol Audit and the team at Archway Publishing from Simon & Schuster. Thanks to my publicists Olivia McCoy and Shannon Donaghy, and the team at Smith Publicity, for believing in the message of hope for animals.

I am thankful to the leaders and trailblazers who paved the way and continue to inspire me in this cause. Also, I want to acknowledge animals in shelters, rescues, sanctuaries, billions of farm animals, animals in laboratories and vulnerable wildlife. To give them a voice through the words of this book is a privilege. I am truly honored to be a voice for our animal friends. Lastly, thank you for choosing to read this book. I hope that you will find it interesting and that it will motivate you to take care of animals.

INTRODUCTION

We Need Companion Animals, and They Need Us Too

When I first sat down to write this book, I was trying to fill a void in my life. My beloved dog and furry baby, Charlie, had passed away. He was my constant companion. After he was gone, everything in my life changed. I felt alone in my grief, and I was looking for a way to cope with this heavy loss. The special bond that I had with Charlie was like no other. He was more than *just* a dog; he was part of the family and my best furry friend. I was deeply affected by this loss. I decided to do something in honor of his memory and as a way to cope with his passing. I sat down to write *A Voice for Animals*.

Sharing My Story with You

My personal journey into animal rights begins years before I decided to write this book. I had a childhood passion and love for animals. I volunteered at an animal shelter. I eventually became an animal-rights lawyer, which turned into a lifelong passion of animal advocacy. I am deeply honored to be able to provide a voice for these beautiful creatures.

My childhood consisted of visiting pet stores and animal shelters, feeding and taking care of stray and feral cats in our neighborhood, and horseback riding. When I was six, we adopted a small dog named George. He was a friendly Chihuahua, who quickly became my puppy love and an important member of our family. We spent so much time playing together. I would run home from school to hang out with George because he was my best friend.

One day, I came home from school, and he was gone. My mother had the sad responsibility of telling me the heartbreaking news: dogs were not permitted in our building. George had to go. I was devastated. Thankfully, my mother had found him a new loving family and home. However, I railed against this injustice. It brewed inside me for years and fed my commitment to contribute to animal welfare. When I grew up, I knew I would be committed to making changes in laws that hurt animals, such as my best friend, George, who had no legal rights, and help owners (guardians) keep their companions. This desire was strong enough to fuel my growing aspiration to turn this passion and dedication to animals into a profession.

My commitment to animals continued throughout my teens and into adulthood. While I was a volunteer at a municipal animal shelter, I witnessed kindness from volunteers and some staff, yet simultaneously, I noticed there was a dichotomy in the treatment of animals. I discovered the misnomers that were widely used to shield their true function from the public.

Sadly, some animal shelters should be described as maximum-security animal prisons. The practice of euthanasia takes the lives of millions of companion animals every year across North America and often amounts to socially sanctioned mass execution.

The original idea for this book started a few years before Charlie's passing. It happened in the year 2010 while I was a volunteer dog walker and cat groomer at a municipal animal shelter. I had a chance encounter with a shelter dog. He was a beautiful, beige-colored, friendly Pomino dog breed (Pomeranian mixed with American Eskimo breed) named Fabio.

I started visiting the shelter more often. I walked Fabio regularly. He would start barking as he eagerly anticipated my arrival and wagged his tail when he saw me approaching his cage. I think Fabio sensed that I was going to rescue him and that I looked forward to seeing him. We bonded quickly. I realized that we ended up rescuing each other. We went for long walks together, and this experience taught me that shelter animals are no different from people's pets. They crave companionship and form bonds with the humans who care about them.

Thankfully, I was able to find Fabio (later known as Gucci) a loving home when my mother met him and agreed to adopt him on the spot. She has given him so much love and affection for the past decade, and he's still her furry baby. In return, Gucci has been a wonderful addition to our family and a loyal companion to my mother. He opened my eyes to the antiquated shelter systems that are meant to protect vulnerable companion animals like Gucci.

Animal shelters are supposed be safe places and havens for homeless companion animals, or at least, that is what I thought, but sadly some shelters are places of mass execution. Although many people care about the well-being of others—especially those in vulnerable situations such as homeless animals—they are unaware of what happens to unwanted companion animals that find themselves in the broken animal shelter system. I knew Gucci's time had an expiry date if he was not adopted. Although these shelter practices did not align with mainstream society's values I felt an urgent calling and moral responsibility to speak up for shelter animals. I continued to volunteer at the shelter and even doubled my efforts to find solutions to this animal-shelter debacle. I became more engaged and active as an outspoken animal advocate. I started to volunteer my time to help local politicians whose records showed that they were sympathetic to animal welfare and rights and that they assisted in updating municipal animal legislation.

My interest in companion-animal issues continued after I finished law school and master of laws. That path led to a career in animal rights as a vocation. When I launched the first animal law firm in Canada, Gartner & Associates Animal Law, I learned about the inadequacies of the legal system to protect companion animals. I was determined to defend them. I saw the unwavering love that people had for their pets, especially when their animals were harmed or were taken unjustly. They were not *just* pets; they were part of the family. Being a pet parent myself, I could relate to their cases and empathize with their situations.

The Beginning of a Book

During this time and to my delight, I met many caring people that shared my love for animals. I heard that over half of the population in the United States shared their homes with cats and dogs and for the most part, took good care of them. That was encouraging. The proof was in the billions of dollars spent every year in the pet industry and on veterinary bills.

This book examines the root of society's contradictory treatment of animals—they are viewed as valuable family members when they belong to us, yet they are treated as disposable commodities when we abandon them in shelters. It inspires readers to awaken to this tragedy and want to change this situation. It also bridges the gap between owned-beloved and unowned-disposable companion animals. It evokes empathy and compassion, by illuminating the plight of animals, offering solutions to the shelter debacle, and showing what can be done to protect them.

While the first part of the book focuses on companion animal issues, the remainder of the book explores other species and the broader topic of animal rights. It will open the reader's eyes to the wider spectrum of animal rights and concerns, as domesticated, land, farm, and wild animal species are considered. It examines the mistreatment of animals resulting from a consumer-oriented, western, materialistic culture, which values possessions and objects for self-gratification over compassion and empathy. This unfortunately leads to a culture of disposability, as innocent animals are treated as inanimate objects and lose their lives.

My hope is that this book inspires readers to understand that the mistreatment of animals is a determinant to humanity's social moral progress. It explores the underlying reasons why society condones the mass extermination of animals and permits animal cruelty and abuse to go unnoticed. It also offers hope and optimism for a better future, as it highlights animal victories and shows the momentum that is happening and provides readers with tools.

This book is written for anyone interested in helping animals—pet parents, animal lovers, rescuers, volunteers, fosters, donors, animal defenders including advocates, and activists, behaviorists, veterinarians and staff as well as those involved in animal organizations. Readers learn that there is a biological need for us to share our lives with animals. We realize the many ways that animals contribute to our well-being—emotional, health, mental, psychological, physical, and spiritual—as they help humans cope with diseases and psychological conditions.

Throughout this book, I share real-life; heartwarming stories of many ways that animals have helped humans. I will show that animals need us too. As a former animal law attorney with specialized expertise in animal law issues and animal advocacy, I believe that I am in a unique position to provide insight into the cause, as I journey into animal rights.

At the root of the problem is disposability of animals, which extends beyond a concern for animal rights and has a greater implication for the future of our planet. Our relationship to animals is mutually beneficial. They rely on us and need our voices, in order to make progress. Viewing animals as owned possessions or property is no longer socially acceptable. People are speaking up to defend animals, and most of us can agree that animals are not objects or things; they are living, breathing, complex, sentient creatures with feelings and emotions.

Humanity has united for other important social-justice causes. There is more tolerance and protection for once exploited and marginalized communities. These social movements, which began in the twentieth century, stimulated change after years of slow incremental gains. The Me Too Movement shines light on the dark secrets in Hollywood. The Environmental Movement has made gains over the years. The moment has arrived for the Animal Rights Movement to take center stage. There is a united front of animal lovers, advocates, and activists in social networks, as the ground swells under this next great social-justice cause for humanity.

Better treatment of animals is a social justice concern, and it is linked to humanity's moral progress. Readers gain insight into the plight of animals, from an examination of the animal-shelter debacle to finding solutions and ways to reduce the suffering of farm animals and protect wildlife. Readers gain practical tools on how to participate and take action for animals through advocacy, activism, and joining forces in this movement. The human-animal bond is a special, sacred and mutually beneficial relationship, which benefits human and nonhuman animal species. Readers will learn throughout this book that animals are here *with* us and not for us.

CHAPTER 1

How Companion Animals Transform Human Lives

When I look into the eyes of an animal, I do not see an animal. I see a living being. I see a friend. I feel a soul.
—A. D. WILLIAMS

Companion animals are closely connected to humans. They teach us about unconditional love, friendship, loyalty, and even bravery. Heartwarming and uplifting stories about animals strike a chord within us and have a noticeable positive effect on our well-being, mood, and outlook on life. We are clearly interested and invested in animals. The reverse is also true: Animals are invested in us, whether they know it or not.

Animals as Teachers and the Human-Animal Bond

There was a time in history when domesticated animal species such as cats and dogs did not exist. For instance, man's best friend, the loyal, brave, and beloved canine, descended from wild wolves. The unique, loving bond and special relationship have histories that go back over fifteen thousand years, when humans lived as hunter-gatherers.

It is thought that friendly and docile wolves first started to approach humans for food, and in exchange, these wolves helped humans hunt and offered them protection from predators. Eventually, this interspecies partnership developed into trust, and a sacred relationship that began as an alliance for survival turned into a special friendship that deepened over time. In an interesting article in the *Good News Network*, new research from Japan showed that dogs became human companions due to a gene that lowered their stress and made them more relaxed around people. Dogs' special relationship with humans began with domestication, after they had descended from wolves. The gene MC2R mutated twice in dogs and produced cortisol.[1] The domestication of dogs was the first time that humans took evolution into their own hands. Our ancestors began breeding certain wolves for more desirable characteristics, and artificial selection eventually led to today's many beautiful dog breeds.

Cats have a long history and an ancient connection with humans. Wildcats helped protect farmers' crops from rodents, and as a result, humans began to befriend and domesticate them. Scientists have hypothesized that the domesticated species of the cat originated around nine thousand years ago, when humans started feeding wildcats as a reward for protecting their crops. In ancient Egypt, cats were initially brought into their homes as predators and gradually became protectors. They were also believed to be sacred animals, so keeping cats in homes was considered wise. Egyptians believed that cats would bring them good luck.

Cats are popular companions to humans and more than just pets. They can form bonds with their caregivers and have different personalities. Getting to know cats can enrich our lives. In fact, they can form deep connections with humans, and they are smarter than most people give them credit for. Most feline parents who share their lives with cats can agree. Cats can even form bonds with other cats. For instance, another interesting recent study from Japan shows that cats can learn their own names and even the names of their feline friends.[2]

---

[1] "Dogs Became Perfect Human Companions Due to a Gene that Lowered Their Stress," Good News Network, (June 2022), https://www.goodnewsnetwork.org/dogs-became-human-companion-due-to-gene-that-lowered-stress/.

[2] Saho Takagi, "Cats Learn the Names of their Friend Cats in Their Daily Lives," *Scientific Reports,* volume 12, Article number: 6155 (2022).

Horses, too, have a long history of service and loyalty to humans for warfare and sports and companionship. Horses have fought in wars with soldiers. They have saved people's lives. They are known as wise, brave, intuitive, trustworthy, gentle, majestic, and intelligent animals. Over the evolution of humanity, our relationships with them has deepened, and it has developed to the point where many of us actively choose to spend time with horses as companions, therapists, confidantes, trusted work partners, protectors, friends, and loved family members.

The human-animal relationship and bond has been studied since the early nineteenth century. More recently, scientific studies with quantifiable research have been conducted to back up these findings. These studies have concluded that companion animals can help humans fill their biological needs for social interaction and connection. Humans are social creatures who benefit from connection and companionship. In fact, some of these biological benefits include improving a person's emotional, mental, and physical well-being and psychological health. For instance, sharing a home with a fur friend can help to make a person feel less alone and lonely.

The human-animal connection is based on mutual trust, respect, and reciprocity. Even the voluntary aspect of the relationship—a human choosing to adopt an animal and integrate that animal as a member of the family—is special and unique. In turn, the animal becomes dependent on his or her human parent (guardian) for survival and basic needs such as food, shelter, enrichment, and companionship. In effect, humans have created domesticated species of companion animals that are completely dependent on humans for their survivals and well-beings.

The desire to share one's life with an animal fulfills the biological need for social connection, companionship, friendship, and reciprocal unconditional love. In 2016, *Time* magazine devoted a special issue regarding the history and myriad benefits of this human-animal relationship. It was titled "Animals and Your Health: The Power of Pets to Heal Our Pain, Help Us Cope, and Improve Our Well-Being."[3] The issue delved into the history of domestication and explored the extraordinary benefits of this sacred relationship for both humans and companions.

Extensive evidence demonstrates that this unique and special

[3] Nancy Gibbs, *Animals and Your Health: The Power of Pets to Heal Our Pain, Help Us Cope, and Improve Our Well-Being* (New York: Time Inc. Books, 2016).

relationship is mutually beneficial and that this sacred human-animal bond is even beginning to get noticed and garner legal recognition. For instance, in the last decade, new legislation was passed by the United States Congress to recognize the biological bond that humans share with their animal companions, by the passing of stronger animal-law protection.

In 2005 during Hurricane Katrina, when rescuers in helicopters and boats arrived to rescue people, some boats refused to accept people's pets. It was reported that more than half of those people decided to remain with their family cats and dogs and that many of them ended up losing their lives. As a result, the US Congress passed the Pets Evacuation and Transportation Standards Act (PETS) to protect dogs and cats as well as humans during natural disasters. *Time* magazine said, "The government had come to realize what its citizens already knew: Cats and dogs are not merely our animal companions. They are members of our families."[4]

Interdependence: It Is a Two-Way Relationship

In the special human-animal relationship, the animal depends on the human for the necessities of life—food, shelter, care, and companionship. In addition to basic needs, companion animals also rely on their human guardians for their emotional fulfillment—that is, a relationship that is based on fulfilling the need for connection, unconditional love, and trust. Most domesticated species are social creatures that crave close connection.

Whatever the species may be (dogs, cats, horses, rabbits, tortoise, parrot, etc.); animals have complex feelings and emotions. They also have health concerns and survival needs like our own. For example, a dog can get lonely if left alone or ignored for long periods. They can feel jealous, get sick, and display affection. Dogs can also experience joy, love, loneliness, and sadness. They are known to seek out social connection and interaction with others.

Scientific research has indicated that the first moments of isolation after a dog's guardian has left is the most stressful on them. The reason is that like humans, dogs become accustomed to habits and behaviors and they crave routine and stability. The simple act of getting ready for work, picking

---

[4] Ibid., 4.

up keys, or putting on your coat is a cue to your dog that something bad is about to happen.[5] Researchers have suggested that your dog may howl or whine for hours when you leave the house, stopping only to listen for your return home. One possible solution that was proposed by researchers to alleviate the dog's suffering is for dog parents to feed and exercise their dog before leaving the home. Researchers conclude that the dog is more likely to relax once his or her needs have been met, so even a brisk walk around the neighborhood can be helpful.

Pets Are Members of Families

Most pet parents agree that our beloved fur friends are more than pets. Dogs, cats, and other animals kept as pets become integral members of the family. They are deeply loved family members. Even children can form deep bonds with their family pets and love them. This sentiment became clear when I was on my daily walk in the forest and overheard a conversation between a young boy and a man that put a smile on my face. The boy was probably five or six years of old. He was talking to what appeared to be his father. They had to stop so that their senior dog could rest, and the boy gave the dog water to drink. The boy referred to his dog as his brother and said, "My brother has to take a rest." The father agreed with the boy but immediately corrected him by explaining that the dog could not be his brother because he was a dog; however, he did say the dog was part of their family.

Pets Have Unique Personalities

Companion animals are viewed by most pet parents as valued and beloved family members, and they are far more than just people's pets. They have feelings similar to our own, and they have individual personalities. Anyone who has shared their lives with a dog or cat will agree that they

[5] Daisey Dunne, "What Happens When You Leave Your Dog at Home Alone: Scientists Reveal the Stress Pets Go through When Isolated," Daily Mail Online: Associated Newspapers, (21 Apr. 2017), http://www.dailymail.co.uk/sciencetech/article-4432134/What-happens-dog-leave-alone.html.

are all unique and have distinct personalities. I know that each dog or cat that I have had the privilege of encountering in my life had a personality that was unique from the previous dog or cat. I have met shy and outgoing dogs of the same breed and feisty and affectionate cats. This realization that animals are unique individuals is the first step to elevating their status in society and eventually granting them the legal protection they deserve. Through our relationships with individual family pets, we can have empathy for other animals.

The Power of Authentic Connection, Friendship, and Unconditional Love

People who share their intimate lives with animals report how grateful they are for the unconditional love that comes from their beloved companions. Simply put, a dog or cat can put us at ease. They do not judge us or place unfair expectations on us. They do not relate to us through the roles and personas that we have created so that we can interact with the superficial outside human world. It seems that our animal friends can connect with us on a deeper level of existence and can put us at ease so that we can truly relax, live fully, and be ourselves.

Animal bonds are real, authentic, and not superficial. For instance, your dog or cat does not care about your physical appearance or the clothes you wear, but they can sense how you feel and be in tune with your emotions. They can lift our spirits and make us feel less lonely and more loved, wanted, accepted, and needed. As the spiritual teacher Eckhart Tolle stated in his book on animals and human spirituality, *Guardians of Beings*, "Dogs offer precious opportunity, even to people who are trapped in their egos, of loving and being loved unconditionally."[6]

In turn, we can relate to our beloved animal companions from an authentic state. Our dogs and cats can help deepen our connection with the part of us that exists beyond the material and external world—what some call our true selves. This might explain the powerful need to share our lives

---

[6] Eckhart Tolle and Patrick McDonnell, *Guardians of Being* (California: New World Library, 2009) 86.

with companion animals. They can help us discard the false personas we carry with us in public and be our true selves when we share their company.

In this sense, the human-animal bond and relationship has a spiritual element, according to Eckhart Tolle. As Tolle further states in *Guardians of Being*, "Everything natural—every flower, tree, and animal—has important lessons to teach us if we would only stop, look, and listen. When you pet a dog or listen to a cat purring, thinking may subside for a moment and a space of stillness arises within you, a doorway into being."[7]

The sacred human-animal bond can be more loving and deeper than some of the human relationships in a person's life. We've all seen bumper stickers and coffee mugs that say, "The more I get to know people, the more I like my cat." For people who live with social anxiety or whose social networks are limited, that intimate relationship can literally be a lifesaver.

Many of us living in big cities have probably witnessed a homeless person, with a devoted dog lying by his or her side. Although society may have rejected that human and perceived that individual as a social outcast, his or her dog is accepting of that person. Day after day, the loyal dog sits on that street corner and does not judge that person. No matter what the humans' circumstances are, our beloved fur friends have no regard or sense of our personas or material, external appearances and possessions—or lack of them. Their needs are as basic as ours are: sustenance, shelter, love, comfort, and companionship.

The sacred relationship between humans and animals comes from a fundamental, natural state. Humans are not required to bring a companion animal into their lives. Adopting and interacting with an animal are deliberate undertakings and conscious choices. Many of us seem to need to bring animals into our homes and make them an integral part of our families.

There are Health Benefits of Spending Time with Pets

Numerous scientific studies over the years have linked pets with positive health benefits: getting outside for a walk, participating in physical exercise, and helping people recover from illnesses. For example, The October

---

[7] Ibid., 30.

2015 *Harvard Health* newsletter supports this claim with evidence that was reviewed by the American Heart Association. It indicates, "Dog owners are more likely to exercise, have a better cholesterol profile, have lower blood pressure, are less vulnerable to the physical effects of stress, and more likely to survive a heart attack."[8] In another scientific study, it was concluded that heart-attack patients were found to have recovered and healed better from their disease when they had a pet at home, versus those without pets.[9]

Similar research studies have shown that dog owners—rather, I prefer the terms pet parents or dog guardians—have lower blood pressure than people who do not share their homes with dogs. Dogs have a calming and soothing effect on people, and dog caregivers tend to get more physical exercise. In a recent study, pet parents said that they relied on their pets for stress relief. In fact, in this study, ninety-five percent of pet parents agreed.[10] As well, blood pressure has been found to decrease when a person strokes a dog. Further research shows that dog companionship is associated with lower cholesterol and triglyceride levels than in non-dog owners and that these differences were not explainable by diet, smoking, or body mass index. The *Harvard Health* newsletter even has a special edition of their publication available for purchase titled "Get Healthy, Get a Dog," which can be ordered from their website. It also discusses the numerous health benefits of getting healthier with a dog and pet ownership.[11]

Research from the University of Missouri-Columbia concluded that the hormonal changes that occur when humans and dogs interact could help people cope with depression and certain stress-related disorders. For example, spending a few minutes stroking a pet prompts a release of good hormones in humans. These hormones include serotonin, prolactin, and

---

[8] Daniel DeNoon, "A Dog Could Be Your Heart's Best Friend" Harvard Health (29 Oct. 2015), https://www.health.harvard.edu/blog/a-dog-could-be-your-hearts-best-friend-201305226291.

[9] Mwenya Mubanga et al, *"Dog Ownership and the Risk of Cardiovascular Disease and Death—A Nationwide Cohort Study,"* Sci Rep 7, 15821 (17 Nov. 2017), https://doi.org/10.1038/s41598-017-16118-6.

[10] American Heart Association, "New Survey Finds 95 Percent of Pet Parents Rely on Their Pet for Stress Relief," Newsroom (June 2022), https://newsroom.heart.org/news/new-survey-95-of-pet-parents-rely-on-their-pet-for-stress-relief.

[11] Harvard Medical School, "Get Healthy Get a Dog," Harvard Health (2015), https://www.health.harvard.edu/staying-healthy/get-healthy-get-a-dog.

oxytocin. Furthermore, the Missouri-Columbia study on the health bene-fits of dog ownership states, "In addition, petting our pooches resulted in decreased levels of the primary stress hormone cortisol, the adrenal chemical responsible for regulating appetite and cravings for carbohydrates." This is additional documented evidence that spending time with a dog can help humans to alleviate stress symptoms (fight or flight).[12]

Well-known psychologist Abraham Maslow described a human's need for companionship with cats and dogs as being innate. He suggested that dog owners live longer, report better life quality and satisfaction, and even have better eyesight. In addition, Maslow noted that pets are often used as a substitute for meaningful relationships with others. He suggested that humans have an innate longing for social companionship with others and needs that are beyond the basic physical and psychological requirements.[13]

Humans crave the company of other living beings and benefit from spending time with others, including animals. There is an innate biological need to share our inner lives with others. Age does not seem to be a factor. Humans are hardwired for social connection at any age.

Animals Are Good for a Human's Mental Health and an Antidote to Isolation

Our need for companionship is more urgent than ever before in the history of human evolution. There is a reason that companion animals are called companions. This became apparent during the Covid-19 pandemic, when people were isolated and spending more time with their pets. Despite the pandemic, social isolation is prevalent in modern-day society, particularly in big cities where people are less connected to their communities and even neighbors. As people spend more time indoors staying connected on social media, they spend less time outside connecting with other people in real life.

For an increasing number of people, an animal's companionship can help ease the feelings of loneliness. They help to fill the lonely void. As the

---

[12] Jeff Sossamon, "Senior Adults Can See Health Benefits from Dog Ownership," University of Missouri News Bureau (20 Apr. 2016), https://munews.missouri.edu/news-releases/2016/0420-senior-adults-can-see-health-benefits-from-dog-ownership.

[13] Abraham H. Maslow, *Motivation and Personality* (Harper & Row Publishers Inc., 1954).

special *Time* magazine issue noted, "More than a third of all Americans and half of all singles say they rely more on their pets than on other people for companionship. Our companions are the glues that keep us together and the presence that keeps us healthy."[14] In the absence of a supportive and loving human-to-human relationship, companion animals keep us socially connected and help us feel unconditionally loved by another living being.

Animal Friends Offer Humans Emotional Support

For the elderly, cats and dogs offer a form of therapy that eases the feelings of isolation in retirement. More than half of seniors in Canada and the US share their homes with animals.

Children also benefit greatly from sharing a home with a furry friend. For instance, children living in a house with a dog suffer less from allergy symptoms. Researchers determined that when a child and a dog shared a household, the child enjoyed reduced allergic sensitization and fewer allergy-related skin rashes. Researchers found a similar effect when cats and children shared households. In addition, children's immune systems were strengthened from this early exposure to pets.[15] Further research from Cambridge provided evidence that pets have a positive influence on children's well-beings and help to reduce their feelings of loneliness and isolation and to gain the self-esteem to become more confident social adults later in life. This study even revealed that children can feel closer to their cats and dogs than their siblings, as they can share their feelings and frustrations with their pets without feeling judged or criticized.[16]

Children with autism spectrum disorders benefit significantly from interactions with animals such as cats, which are known to ease anxiety and stress. Also, therapeutic horse-riding lessons have been offered for decades as a form of therapy for autistic children. Further scientific research

---

[14] *Supra*, n1, 5.

[15] James E Gern et al, "Effects of Dog Ownership and Genotype on Immune Development and Atopy in Infancy," (American Academy of Allergy, Asthma, and Immunology, 2003).

[16] Matthew Cassels, et al, "One of the Family? Measuring Young Adolescents Relationships with Pets and Siblings," *Journal of Applied Developmental Psychology*, volume 49 (2017).

reveals that these children can relate to horses on a unique level. In turn, the horses are in tune with these children, and they offer soothing and calming benefits.

Nowadays a variety of animals including dogs, cats, horses, rabbits, and other types of domesticated animals are essential for a human's emotional and psychological well-being. For a long time, it has been recognized that certain animals—mainly dogs—can be trained as service animals to help humans with physical disabilities perform specific everyday functions, such as opening doors, picking up dropped objects, or assisting with household tasks. For instance, blind people have had Seeing Eye guide dogs for years to assist them with wayfinding and safety.

Another important function of companion animals is to offer emotional and mental comfort and support to humans who are suffering from psychological conditions like depression, anxiety, and panic attacks. Recognized as emotional support animals (ESA), these types of companion animals can offer not only companionship but also relief to their human handlers. This bond is so crucial that in many provinces across Canada and the United States, ESAs are legally permitted to enter public buildings with their humans.

Dogs have been trained extensively to help individuals cope with post-traumatic stress disorder (PTSD). For example, returning war veterans report relief from PTSD symptoms when they bring home a companion or a dog is provided to them for emotional support. It is also reported that dogs can provide relief from stress, give emotional and mental support, and provide companionship to soldiers overseas. In fact, in brainwave studies, soldiers suffering from PTSD were shown to have higher levels of oxytocin (the feel-good chemical) when they were interacting with a dog or cat companion rather than when they were spending time alone. Some soldiers reported that they formed a bond with the stray dogs that they encountered in war-torn countries, and many went to extreme lengths to have them transported back to the United States with them.[17] Other soldiers developed strong bonds with the military dogs that accompanied them into war zones. They wanted to adopt the dog when they came home.

---

[17] "Dogs and PTSD", US Department of Veteran Affairs, https://www.ptsd.va.gov/gethelp/dogs_ptsd.asp.

Animals Help Us Heal

Companion animals can lift our spirits and help us recover from or at least manage medical conditions. In some unusual cases, animals have been known to diagnose illness and help humans' recover from illness.

In Susan Chernak's *Animals as Teachers and Healers*,[18] she relates the story of a woman named Susan McElroy, who was diagnosed with cancer and was told that she had one year to live. Susan lived alone, and one day she let in a stray cat who visited her to give her some company. She took the cat, which she named Flora, to the vet for a routine checkup. To Susan's grief and dismay, the vet diagnosed the cat with leukemia and told Susan that Flora would likely only live for another year. Susan was very depressed by this news, but she noticed that Flora was not. *Maybe the cat knows something that I do not*, she reasoned. She decided to act more like the cat—taking naps, resting more, and so on. Remarkably, Susan and Flora both recovered from their illnesses. Susan asserts that Flora taught her a valuable life lesson about health and helped her heal from the disease.

As I was finishing this book during Covid-19, my family adopted a dwarf, white, beautiful bunny named Sassy (we named her Zoey) from Coveted Canines Rescue and Sanctuary. She came into our lives by chance! At the time, we didn't know that Zoey was there to help us to cope better. We were dealing with the uncertainties and challenges of the pandemic, which made life more stressful. I was a full-time working mom with an animal law firm in my home. I managed online school for my kids and tried to finish writing this book. Looking back, I realize now that I was juggling too much. I was stressed out to the max like most of us and not eating well or thinking about myself, health, wellness, or self-care. When Zoey arrived, something inside me shifted. I found that I was spending more time with this bunny, which was an enjoyable, relaxing, and soothing experience. It took my mind off the pandemic.

I learned from this tiny creature to take better care of myself. It was a transformational experience for my entire family. Since rabbits are natural herbivores and plant eaters, I bought more greens, such as spinach and kale, to feed Zoey. To my delight, my family started integrating and eating more greens as a habit. It was especially satisfying to see the kids eat more

---

[18] Susan Chernak, *Animals as Teachers and Healers: True Stories* (Thorndike Press, 1997), 312.

vegetables. I believe that Zoey's timing was perfect for my family. I also believe that animals come into our lives for a reason and that they are there to teach us. For instance, my kids had a great time playing with the bunny, feeding her, and cuddling with her to gain her trust. In other words, this tiny creature helped us to find joy and contributed to our well-being and even healing during a challenging and somewhat difficult time in our lives.

When we took Zoey to the veterinarian (who was an exotic vet) for the first time for a routine checkup and nail trim, I became aware that she was no different from the other pets that were part of our family. She was timid, scared, nervous, and shaking as she clung to us (her family). In that moment, it was clear to me that she needed my husband and I to comfort her while the vet examined her. I asked the vet what we could do to give Zoey the best life. We talked about nutrition and diet. Then the vet turned to us and said something that put a smile on my face and that has stayed with me. He said, "Love your beautiful bunny." It seemed so simple yet so profound, and I have thought about those kind words often.

Animals and Spirituality

Animals can help humans stay more fully present in the moment and connected to nature and our own deeper inner selves. For example, dogs comfort and bring us out into nature, which is in the natural world. We spend more time outside when we take them out for daily walks. It encourages humans to connect with nature and others as well. When we are outside with our dogs, we are more likely to engage in social interactions and conversations with other dogs and their human guardians, leave our busy lives and worries behind for a while, and simply enjoy the tranquility and peace of the outdoors and natural world. Also, cat lovers know the relaxing feeling of their cats' purrs when they are rubbed. Dr. Bernie Siegel wrote in *101 Exercises for the Soul: Simple Practices for a Healthy Body, Mind & Spirit*, "Animals live in the moment and can help us to do the same, to let go of our fears and our worries about tomorrow. Our pets know that worrying does not solve anything, while a tummy rub, or a nap can do a great deal."[19]

---

[19] Bernie Siegel, *101 Exercises for the Soul: Simple Practices for a Healthy Body, Mind and Spirit* (New World Library, 2010), 106.

Dogs Are In Tune with Human Emotions

It probably doesn't come as a surprise that our most loyal companions, dogs, are in tune with our human emotions. They can respond to our facial expressions and moods. They know what we are feeling. Most people that have shared their lives with canine companions can attest to this. When I am happy and excited, my dogs are in tune with my emotions, and they literally start wagging their tails and jumping around as if to communicate that they share my joy and excitement. When I am sad, I can sense that my dogs will come over to give me their affection in gentle ways, such as lying beside me. They seem melancholy too. It is an extraordinary relationship that is like no other and that shows us there is a deep emotional connection with our dogs. They are known as great protectors and loyal friends. They sacrifice their own lives for humans. There seems to be nothing more important to dogs than to please their pet parents and give love.

Rescue Dogs Can Save Humans

One night during the weekend, my family gets together for movie night. Each of us gets to select a movie, and it might not come as a surprise to learn that I chose a dog-friendly movie. I am an admitted dog geek (My kids have joked with me about it), and I especially love tear-jerking real-life stories about dogs. I selected the movie *Rescued by Ruby*[20] based on a real-life story of a shelter dog named Ruby, which was surrendered to an animal shelter in Long Island several times for unruly behavior. At that point, she was still a mischievous Australian-shepherd and border-collie mix puppy (Both of these are both working dogs). She had not been given a chance to shine and show her true potential yet.

Fortunately, there was a volunteer and dog behaviorist named Patricia Inman, who would not give up on Ruby. She worked with the dog to correct these unwanted behaviors. She also was Ruby's advocate. Just a few hours before Ruby was to be euthanized at the shelter, she was rescued and given a second chance at life. Ruby was assigned to train with the Long Island K-9

---

[20] Jennifer Borget, Netflix Movie: *Rescued by Ruby* (2022), Commonsense Media, https://www.commonsensemedia.org/movie-reviews/rescued-by-ruby.

unit as a police dog with Corporal Daniel O'Neil, who decided to adopt her. She became a family member and loyal, brave friend. It was touching to see the two bonding and clear that Ruby helped this corporal learn to be more patient and in tune with himself.

In a strange twist of fate, Ruby ended up saving a boy's life when he got lost in the woods, and she found him (when no one else could). He was barely conscious, and she barked loudly to get the attention of others because they were deep in the woods. It turned out that the boy's mother was Ruby's angel and advocate, Patricia Inman, in this happy, miraculous ending. Both Ruby and Corporal Daniel O'Neil went on to save more lives over the years. They are still together as best friends and working partners eleven years later. This uplifting story gives us hope and provides a needed voice to shelter dogs. It shows us how remarkable they are and that giving up on them is a tragedy. Another interesting detail from the movie is that the actor dog that played the role of Ruby was named Bear in real life. He was also a shelter dog that was close to being put down for unmanageable behavior. He was similarly given a second chance at life when he was saved by dog trainers and played the part of Ruby beautifully.[21]

It is a touching tribute to Ruby and all shelter animals, which deserve to live. There are many touching stories of dogs saved from shelters that go on to do great things. Given the chance to prove it, they can live up to their true potential. These dogs can give so much devotion, unconditional love, loyalty, and companionship beyond anything that is imagined. It's as if they can sense they were given a second chance at life.

The Dog's So-Called Sixth Sense

In another example, a small shelter dog named Peanut was credited with saving the life of an abused child. Peanut came to the Delta Animal Shelter in Michigan after being severely abused in her former home. At two years of age, she was found with broken ribs and legs and carpet burns on her body. Her former human owners were later charged with animal cruelty. Peanut was ultimately adopted into a new, loving home. One cold winter

---

[21] Ibid.

morning, Peanut began barking uncontrollably and pacing around inside the family's home. The husband took Peanut outside, where she led him to an open field behind their house. There in a ditch, they found a naked three-year-old girl, who was shivering and crying for help. Somehow, Peanut had sensed the little girl was in danger, called attention to her, and saved her life. Among the girl's first words to her rescuers was "doggie." Afterward, police investigated the girl's family and found that she and her sister were living in deplorable conditions. The children were placed into foster care. Peanut was widely praised for her so-called sixth sense.

There are countless other heartwarming news stories of animals saving people and their remarkable abilities to detect when humans are in danger. We can learn much from their bravery, courage, and selflessness; however, perhaps more fascinating is their *desire* to help humans. Not only can animals somehow sense danger but also communicate with humans to alert us to impending harm, sometimes at the risk of their own lives.

Dogs have evolved an extraordinary sixth sense and innate ability to detect when humans are in danger. Peanut, for example, was able to pick up on cues that her humans were not able to detect. Perhaps it was the faint high-pitched sounds of a child in distress or something else entirely. It may not have been a coincidence that both Peanut and this little girl had been victims of horrible physical neglect and abuse. Perhaps Peanut was more in tune with sounds of suffering because of her experience. Research may tell us more about this so-called sixth sense, but it is undeniable that animals such as Peanut can teach us about bravery, unconditional love, and the strong emotional connection humans have with animals.

Cats as Companions

I admit that I was a huge dog-loving person before I adopted a cat. I deeply cared about our feline friends too, and during childhood I fed feral cats in my neighborhood and even brought some cats home, as well as other creatures. That being said, I had a special connection to dogs. I have always loved all canines, no matter what their sizes, breeds, or personalities were. It still amazes me that my senior-citizen eleven year old German shepherd dog Lily still gets excited and greets me at the door, even if I am only gone for a few moments. She loyally follows me around the house. Wherever I go, she is by my side.

As I sit here to write this book, Lily's companionship, and loyalty are unwavering; they serve as a reminder of how special dogs are and how tuned into our emotions they are. It's as if she senses that her presence is needed for me to finish writing and that she eases the loneliness of the isolation required while writing. I feel her unconditional love. I am fairly certain that most dog parents can relate to this.

But there is something special and unique about cats as companions to humans and the way cats sit back and seek out our affection. They are more discerning and subtle than dogs are in their expressions. Although they might not jump up with excitement to greet us when we walk through the door, cats form special bonds, become very attached to their human pet parents and caregivers, and show their affection. I learned about cats through my personal relationship with my first feline friend, Jackson. He was a handsome and cool cat. We adopted him as a kitten and he was a constant source of soothing comfort for many years. I am very sad to share that he has recently has passed away as I was finishing this book. When he was gone, it felt like a part of my heart was taken. I cried every day when he left and I miss him deeply.

When I think about what made Jackson so special, there are so many memories. It was his loyalty and companionship to our son, Brad. I fondly look back to when he was dropped off at our home by a family friend. He was a feral kitten found. He was tiny, just three weeks old, a fur ball with a beautiful black and white coat, a few pounds, and a little helpless creature. He was a baby that needed a loving home. Brad was home from preschool that day (it was meant to be), and he is a HUGE cat lover. Coincidentally he had been asking us for a pet cat, as he would play with the neighborhood cats! The moment my son laid eyes on this kitten they became friends.

When we met this kitten, and held him in our arms we fell in love. He became an instant companion to our son, slept in his room, and was a great friend. Jackson was a friendly, laid back cat, who behaved more like a dog, and would greet visitors and liked to be around us. He had warm yellow eyes that people admired. He loved attention (and he would purr as soon as we pet him), but he happily retreated from the rest of us, when he needed his time away or sensed we were distracted. I had never had a family cat before

Jackson. I was intrigued to learn that cats too can be such friendly, loving, cozy, and affectionate animals. Jackson had a calming energy. He was smart too and would sit in my suitcase whenever I was packing for a trip as if he knew I was leaving and he would wait by the door when I arrived. He was all of that and much more!

A 2019 study suggests that cats can form bonds with their human families. This study was conducted by Oregon State University and was published in the journal *Current Biology*, which looked at seventy cats. The cats were put in a room with their owners for two minutes. Then they were left alone for two minutes before the owners returned. Sixty-four percent of the cats displayed what the researchers classified as "secure attachment" to their guardians.[22]

Cats can be such cozy and cuddly companions. If you've ever shared your home with a feline friend, you know that there is something special about their purrs. Whenever I stroked my cat, I found it relaxing when Jackson purred. Cats are curious and playful and loveable family members, so they are great for the entire family. At the same time, you can leave a cat alone for longer periods. They are independent. Our beloved family cat Jackson always knew when we needed his comfort; he sat next to me whenever I would mediate, and he softly purred.

He was a constant source of comfort and important family member. His purrs would ease my daily stress and his bright yellow curious cat eyes watched us as he eagerly waited to play. He was patient and never forceful. He was kind to children and let them play with him. Jackson brought happiness and joy into our lives and brought us into a cozy, quiet, and calm inner peace.

Sadly, he was diagnosed with cancer this year. It was unexpected and it felt like it came out of nowhere. I thought he would live until he was twenty years old. He was easy to care for and healthy (a little overweight from being indoors and getting treats). I never imagined that he would get sick and pass away so suddenly. It felt like a huge tidal wave came over us and I could not imagine he would not be with us for many more years. I remember hearing the saying 'cats have nine lives' and he certainly seemed

---

[22] Jessica Booth, "9 Studies That Prove Cats Make the Best Pets," Insider (16 Dec. 2019), https://www.insider.com/studies-about-why-cats-make-good-pets-2019-12#cats-are-attached-to-their-owners-just-like-dogs-are-researchers-say-1.

to. When my family found out about his diagnosis, we immediately took the necessary steps to "save him" from this illness. If any cat could beat cancer it would be "our cat", the survivor, Jackson. After all, he was the only survivor of a kitten litter and when he escaped the backyard a few years ago in the middle of a cold Canadian winter and found his way home days later, he would beat this too.

Both of my sons Andrew and Brad were amazing helpers and we drove him to chemotherapy and we administered his medicine. We cheered him on as he fought bravely. He was a survivor and took his treatments well. We remained hopeful knowing this little guy was a fighter that he would conquer cancer. But to our surprise, after a few rounds of chemo (which he handled like a true gentlemen), we found out the cancer had spread to his lungs and metastasized. That was devastating news for all of us. Jackson was not *just* a cat; he was part of our family, eleven years of fond family memories; feline friendship with Brad, and always there during happy and sad occasions. We miss him terribly but choose to be grateful to have shared our lives with such an incredibly friendly, cozy, affectionate, sweet, caring, loving, and brave warrior cat. Anyone that ever met Jackson would comment on how friendly and handsome he was. I will always remember him and keep his loving memory close to my heart. After all he was my first family cat and younger son's best fur friend and there will never be another cat like Jackson.

This chapter has highlighted the many ways cats can be wonderful, caring, and loving family members and easier to care for when compared to dogs, which can require a lot of care.[23] If you have a busy schedule or travel frequently, a cat can make a great companion. You don't have to take cats outdoors for daily walks. If you live in a cold climate, you can stay indoors during the winter and cuddle with your cat. Cats as companions can be ideal for seniors or the elderly, as they don't bark, and they are quieter. They are less likely to disturb the neighbors.[24]

Cats can make loving companions to children too. They can teach children to care for another living creature in the home and have a companion friend to keep them company.

---

[23] "Thinking of Getting a Cat?" International Cat Care (7 Oct. 2019), https://icatcare.org/advice/thinking-of-getting-a-cat.
[24] Ibid.

Horse Sense and the Human-Horse Bond

Alongside the close bond that humans share with domesticated species, such as cats, dogs, parrots, tortoises, rabbits, hamsters, etc., horses deserve special mention and praise for their dedicated service to humanity throughout history. Although many people have grown up with smaller animals, such as dogs and cats, some people have been lucky enough to share their lives with horses, the gentle giants. They are known for their remarkable intuition and ability to develop strong bonds with their human caregivers. In fact, many people regard horses, burros, and other equines in a similar way to other pets. If you or someone you know cares for a horse, you understand the deep human-horse bond that develops from this unique relationship, which is nurtured through care, and a great deal of trust on the part of the human and the horse.

Although horses are strong and large, and they have imposing physical features, they respond favorably to humans who provide them with tender care, food, veterinary care, and enriched social and living conditions. They return this with their unconditional love. Like cats and dogs, horses, too, have a long history of service to humans—warfare, sportsmanship, and companionship. Humans who interact with horses attest to the close human-horse bond, which develops over time. Horses can recognize their human caregivers, and they have been known to cry when they are absent. Also, horses can mourn the deaths of their human caregivers; in the following section we learn the story about a horse named Sereno which offers one powerful example of the strong connection that exists between humans and horses.

Another example of the horse's remarkable abilities is depicted in the Hollywood movie *Dear John*. It shows us the strong human-horse bond and an example of helping an autistic boy. The term *horse sense* is used in this movie to describe a horse's intuitive ability to connect and help autistic children to relax and feel more comfortable around horses, without judgment or pressure through their extraordinary senses.[25]

---

[25] Cristy Lytal, "Autistic Boy Saddles Up 'Dear John,'" Los Angeles Times, (February 7, 2010), Https://Www.Latimes.Com/Archives/La-Xpm-2010-Feb-07-La-Ca-Workinghollywood7-2010feb07-Story.Html>

Despite horses' remarkable abilities and service to humankind, their status is similar to other animal species. Sadly, horses are regarded as chattel and are owned as property. For example, take the story of Justice, an eight-year-old American quarter horse from the state of Oregon, which was discovered severely malnourished, after he had been neglected by his human owners. He was three hundred pounds underweight, starving, and suffering from severe penile frostbite because he had been left outside in the extreme cold. The heartbreaking story sparked outrage on social media, and as a result, the American Legal Defense Fund (ALDF) commenced a litigation proceeding and sued Justice's former owners for one hundred thousand dollars ($100,000) for his neglect and mistreatment.

The legal claim's estimate is based on the projected future costs of covering his ongoing medical care. Since the state of Oregon has strong anti-cruelty laws, ALDF argued that his legal owner's criminal negligence should not be compensated only with restitution but also should go beyond financial restitution. This was a precedent-setting case in the US's judicial system. The horse's court case was based on the premise that animals have legal standing in court rather than simply being viewed as property. Horrifying though it is, this story is a noteworthy example of humans' concern for animals and the huge strides that are being made in the arena of animal protection legislation.

In my hometown of Toronto, another horse-related tragedy made the news. In the early hours of May 20th, 2018, the city's renowned Sunnybrook Stables burned to the ground in a suspicious fire that was started either by arson or fireworks. Sixteen beautiful horses perished, and thirteen others were injured in the fire.

Although this loss was devastating, the public outpouring of support from the community was heartwarming. Hundreds of people visited the memorial site, placing flowers, carrots, and cards near the stable, and attended a memorial service to show their respect for the horses that had been injured and those that had lost their lives. Also encouraging were the efforts of the first responders. Firefighters and police officers did their utmost to contain the fire and move as many animals as they could to safety. The Toronto police's mounted unit offered their own stables to house the surviving horses.

This is a powerful example of the enduring strength of horses and the horse-human bond—the special connection to these noble creatures. Many of the people who were deeply affected by the deaths of these horses were not regular riders at the stable or even staff or volunteers but were merely ordinary people like you and me, who had derived joy and comfort from visiting the premises and spending time with these majestic animals. They had mourned their loss as keenly as they would the loss of a human friend or family member.

Death and Grieving Pets: A Deep Loss

Our beloved companion-animal friends are part of our everyday routines. They spend more time with us than others do and share our intimate lives. We can become more bonded and connected to them than we are to some human relationships. When we lose them, we grieve them deeply.

I know that losing a beloved dog, cat, and any other furry family member can be a devastating and lonely time. Their shorter life spans mean that they usually die before we do. This is sometimes cited as a reason not to adopt an animal ("I couldn't stand the heartbreak"). It also provides a unique opportunity to learn that life is precious and that we are able to find joy living in the present moment. When pets pass away, we can learn about the significance of their lives vis-à-vis our own. We grieve the loss of our fur friend in the same way that we may mourn the loss of other human family members; so much so, that there are numerous grievance support groups that are available for human guardians. When I lost my best fur friend, Charlie, I cried every single day during the months before he passed on and for a long time after he was gone. I still miss Charlie dearly. I found that reading books and blogs and connecting with other grieving pet parents helped me to cope better and feel less lonely in the grief.

On a deeper level, my beloved dog Charlie's passing and more recently my beloved cat Jackson's passing has reminded me of how fleeting life is. I had to regain my strength after both of these losses for my family. I did so through a period of grieving and eventual acceptance of the full circle of this dog's life and story. Charlie's legacy goes on, and his memory lives on in my heart. He's that heart dog that will remain part of me for the rest of my life. Jackson too holds a special place in my heart and is dearly missed and remembered.

I know there will be more fur babies, along the way, that will become part of the family, and I will love them too. I know that each companion I get to know will never be forgotten. Each one of them will hold a special place in my heart. There will never be another dog like Charlie, or another cat like Jackson. Each one of them is unique and special. Each of them remains etched in my heart and memory, just like your fur babies that passed away.

Animals Grieve Us Too

Animals can teach us that we are not a unique species in grieving lost loved ones. Remarkably and perhaps unsurprisingly to anyone reading this book, animals also grieve the loss of their human caregivers. Dogs are prime examples of this. I will always remember the moving story of Hachiko. His legacy lives on at Shibuya Station in Japan, where there is a bronze statue of this dog. He was abandoned at the train station as a puppy in the early 1920s, and subsequently, he was befriended by Eizaburo Ueno, a professor at Tokyo University. It is a touching story of unconditional love and a strong human-animal bond. Every day, the professor and Hachiko would walk together to the train station. Remarkably, he would return and wait for the professor, greeting him with the sheer excitement and deep affection that only a dog can display.

One afternoon in May of 1925, the professor did not return to the train station. Unbeknownst to the dog, the professor had suddenly died at work from a cerebral hemorrhage. For the next ten years of his life, Hachiko went to the station faithfully every morning and evening, at the time the train was due to enter the station. He waited in vain for the return of his beloved guardian. In 1932, a newspaper reporter published this remarkable story of Hachiko's loyalty, and the dog became a legend in Japan and around the world.[26]

More recently, I saw a photo on social media that was shared about

[26] Maria Wulff Hauglann, "The Amazing True Story of Hachiko the Dog," Nerd Nomads (13 June 2017), https://nerdnomads.com/hachiko_the_dog.

a horse named Sereno, from a small rural community in Brazil, who was shown grieving at the funeral of his guardian, thirty-four-year-old Wagner de Lima Figueiredo. At one point during the procession, Sereno sniffed the coffin, laid his head on the lid, and whimpered. In an interview, Figueiredo's brother stated that the two had shared a very deep bond and connection for many years. Figueiredo had been so attached to Sereno that he would often save food for the horse to make sure he ate, often going hungry himself.[27]

Conclusion: Animals Make Us Better Humans

During this time of uncertainty in the world, our furry friends can bring us comfort, joy and love. They offer friendship, support and unconditional love. While there is more political division among North Americans than ever before, we find that our love for our beloved animal friends can unite us and even bring us closer together. Our love for animals transcends cultural borders and boundaries, political and religious beliefs, age, gender, and social class. This uniting social-justice issue brings people together for a kinder, gentler, and more compassionate human species.

This chapter has outlined the many ways that animals can transform human lives: biological needs, a mutually beneficial human-animal bond, and ways they can enrich human lives. In turn, it has also discussed how humans bring happiness, love, and joy to their animal friends. All of us—humans and nonhuman animals alike—can benefit from this special, sacred human-animal bond and unique relationship. We share similar biological needs for acceptance, love, companionship, friendship, trust, happiness, affection, attachment, and social connection.

Ordinary citizens, politicians, and those in the spotlight such as famous people and many celebrities have relationships to animals that are like no others. The special bond that exists between human and animal is unique and remarkable. I found this celebrity quote very endearing. As British actor Patrick Stewart (*Star Trek* and *X-Men*) states of his personal experience fostering a pit bull named Ginger, which he eventually adopted,

---

[27] "Heartbreaking Moment Horse Cries at Owner's Funeral," *USA Today* (8 January 2017), https://www.usatoday.com/story/news/humankind/2017/01/08/heart-breaking-moment-horse-cries-owners-funeral/96256444.

I find that my relationship to the world, and to the news every day in the papers and on the television, has been changed by Ginger, because she has brought such a quality of patience and tolerance and fun into our lives. It has, in a very short space of time, shifted my sense of where our world might be going.[28]

---

[28] Kelli Bender, "Patrick Stewart Inspired to #GetTough on Dog Fighting after Fostering a Pit Bull," PEOPLE.com (8 Apr. 2017), https://people.com/pets/patrick-stewart-foster-dog-anti-dog-fighting.

CHAPTER 2

Unintended Consequences:
Animal Disposability

A dog is not a thing. A thing is replaceable. A dog is not. A
thing is disposable. A dog is not. A thing doesn't have a heart.
A dog's heart is bigger than any "thing" you can ever own.
—ELIZABETH PARKER

As I often say, animals are here *with* us and not for us. They are not disposable items. Animals are living, breathing, complex creatures that deserve to be treated with kindness and respect. Companion animals form strong bonds with their pet parents and become integral members of families. They are capable of a plethora of emotions, yet far too often, they are treated as disposable commodities when they are abandoned in shelters. People who purchase their pets from breeders are unknowingly contributing to the endless cycle and tragedy of throwaway pets.

When more humans adopt animals from shelters and rescues and stop dumping them, this vicious cycle will end. Animal disposability is condoned when irresponsible humans dump their unwanted dogs and cats at shelters.[29] This repetitive and vicious cycle often results in tragic endings

---

[29] Craig Brestrup, *Disposable Animals: Ending the Tragedy of Throwaway Pets* (Camino Bay Books, 1997), 18–19.

he could find his cat a loving home, but the disinterest in his eyes prevented me from disrupting the cold exchange. I innately felt sad and knew that animals should not be treated this way—as disposable commodities and replaceable items. I thought that perhaps this type of situation would not happen so frequently if people took the time to understand what happens at shelters to their companion animals when they are left behind.

It would be helpful for there to be more resources offered to pet parents who are thinking of surrendering their pets to shelters. As noted above, some people can no longer look after their cat or dog due to expensive veterinary bills or losing a job or illness. Life happens and there are circumstances that lead people to have to give up their pets. There should be solutions for these types of circumstances: temporary shelter and foster care for extended times rather than shelters easily taking people's pets at the surrender counter when they are overcrowded.

Designer Dogs, Puppy Mills, and the Purchasing Mentality

We live in a society that values materialism and possessions in a western culture that gathers items for instant gratification. Some people consider beloved pets as part of these consumer possessions. For example, designer dogs are worn by some celebrities; they are spotted at parties in photos, and have become popular status symbols. I am not suggesting that these animals are not loved; however, sometimes these fashionable designer dogs are viewed as status symbols or accessories because of their cute physical appearance.

The truth is that most of these designer dogs often came from breeders and in some cases, puppy mills, born of females living in horrific, deplorable, and confined conditions. In fact, puppy mills are the result of the supply and demand for designer dogs. These puppy mills overbreed dogs to produce beautiful, posh-looking puppies to satisfy the demand for stylish purebred dog breeds that match designer bags and status symbols. This is a business transaction, and it sends a contradictory message to mainstream society that animals have no intrinsic worth or value. Sadly, puppy mills contribute to the endless cycle of throwaway pets and overpopulation in shelters when they are no longer wanted.

WHERE DO DOGS COME FROM?

The Truth about Disposable Dogs from Puppy Mills

If humans continue to purchase their dogs from puppy-mill operations, which include pet stores, breeders, and some online websites, animal mistreatment and disposability will continue. We need stronger regulations to prevent the purchase of companion animals from unethical breeders and pet stores. I learned that unethical breeding contributes to this endless cycle of shelter killing due to the overpopulation of cats and dogs.

I am not trying to make people feel badly or guilty about their past experiences, choices, or decisions. I hope to share information and inform others on what I have learned. I am still learning as well. I have made bad decisions and acted impulsively in some cases. It is an emotional experience. I was unknowingly a contributor to commercial puppy mill operations. I shared my life with two of these dogs. The first dog was Sasha, a sweet, smart, loyal, loving, and elegant looking black and white purebred Papillion dog. My mother purchased him for me as a gift when I was in high school. After my first childhood dog, George, was given away when our building did not allow him to stay with us, we did not adopt another dog. I frequently pestered my mother to adopt another dog. Years went by with no success. We continued to live in the apartment building that did not permit dogs or cats. My determination finally paid off when we moved out of that place. When I was sixteen years old, my sweetie Sasha finally arrived.

The dogs and other fur friends that came into my life offered many great lessons. I am grateful for them, for they touched my life in many ways. I will remember all of them fondly.

Sweet Sasha

In high school, I went on a school trip to a farm, where I contracted German measles and was hospitalized. While in the hospital, my mother tried to cheer me up and asked if there was anything that I wanted while I recovered. I had just started driving, and my mother later revealed that she was certain I was going to ask for a new car. Instead, I looked up with excitement and told her that I wanted to adopt a dog. As promised, the day I was released from the hospital, we went to the local pet store to find a puppy. I think that in those days, most people got their dogs from shopping malls. I do not think most people (including myself) thought about where the dogs originated. I assumed the dogs displayed in pet stores derived from animal-loving people.

As soon as I laid eyes on this tiny black-and-white fur ball, who was three pounds and three months old, I wanted to take him home. This Papillion puppy was energetic, sweet, playful, and smart. He made eye contact and held a gaze as he seemed to say, *pick me.* I was ready to take him home, but my mother reassured me that if he were meant for us, he would still be there. We went to a few more pet stores, but Sasha remained in our minds because he had stolen our hearts.

To my surprise, my mother went back for him the next day while I was at school and surprised me when I came home. Vividly, I still remember the day when he jumped into my lap and instantly became part of the family. Sweet Sasha lived a long life and was with me through high school, college, law school, marriage, and even my firstborn child, Andrew. Sasha was a joy. He was so smart and learned tricks easily, knew of our names. He loved snacking on sliced apples, and he did not mind performing tricks for his treats. He lived a full life well into his golden years and almost twenty years. He lived with my mother when I went away to law school, which I later realized helped her better cope with the change. Sasha was our faithful and loyal companion. He was a wise teacher who taught me to be less selfish (After all, I was a teenager when he came into my life), to be more responsible, to better understand the needs of caring for another living breathing creature, and to appreciate the deep connection and human-animal bond.

Charming Charlie

After this joyful experience, my next canine companion was Charlie. He was charismatic yet another designer dog born in a puppy mill. Charlie was a charmer and a beautiful looking dog, with a silky beige coat. He was a Pomeranian breed that my husband and I noticed for sale at the local pet store. He was a gift from my husband for our first-year wedding anniversary.

Charlie immediately grabbed my attention because he was no longer a puppy. He was almost a year old. His perceived worth and value had dropped in the eyes of the store's owners. I was stunned to see that he was listed as "dog for sale" and that his price had dropped by fifty percent. I was perplexed, slightly disgusted, and very sad to see this dog confined to a tiny cage and advertised for half the price. I was eager to bring him home. I fell in love with Charlie the moment I held him in my arms. He licked my earlobe as if to thank me for removing him from that small, crowded space. I learned so much from this dog. I instantly felt loved and needed. He put a smile on my face, and he filled my heart with happiness and hope for many years.

From our first chance encounter and for many years after that, Charlie was a constant companion. I did not have children when we adopted Charlie, so he was my furry baby boy. He was always there to help me cope better with life's ups and downs and twists and turns. He was loving, fun, adventurous, and very adaptable. We traveled a lot before we had kids and moved several times with him from Toronto, Ontario, to Corner Brook, Newfoundland.

A year later in 2005, we moved to the United States to New Port Beach in California. As we navigated life's challenges together, he helped me realize the unconditional love a human can feel for an animal. Charlie had a unique personality. He loved to meet new people and charmed them with his friendliness, and he was a real foodie. I loved to cook for and take care of him. In turn, he provided me with much comfort after I suffered two miscarriages early in my marriage.

Charlie could not be replaced. I was bonded to him for many reasons; perhaps because it was the first time that I was responsible for another living creature or felt his unconditional love. Although taking care of Sasha had been an amazing experience, he was really my mother's dog, and she was responsible for him. On the other hand, Charlie relied on me for his daily needs—food, walks, and vet checks. Beyond that, we kept each other company while my husband Peter who is a surgeon worked long hours at the hospital. When we moved, he helped ease my loneliness. I took him for walks and noticed my surroundings, met other dog parents, and we had a great time together. I felt comforted by my furry best friend. He was in tune with my emotions. He helped me get through those moves and cope better with life's ups and downs.

Charlie passed on in 2018 at almost sixteen years of age. When he died, as I shared, it was one of the most difficult losses in my life. Initially, I was unable to imagine not seeing him every day. I think most pet parents can agree that the life of a dog is far too short. I am convinced that most animal lovers can relate to that empty feeling and loneliness that is brought on by this heavy loss. The veterinarian diagnosed him with congestive heart failure and advanced kidney disease—a bad combination and a terminal medical condition. There was no cure or hope that he would ever recover. On top of that, he was suffering with daily seizures.

Although Charlie had a long life in dog years, his passing left a big void in my life. I am grateful to have shared my life with this spirited dog. Somehow in the depths of my grief and sorrow, I felt more motivated than ever to dispel this notion of animals as mere things or inanimate objects and to make a difference. I wanted to educate people on the dangers of buying pets from puppy mills, which as I said was something I had unknowingly contributed to.

I cannot imagine what breeding females must endure while living in such unthinkable conditions. Dogs bred in puppy mills are kept confined in tiny cages, not taken for walks, are treated like inanimate objects, and are eventually discarded. Thankfully, the laws are changing and cracking down on unethical breeders, and more puppy mills have been forced to close.

To honor Charlie's memory, we planted a tree at Thistledown Pet Memorial and buried his ashes. While visiting there, I saw other people who were grieving the loss of their animal companions. In that moment, I realized that this experience was to give some closure.

Revolving Door at Shelters: A Vicious Cycle

Animal shelters unwittingly contribute to the endless cycle of animal disposability. I have witnessed potential adopters being rejected during an interview process and forced to walk away from a particular animal due to an unpleasant encounter with a shelter worker. I remember one specific situation when I was a shelter volunteer at the local municipal pound. A young, happy couple grew fond of a young husky. He was an adorable and stunning dog that was full of life and energy. This couple would visit the dog often.

Their adoption process was a failure from the outset. I witnessed an awkward encounter. The shelter's intake worker rejected their adoption application because the couple worked full-time. Afterward, watching the couple walk away with their heads down, defeated, I felt sad. The shelter denied their application and the couple left and did not return. This couple had interacted well with the dog. I could see the joy in their eyes, and similarly, the dog was happy when they visited and clearly wanted to be loved. I believe that they would have been caring pet parents; however, they were not given this chance. Instead, this spirited husky puppy was sent back to his lonely cage. I do not know how this beautiful creature's story ended. Hopefully, this dog found a loving family to care for him.

Animal Shelters Stop Doing Society's Dirty Work

Animal shelters can do better and prevent the untimely deaths of innocent companion animals. This cycle of disposability by taking people's pets without reason is unjustifiable. By accepting unwanted dogs, cats, and rabbits without consequences to the human and not asking probing questions, shelters make it easy for people to give up their pets and relinquish responsibility for these living beings. For example, the drop-off relinquish-and-surrender counters at shelters can be replaced with a help desk to assist human guardians in resolving their animal issues.

The onus should be put on the person who is giving away the animal. They should prove that they tried to resolve their unwanted situation prior to dropping their animal at the shelter. In other words, animal shelters can offer support and educate caregivers to help them keep their pets or find other suitable adopters. The animal shelter should be a last resort for dumping a pet.

Ban Puppy Mills

Puppy mills are the sad result of a consumer-oriented society. The demand for designer dogs directly contributes to the cruelty and exploitation of animals. When prospective adopters do not exercise due diligence when researching an animal companion, they further contribute to the inhumane treatment of innocent companion animals.

There are puppy mill operations on a large scale and smaller scale with backyard breeders. I recall the story from a shelter worker of an elderly couple that surrendered a dozen dogs to the shelter. Sadly, the dogs were being held in deplorable conditions and the couple profited from selling them. When they came into the shelter, the dogs looked frail, unwell (they hadn't been to a vet), and hungry. This couple did not keep these dogs as companions but as commodities.

Since the laws treat animals as property, the legal system perpetuates this problem by creating weak animal-protection laws. Animals are viewed as objects and are owned as property, which often means that there is a lack of attachment. Instead of legal ownership, I prefer the term guardianship to describe the relationship between humans and their companion animals. By changing the term from *ownership* to *guardianship* our relationship to them improves.

Loyal Lily

Another instance of my unknowing experience with unethical backyard breeders was when we decided to adopt our next family dog. My husband wanted a larger breed of dog, and he did his homework. Based on hours of online research, he concluded that German shepherds were a good fit for our family. They had a good temperament and so he found a reputable breeder.

I reluctantly agreed to visit the dog breeder's home. Even then, I knew in my heart that adopting from breeders felt wrong. I was worried about the dog's temperament, as we had two small children at home and two pets. At that time, I had some knowledge that adopting dogs from breeders was probably not the best choice, but I didn't know enough about this topic to make an informed choice. I can admit that I was somewhat naïve. I wanted to believe that there were breeders (and there probably were) who cared about these dogs.

When we arrived at the breeder's home, I was shocked at the filthy living conditions. There were dozens of adult dogs and puppies that were kept in unsanitary kennels. It felt like a barn instead of a home. Nonetheless,

I noticed from the corner of my eye an adorable-looking, friendly female puppy with floppy ears, which happened to be the only girl in the entire litter. I was immediately captured by her. She was a beautiful beige-and-black German shepherd puppy. She was full of life and had a gentle personality. The breeder wanted to show us how obedient she was. She sat for a small carrot, and she was focused on pleasing the lady. She seemed more attached to the breeder rather than the dogs in the pack. I sensed the breeder did not reciprocate this affection, and she seemed overly eager to sell us the female puppy. It seemed like a business transaction that was no different than shopping for other consumer items. We took Lily home with us that day and never looked back. Lily has been an amazing, protective, and loving dog.

I was unaware that I was supporting dog breeders while shelters were overrun with animals waiting for loving homes. I am making better decisions now. I realize that more people are learning about the sad reality of puppy mills and breeders and that they do not condone them. By letting others know, we are educating people about bad conditions and encouraging others to adopt their companion animals from animal shelters instead of purchasing them from breeders.

Lily is a loving dog and an adored member of our family. She is also an impressive guard dog. She sits beside me and keeps watch, even as I write this book. Lily senses when I need her. When we bought our home, we temporarily stayed in a condominium before taking possession of the house. We later discovered that Lily was not allowed in the rental. It was too late to find another temporary residence for the family. We found a dog sitter for her, but she hopped a fence and escaped his facility after a few days.

Lily was found on the side of the highway by an elderly couple while she was trying to make her way home to us. Lily's instincts and journey home remind me of a television show I watched as a child called *The Littlest Hobo*. I will always remember the joy of being reunited with her. It was clear that Lily wanted to come home. It has been over a decade since we brought Lily home, and she is irreplaceable. That being said, she is a large dog, she is very protective, and she wants attention. As well, she's not the friendliest dog in the neighborhood with other dogs, and gets jealous so she was not overjoyed when we adopted our next fur friend, Freddie!

Fabulous Freddie

Freddie is an adorable, black, four-year-old, miniature rescue poodle. We named him after the famous lead singer of the British rock band Queen: Freddie Mercury. He has a fun and feisty personality to match his name! Coincidentally, he has the loudest bark. He thinks he is a rock star and a doggie diva. He is also a sweet and shy boy. A small dog breed rescue Button noses took Freddie and saved him from a puppy-breeding operation.

I was grieving the loss of Charlie when I met Freddie. He was born with a luxated patella, a common genetic condition found in puppy-mill dogs. I quickly bonded with this little fur baby and fell in love with his spunky and magnetic personality. He does tricks for us and lies down on his back to be petted. He has quirks like putting his chin on the counter when he is tired. He loves playing games like hide and seek and loves to be carried and being held in our arms.

Unfortunately, Lily was not initially enthusiastic when we brought Freddie home. She was curious but was protective of her food bowl. Freddie was an innocent, small puppy, which did not know boundaries and wanted to play. I worried that she would hurt this small fragile puppy. We worked with a dog trainer and decided that Freddie should not stay home alone with Lily, based on the trainer's advice. At that time, Freddie weighed only three pounds, and Lily weighed close to eighty pounds. Even if Lily unintentionally hurt him during play, it was not worth taking the risk. It took many months and a lot of patience before I was comfortable.

My mom loves poodles and fell in love with him, so they bonded. She happily spends time with Freddie, and we agreed to share him, so he has two moms. My favorite time with Freddie is going for long walks in the forest and then cuddling on the coach afterword.

Every animal is special, with individual needs and a unique purpose. Freddie came into my life, out of the blue; three months after Charlie passed away and helped me cope with this loss. Although Freddie is a rescue dog, he looks like a designer dog. People often compliment him on his looks, and I frequently get asked about his breeder. I am eager to share his rescue story of adoption from a small breed dog rescue. I enjoy interactions with people and share his story to show them that there are lovely animals waiting in animal rescues and shelters. They don't have to purchase their next pup from a breeder.

Pandemic Pets

During the COVID-19 pandemic, many people began to work from home, which resulted in more people fostering and adopting animals. Those who thought they did not have time to help an animal in need reconsidered and opened their hearts. During this unprecedented time, animal shelters got creative in the way that they let the public know about animals that were available for adoption because it was not possible to meet them first and form a physical connection. Video conferences, live streams, and social-media platforms were successfully being used.

Although this pandemic was a challenging time for humanity, there is some good news. People were sharing uplifting animal stories on social media. Perhaps this moment in time was an opportunity to move away from the Western culture of materialism, find more balance in life, form bonds and deepen connections with furry friends, and become more compassionate.

Puppy-mill breeding is a step backward for animal rights and society's moral progress. By condoning it, society is unconsciously devaluing not only animal life but also all life. Social change precedes legislative change. A societal shift needs to occur before there will be enough support for the revision of the applicable laws. Please encourage family and friends to adopt animals in need from animal shelters and rescues. Educate the community on the benefits of emptying a shelter cage and not supporting breeders and puppy mills. The realization that shelter animals are living creatures and sentient beings, which crave love and companionship just like humans do, is crucial for meaningful changes to adopt from shelters and revise legislation.

Pandemic Pet: A Beautiful Bunny Rescue Story

As discussed earlier, the real-life story of finding our beloved, beautiful bunny, Zoey, happened during the COVID-19 pandemic. She is a pandemic pet. I had a bunny when I was a young child. She was a big, friendly bunny with a grey and silver coat. I named her Susie (after me), but she was given away. Much like dogs and cats, rabbits are amazing, smart, loving, and social creatures. They crave company, love, and affection, so keeping them on your own is hard.

One true, touching story in the *Washington Post* was about a bunny rescue during the pandemic, which warmed my heart and put a smile on my face. It was especially endearing as we had rescued a rabbit, and I could somewhat relate to the story. A woman, Sarah Garone, who also happens to be a writer for the *Washington Post*, was asked to take care of a bunny for a few months. Here's the headline: "I Never Liked Animals. Then I Got a Pandemic Pet Bunny."[31] There was a nice photo of the author, Sarah holding her beautiful, black bunny named Nibbles and smiling. Sarah shares that Nibbles brought so much joy and comfort to the Garone family during the coronavirus pandemic. She had never shared her adult life with pets and hadn't grown up with animals. Sarah says that she had no idea how to care for a bunny.

Convinced by her children, who were feeling cooped up during the pandemic; she reluctantly agreed to take care of the bunny. As time went on, Sarah grew closer to Nibbles. While working from home, she realized that she enjoyed and needed the bunny's companionship. She found it easier to take care of a rabbit than dogs and cats. Also, Nibbles was very quiet and slept most of the day (rabbits are usually awake between dusk and dawn), so she was able to do her work. Ultimately, Sarah decided to keep the bunny. Even though she had a family (she was a wife and mother), she confessed that the authentic relationship with her bunny was less complicated than other relationships. It seems that Nibbles fulfilled a part of her that craved and needed uncomplicated love and made her feel less lonely and isolated.[32] More people are opening their hearts and homes to rescuing domestic rabbits.

Horses Are Majestic and Worthy Creatures

Although horses are known as gentle giants and can be trusted companions to their human caregivers, they are treated as disposable items when they are no longer able to serve human needs. For instance, racing horses are used for

---

[31] Sarah Garone, "Perspective|I Never Liked Animals. Then I Got a Pandemic Pet Bunny," *The Washington Post* (2 Apr. 2021), https://www.washingtonpost.com/lifestyle/2021/04/02/pet-bunny-pandemic.
[32] Ibid.

human entertainment, and then shipped to meat-slaughter facilities when they are past their primes. There is promising news on the horizon. The racing industry is losing ground, and the horrific horse-slaughter industry is being exposed.

In fact, a recent poll conducted by the American Society for the Prevention of Cruelty to Animals (ASPCA) has revealed that the majority of Americans oppose horse slaughter and that eighty-three percent of Americans oppose killing horses for human consumption.[33] This public sentiment is reflected in the laws of numerous US states, including California, Texas, New Jersey, and Illinois, which have passed legislation against this cruel practice and have placed a temporary ban on horse slaughter; but this is only a temporary solution.

Proponents of this horrific practice argue that a growing population of unwanted horses is a reason to allow their slaughter. Thankfully, horse lovers, enthusiasts, advocates, and activists have taken a stand against this practice. There are more humane and compassionate ways of dealing with this situation, including adoption, fostering, donating to help care for homeless horses at rescues, and expansion of horse sanctuaries. More work and advocacy efforts are needed to ensure that unwanted horses are not disposed of or sold for slaughter. By removing horses from their natural habitat, we have made them dependent on us for survival. They rely on our efforts to help save them. Companion animals, which include horses, are vulnerable members of society. Humans bred and raised these animals into a situation of dependence where they are unable to defend themselves from the institutions and methods that take their lives.

Chance Encounter with a Stray Dog

On a long day during my first year of law school I was on my way back to my apartment. My friend and I encountered a stray dog wandering the streets. He was a friendly, small, mixed-breed, beige-colored dog, but he seemed lost. He looked as though he needed a bath, as his fur was matted

---

[33] "New Poll Confirms That Overwhelming Majority of Americans Oppose Horse Slaughter," ASPCA, (February 9, 2022) https://www.aspca.org/news/new-poll-confirms-overwhelming-majority-americans-oppose-horse-slaughter.

and in knots. We couldn't leave the dog alone because night was approaching, so my friend offered to keep him at her place until the next day.

I called the local humane society and municipal animal shelter to find out if there was anyone searching for this sweet dog. As days passed and no one claimed him, I noticed that my friend and the dog were forming a bond, and there was a special connection. She decided to adopt the dog she called Benji and went on to live happily for many years. This personal story is another example of our responsibility to help and do something if we witness an animal in need. It was clear that Benji could not survive for long on the streets, and he relied on our human hearts to open and show compassion and love.

We can work together to do better for these vulnerable and silenced animals. There is opportunity to bring more education and awareness to the plight of animals. This is an important social justice cause. Thanks to powerful tools, such as social media, caring people are uniting to form stronger networks, and positive change is happening. However, a clear strategy for igniting change through larger community efforts is still missing. Although posting animal stories on social media does help, even greater impact is made if people gather in their communities in larger groups to start petitioning and creating publicity campaigns to garner broader societal support. For example, being vocal and lobbying politicians are crucial things to do so that more positive steps can be taken for progressive laws to be codified for stronger animal protection.

CHAPTER 3

The Animal Shelter Debacle: Change This Inconvenient Truth

Being a hero to someone, even if it is a dog, is a feeling like no other. Though it can be frustrating, it can be the most rewarding thing to give someone a second chance at a happy life.
—ELIZABETH PARKER

What *Really* Happens to Animals at Shelters

As I often say, animal shelters are supposed to be temporary places of protection, safety, and care for homeless companion animals while they wait for a loving family to take them home. To put it bluntly, that is not always the case. As a volunteer at a municipal shelter, I was made aware that healthy and adoptable animals lost their lives. I witnessed the sad reality that the lives of animals in shelters are numbered and taken too easily. It is a beauty contest and age matters. Those younger, cuter, cuddlier, friendlier, and better-looking animals had a chance of getting out of there. They were the lucky ones. Unfortunately, others were not so lucky. Senior pets, especially with medical issues, were often overlooked, and their lives were considered less worthy. With a simple injection of sodium pentobarbital ("the pink stuff," as they call it), yet another precious life was lost.

The typical animal-shelter story goes something like this: An unwanted dog or cat has been waiting in the shelter until his or her time is up. When the day finally arrives, that animal is taken out of the kennel—sometimes with tail wagging as the animal is happy to be taken out of the cage. Someone put on his or her leash for the last time. As that animal enters its destination—the room where it will die—that innocent animal begins to panic, as if he or she can sense death in the room. That animal's life was not treated fairly or regarded as worthy. Yet that is not true. Every animal's life is precious, and there are solutions to increase the chances of adoptions and to have happy endings.

Although it is more typical for elderly animals to be put down, younger animals and even puppies and kittens as well as shelter rabbits lose their lives too. I remember hearing one shelter worker's story about a kitten that was taken from her cage. She purred when one the shelter's staff held her. Apparently, it was kitten season, and the shelter was at full capacity.

A shelter technician (sometimes a veterinarian) has the job of administering the deadly injection, and sometimes the animal suffers before it unwillingly dies. When the dog or cat is finally killed—sometimes it takes a while—the body is stacked in a freezer with others. These helpless animals' corpses do not receive a burial. They are treated like trash and as if their lives are not worthy of any tribute.

Most troubling and heartbreaking in this broken animal-shelter system is that the humans who surrender their unwanted pets do not have to think about the almost certain fate of their animals if they don't get adopted. Drop off is easy street for most people. This reinforces society's collective perception that animals are disposable and replaceable items. They are commodities to be used and discarded rather than living beings.

I reiterate that animal shelters are supposed to be safe places that provide food, safety, and protection to homeless shelter animals. It is not always the case, and sadly, many innocent animals have lost their precious lives in these institutions. This is unacceptable, and every time an animal's life is taken, it is a failure of society. This was a difficult chapter to write. If more people adopted from shelters, more animals would leave these places alive. Therefore, it is not my intention to blame only animal shelters for their faulty institutions. Rather, the intent of this chapter is to awaken readers to the dire situation of shelter animals and to help them realize that it's a community-wide responsibility and societal problem, which requires motivation and effort to change the shelter system. There is ripe opportunity for change, and the good news is that the shelter situation is improving. My hope is to motivate readers to learn more and be involved so that we can turn animal shelters back into places of protection.

Currently, no government institution or animal organization is obligated to tabulate animal statistics. However, if you check the American Society for the Prevention to Cruelty Act's (ASPCA) website, you will find the latest euthanasia statistics, which is based, in part, on Shelter Animals Count data and other known and estimated sources from 2019.

> Approximately 6.3 million companion animals enter U.S. animal shelters nationwide every year. Of those, approximately 3.1 million are dogs and 3.2 million are cats. We estimate that the number of dogs and cats entering U.S. shelters annually has declined from approximately 7.2 million in 2011. The biggest decline was in dogs (from 3.9 million to 3.1 million). Each year, approximately 920,000 shelter animals are euthanized (390,000 dogs and 530,000 cats). The number of dogs and cats euthanized in U.S. shelters annually has declined from approximately 2.6 million in 2011.[34]

We can see from these ASPCA statistics that the situation is improving. However, there are still far too many cats, dogs, and other vulnerable animals losing their lives daily. The numbers are too high, somewhat shocking, and totally unacceptable. We will win when there are no healthy and adoptable animals left in the shelter system. Before that time comes, we can double our efforts to find solutions and save their lives. I dedicate this chapter to shelter animals. I want to give those animals that are sitting in their lonely cages and waiting for a loving home and those unlucky ones that have lost their lives a voice.

It is important to understand the other person's perspective. I hope that

---

[34] **"Pet Statistics," American Society for the Prevention of Cruelty to Animals (2022), https://www.aspca.org/helping-people-pets/shelter-intake-and-surrender/pet-statistics.**

readers can try to put themselves in the place of a shelter animal. What does it feel like for a social creature like a dog to live in solitary confinement? What does it feel like to live in a family's home and then get dumped into an unfamiliar place and left alone? What does it feel like to be uncertain of where you are or if you will ever find a loving home again?

Trying to see their perspectives and to relate to their personal experiences brings us closer to the sad fate of these vulnerable creatures. We can empathize with their challenges, but can we understand their situations? Why have some animal shelters become mass slaughterhouses? Sadly, the animal shelter system is flawed because it permits the lives of animals to be regarded as unworthy, disposable, and easily discarded when they continue to take the lives of shelter animals. For this reason, shelter animals desperately need humans to speak up for them.

The internet has been a helpful place to speak up for shelter animals and increase the chance for their exposure and visibility for adoption. It has also led to challenges with people purchasing their pets online from unethical breeders and puppy mills. It is an endless and vicious cycle. Consider the following scenario. A purebred dog is purchased from an unethical breeder, who hasn't spayed or neutered it. Eventually, a litter of new puppies is born, which potentially creates more unwanted dogs that are left at an overrun and overpopulated shelter.

On the People for the Ethical Treatment of Animals (PETA) website it says, "On any given day in the United States, there are an estimated 70 million homeless dogs and cats struggling to survive."[35] The fact is that shelter animals are still being overbred and then killed, which is deeply troubling. Overpopulation is a huge problem. Every time a dog or cat is purchased online from a pet store, home breeder, or commercial breeder, it means that a shelter animal is losing a prospective opportunity to find a loving family and home. It also potentially faces future euthanasia. Buying dogs and cats as well as other pets from pet stores perpetuates animal-shelter killing and the continuation of overbreeding and puppy mills. It is a vicious cycle. Puppy mills are inhumane, high-volume dog-breeding facilities, which churn out puppies for profit while ignoring the needs of the pups and their mothers.

---

[35] "Companion Animal Frequently Asked Questions," PETA (5 May 2020), https://www.peta.org/issues/animal-companion-issues/companion-animals-faq.

They are commonly sold through the internet, in online classified ads, at flea markets, and in pet stores.[36]

The truth is that mothers in puppy mills are mistreated and often abused as they spend their entire lives in cramped cages and giving birth to litters, with little to no care, affection, or attention. When the dogs are no longer profitable, they are often abandoned or tragically killed.[37] The sad part of this situation is that people purchasing their pets online or from stores don't think about where the puppies' mothers come from. If you feel you must buy a dog from a breeder, please make sure that at least, you are doing your research and choosing an ethical breeder. Ethical breeders usually care about the animals. Often, they will invite you to their house and let you meet the parents of the puppy. You can usually sense that they care and that they are passionate about the particular breed. They will often educate you. Once the animals are no longer able to produce offspring, an ethical breeder will still love and care for them. I maintain that if you are considering a new addition to your family, it is best to adopt an animal from a shelter or rescue organization.

A Shelter Animal's Perspective

To begin to relate to the lives of shelter animals, we must try to see the situation through their eyes. With these new lenses and perspective, we become more sensitive and empathetic. We become aware that shelters can be lonely, scary, cold, and loud places.

In many municipal animal shelters, a surrendered or lost pet has a small window of opportunity—a seventy-two-hour period—to be reclaimed or adopted before potentially being killed. This is a fact that I hope will shock, awaken, and inspire many readers to speak up. Dumping a dog or cat at a high-intake animal shelter may not be the best solution or preserve life. Finding a loving home is a safe and emotionally stable option. Zack Skow, founder of the California-based rescue Marlet's Mutts said it passionately when referring to shelters: "The vast majority of dogs don't make it out

---

[36] "Stopping Puppy Mills," The Humane Society of the United States, https://www.humanesociety.org/all-our-fights/stopping-puppy-mills.
[37] Ibid.

alive."[38] The chance of being adopted drops drastically if they are older, especially if they are seniors or have any health concerns.

Being forced into a tiny cage alone is somewhat like being in jail. In municipal shelters, these vulnerable animals face ultimately deaths within a few days of entering the institution if they are not adopted. They are helpless creatures with no voice as they wait alone in a cold and dark room for a second chance at life—for someone to take them into a loving forever home. Millions of shelter animals do not find that second chance. Instead, their lives are shortened, and their bodies leave the shelter in a garbage bag.

Although some animals might not experience stress while enclosed in an animal shelter, many do. Forced into small enclosures for prolonged periods while being frightened, sad, and surrounded by loud noises, they can experience sensory overload. Shelter stress may negatively alter the animal's true personality. The animal shelter's atmosphere can make that loving dog or cat totally withdrawn and sad or in more serious cases, aggressive and depressed. A seemingly far-from-perfect furry friend might not be itself in the strange and unnatural environment.

A dog placed into a shelter is naturally scared. In turn, this can make the dog seem less adoptable. Shelter animals experience a sensory overload that is far different from what they are comfortable with while in a loving and familiar environment. A fearful dog will not act like itself and may not interact well with other animals or people. The dog may show signs of aggression or fear, even though it may not be aggressive by nature. They are frightened animals, which may avoid human interaction based solely on fear and not because they want to avoid humans.

I recall one shelter's staff member recounting a situation about a sweet, shy, younger dog (eighteen months) that was so scared, it took her an hour to get the dog to take a treat from her hand. After following up a few days later, she was told that he must be put down because he was too scared, and no one wanted to adopt him for this reason. This is a perfect example of how a misconception can prematurely end an otherwise loving dog's life.

There are many similar heartbreaking stories like this one. There are happy endings too. For instance, Amber Carlton shared a heartwarming story of when she blogged about a happy ending after adopting her loving

---

[38] Christian Cotroneo, "If Everyone Reads This, The Shelters Would Be Empty," The Dodo (31 Dec. 2015), www.thedodo.com/dog-shelter-guide-adoptions-1532460278.html.

dog, Mayzie, from the Second Chance Animal Rescue in Colorado. Mayzie had been chained up for the first two years of her life. She had spent her youth living in fear. Kept outside with minimal food, water, and shelter, she spent her life in isolation. Everything terrified her, including hardwood floors, stairs, kitchen appliances, the barbeque, and the umbrella on the patio set, wind, ceiling fans, getting into a car, and getting out of a car. It was devastating. Over time and with a lot of patience from Amber, Mayzie was able to jump out of her fearful bubble and enjoy life.[39]

Temperament tests are typically conducted before allowing dogs to be adopted into families.[40] If a dog fails this test by showing a lack of desire to respond positively to humans and other animals, it can be considered a danger to the public, and it will not be put up for adoption. The dog's lack of a positive response to others may be a direct result of being placed in a shelter, as opposed to being an innate personality trait. Being scared in their small enclosures in the animal shelter or showing signs of food aggression may trigger a failing grade for this test. Food aggression in an animal shelter's environment is a common characteristic in dogs, which would otherwise not possess this trait. For many reasons it is completely out of the animal's control, but it may fail temperament tests, and the result may render it less desirable for adoption.

Who is Responsible for the Animal Shelter Debacle?

The sad reality is that in some situations, a shelter animal's days are numbered. There is an expiration and exit date, especially in municipal government run shelters. The good news is that this reality is changing as more shelters commit to work with rescues, find homes, and not kill homeless animals, even when the shelters are overcrowded. In those cases, foster homes and rescues can be a tremendous help. On the other hand, there are shelters (mostly privately run) that don't kill animals in their care.

To truly comprehend the severity of the animal shelter debacle, we

---

[39] Amber Carlton, "Have a Fearful Dog? These Training Tips Will Help," Dogster (23 Mar. 2021), www.dogster.com/lifestyle/dog-behavior-training-tips-fearful-dogs.
[40] Sheila Segurson D'Arpino, "Behavioral Assessment in Animal Shelters," Maddie's Fund (2007), www.maddiesfund.org/behavioral-assessment-in-animal-shelters.htm.

cannot put the entire blame on the shelters. We must ask the reason why so many companion animals are dumped at shelters in the first place. By understanding the root cause and source of the shelter debacle, we can take action to help reduce the number of incoming animals that are entering the shelter system and stop this vicious cycle. As author Craig Brestrup noted,

> The truly guilty, being the source of the problem, are those who choose to have animals without choosing to do so in a morally responsible way. That way would be to recognize the value inherent in the life of an animal and to actively respect it, to take charge of its reproduction, to recognize that to take in an animal is to take on a relationship of commitment for his or lifetime. When we achieve that vision, the killing simply stops.[41]

The single most reported reason for surrendering a dog is that it exhibits behavioral problems. [42] Although some instances of behavioral problems may be impossible to reverse, in most cases, many simple solutions are overlooked. For instance, some problematic tendencies of our beloved canine friends may include biting and aggression, which can be serious. In many situations, however, pet parents have mistaken the symptoms of a fearful dog for one that exhibits aggressive tendencies.

A frustrated and fearful dog that is scared may show signs of an aggressive or vicious dog, such as biting, showing its teeth, and barking. Biting and barking because of fear are not behavioral problems but are unfortunate reactions to unfamiliar and stressful environments. By identifying that the dog is scared, proactive steps can be taken to help develop the dog's confidence and to avoid future bites.

Many stray dogs end up in the shelter system because of irresponsible humans and overbreeding. Unless you are a certified breeder, dogs and other pets should be neutered and spayed to prevent unwanted litters from filling up animal shelters. A female cat is capable of breeding three times a

---

[41] Craig Brestrup, *Supra*, footnote 32.
[42] *Supra*, footnote 32.

year, with an average of four kittens each time.[43] Female dogs are capable of breeding twice a year, with an average of six-to-ten puppies per litter.[44]

One un-spayed cat and her kittens can produce over 420,000 kittens within a seven-year period.[45] Such a high number would easily exhaust the resources of hundreds of animal shelters. One un-spayed dog and her puppies can produce over 97,000 puppies within a seven-year period.[46] To avoid overpopulation, guardians must get their companion animals neutered and spayed. By taking individual responsibility, we can prevent premature and unnecessary deaths. It takes one irresponsible human to instigate a domino effect and contribute to overpopulated animal shelters across North America.

Based on the 2017 *Animal Shelter Statistics Survey* conducted by Humane Canada, the majority of dogs taken into shelters across Canada were strays (about 41 percent) and surrendered dogs (about 34 percent).[47] Similarly, most cats taken into shelters were strays (48 percent) and surrendered cats (38 percent).[48] In 2017 alone, Canadian shelters took in over 87,000 cats and 33,000 dogs.[49] To respond to the demand of housing strays and unwanted animals, many shelters across Canada and the US operate over maximum capacity, preventing incoming animals from receiving much needed care. Although most of these animals are either adopted or returned to the original guardians, around 9 percent of these dogs and 6 percent of these cats, which are deemed healthy, treatable, or adoptable, are euthanized to make space for incoming animals.[50]

Although this survey shows a decline in euthanasia rates since 2007,[51] any number over zero is still too high. Of the 9 percent of dogs euthanized, 5 percent were puppies. Of the 6 percent of cats euthanized, around 25

[43] "Petfix—Top 10 Reasons," Operation Petfix Northeast Ohio (2007), https://www.petfixnortheastohio.org/spay-neuter/top-ten-reasons.shtml.

[44] "2017 Animal Shelter Statistics—Humane Canada," Humane Canada (2018), https://humanecanada.ca/wp-content/uploads/2020/03/2017-Canadian-Animal-Shelter-Statistics.pdf.

[45] Ibid.

[46] Ibid.

[47] Ibid.

[48] Ibid.

[49] Ibid.

[50] Ibid.

[51] Ibid.

percent were kittens.[52] Regrettably, many healthy, treatable, and otherwise adoptable shelter animals are euthanized simply because their time limit at the shelter has run out. The excuse is that they have to make room for new animals that are arriving. And the vicious cycle continues like a revolving door. Even with minimal efforts, we can change this situation and reduce the number of animals losing their lives at shelters.

High-Kill Shelters versus No-Kill Shelters

High-kill animal shelters often do not result in happy endings for anyone. Based on definitions by those who operate no-kill shelters, they say that high-kill shelters euthanize more than 10 percent of homeless animals.[53] These shelters typically operate beyond their maximum capacity and euthanize animals that are there past seventy-two hours, to allow new arrivals the same chance to be re-homed or adopted.

On the other side of the fence is the no-kill shelter. The main difference between a high-kill shelter and a no-kill shelter is that animals placed in a no-kill shelter will not be euthanized to make space for new arrivals. Typically, to be classified as a no-kill shelter, the shelter must maintain a live release rate of 90 percent or more. In other words, the shelter must not euthanize more than 10 percent of the animals under their care. As such, these shelters simply cannot admit as many animals as high-kill shelters can.

The beginning of the No Kill Movement as we know it today can be traced back to 1858. At that time, Elizabeth Morris and Anne Waln founded the first animal shelter in the US.[54] The descendants of these two women attempted but failed to operate these shelters as no-kill ones due to the inherent complexity of handling the stray dog and cat overpopulation at that time. To combat this problem, widely available sterilization procedures would have to be provided. Fortunately, in 1923, the American Veterinary

---

[52] Ibid.

[53] "Defining No Kill," PAWS Chicago (2019), www.pawschicago.org/no-kill-mission/about-no-kill/defining-no-kill.

[54] Merritt Clifton, et al, "Who Invented No-Kill? (It Wasn't Nathan Winograd)," (28 February 2019), www.animals24-7.org/2015/10/25/who-invented-no-kill.

Medical Association approved surgeries for sterilizing dogs and cats, but it did not become affordable until the mid-1950s.

In September of 1995, the first No Kill Conference was held in Phoenix, Arizona.[55] As a result of widespread implementation, many success stories have been documented. The most prominent early success was in Pueblo, Colorado, where in 2016, a documented animal euthanasia rate of 6.25 per one thousand of the human population had significantly dropped from a rate of 35.7 per one thousand of the human population in 1999 due to no-kill shelters. More remarkable were twenty-three similar drop rates of euthanasia that could be seen across the United States due to the implementation no-kill shelters.[56]

These animal shelters do not come without peril. Since 2007, solely pursuing the 90 percent live release rate resulted in thirty-five humane deaths from sixty-one re-homed dogs.[57] One of the largest failures of a no-kill shelter can be traced to the Las Vegas Lied Animal Shelter in February of 2007.[58] This shelter's attempt to become no-kill too early resulted in an excessive amount of euthanasia. Nearly one thousand of the 1,800 animals had to be killed.[59] "About 150 of the animals were ill, and 850 were believed to have been exposed to both parvovirus and distemper," which negatively affected the health of humans helping at the shelters.[60]

McHugh-Smith, one of the first ever US shelter directors working in Colorado said, "Animal sheltering is ... complex."[61] In other words, besides a fixed release rate number, there are many variables that must be considered when measuring the care provided to animals. Although McHugh-Smith was an advocate for no-kill sheltering early in her career and one of the first to advocate for the no-kill movement, she quickly came to realize that "[looking solely on] a live release rate is not ... socially conscious sheltering."[62]

---

[55] "No-Kill Timeline," Best Friends Animal Society (10 April 2019), bestfriends.org/about/our-story/no-kill-timeline.

[56] Merritt Clifton, "'No-Kill' Debacle: Will Pueblo Bring 'Responsible Sheltering' into Vogue?" (22 Apr. 2019), www.animals24-7.org/2019/04/16/no-kill-debacle-will-pueblo-bring-responsible-sheltering-into-vogue.

[57] Ibid.

[58] Ibid.

[59] Ibid.

[60] Ibid.

[61] Ibid.

[62] Ibid.

Unintended Consequences

Many unintended consequences can result from the well-intentioned no-kill policies at animal shelters that are prevalent across the US and Canada. For starters, many animals in need of safety and protection may be refused entry because of the strict 90 percent live release requirements. In some cases, dangerous dogs can enter the community of no-kill shelters and remain until their death because they cannot be re-homed or adopted. In other cases, animal shelters may refuse entry simply because there is no more space. In other cases, the system fails, and animals are at risk because some no-kill shelters operate beyond their maximum capacity, and they are unable to provide adequate care to every animal. Several unfortunate events demonstrate the unintended consequences of no-kill shelters.

In one case, a dog named River was taken to a no-kill shelter on February 16. Since the shelter had been operating at overcapacity, River was not seen by a veterinarian until February 25.[63] In another case, a dog with a broken pelvis was granted entry to a shelter operating beyond capacity.[64] This vulnerable dog was not seen by a veterinarian for four days or provided appropriate medication until a month after his arrival. The dog was brought into the shelter on January 12, with reports of being hit by a car.[65] Nonetheless, the benefits of no-kill versus kill shelters far outweigh some of the concerns. In these cases (and others), dogs and cats that are brought to a no-kill shelter remain alive and receive medical care and attention.

As mentioned earlier, in the United States, the definition of a no-kill shelter varies. Another term known as vision zero has been "diluted for the sake of convenience".[66] Many animal shelters have agreed to a live release rate of 90 percent while other shelters, such as the No Kill Advocacy Center (NKAC) in California, define no-kill as "saving every animal that is not 'irremediably suffering,'" which is a much better definition. As Nathan Winograd, the NKAC founder, said, "You count all the noses coming in, and you count all the noses going out."[67]

---

[63] Ibid.
[64] Ibid.
[65] Ibid.
[66] Ibid.
[67] Ibid.

Shelter Secrets: Red-Listing

The following story takes place in the summer of 2019 and describes the horrors that shelter animals endure during their short lives. An animal shelter was operating beyond its maximum capacity. Without joining forces with another shelter, animals were being euthanized by the hour to make room for new arrivals. As I write this story, one friendly dog is being held in the shelter and awaiting a new home. Without anyone to adopt him, sadly, he will most likely be euthanized because there is no space to keep him.

Similarly at another shelter, there lives a sweet boxer waiting for a home. Unfortunately, he has been red listed. In other words, if someone does not come in time to adopt the dog and bring him home, he will be euthanized. These two dogs' lives were prematurely ended. This is a daily, if not hourly, decision made for animals in shelters across North America. This is a preventable tragedy.

Pet Pound Seizure

I was shocked to learn that pet pound seizure exists in the province of Ontario, Canada, where I live. I made this discovery when I was finishing my thesis research for my master of law degree on the topic of animal-shelter euthanasia. I stumbled upon a provincial law that legally permits people's pet dogs and cats to be sold to research facilities. In other words, people who surrender or lose their pets might not know that they can be sold to a research facility anywhere in Ontario and under the law.

My research led me to one woman's story, which touched me deeply. Laurie Bishop shared this heartbreaking story of losing her best friend and beloved pet dog, named Royal, who was a gentle senior citizen of thirteen years, a golden retriever, and a family dog. He wandered off the property. Sadly, a concerned neighbor found Royal and called animal control, thinking this friendly dog would get adopted. This is a horrific example of what can happen to our companion animals in shelters. It shows us how vulnerable their lives are. Understandably, Laurie was devastated when she realized that Royal was missing, and she spent countless hours looking for him. She found out that Royal, who had lived with her his entire life, was sold by a local animal-control facility for research. She was devastated by this tragic end to his life. She was upset that animal control had held Royal for the minimum seventy-two hours, which was required by law, but that they did not try to contact her, even though he was wearing ID tags.

When shelter animals are seized by research facilities, they are subjected to painful tests and endure significant stress—emotional and physical pain. It is incomprehensible to think that our beloved companions can be taken from us, subjected to pain and suffering, are used as inanimate subjects for scientific research, and then are killed.[68] I look at my beloved companion animal Lily, a fragile senior citizen in her golden years, as she sits on her cozy bed, and I cannot imagine the terrible feeling that Laurie endured when she lost her dog Royal.

There are too many sad and horrifying stories that go undocumented in the animal-shelter world. Unfortunately, many healthy and adoptable animals are euthanized daily, with no trace of their existence ever to emerge again. When a dog or cat is surrendered to an animal shelter, that animal goes through sensory overload. The impression that they make because of their at-face-value personality can scare away keen prospective adopters. That animal's time limit is reached, and it may be killed and never heard or seen again. We have seen from this chapter that unfortunately, animal shelters are not always safe places and they can be dangerous for vulnerable companion animals that end up there.

The Bright Side: There is Much Hope on the Horizon for Shelter Animals

The good news is that there is hope on the horizon for a better future, where animals are adopted from shelters, and shelters are transformed into sanctuaries and loving places. Although this chapter has highlighted the dark side and unfortunate fate for shelter animals that are not adopted, I leave you with hope. It takes community-wide effort and proactive initiatives to enact positive change in the companion animal world. If we can

---

[68] "No Pets in Research," Animal Alliance Canada (2022), https://www.animalalliance.ca/campaigns/pets-research/.

view every shelter animal as a unique creature with inherent value, it will be easier to take the option of euthanasia off the table and to consider all other alternatives. Saving every life becomes a priority. Every shelter animal gets a second chance and finds a happy ending.

There are shelters across North America doing wonderful work at saving animals. Most of them are private, which means that they do not receive funding from the government but that they are run by volunteers. I started my position with the Etobicoke Humane Society (EHS) as the executive director of operations and programs. I am responsible for managing the entire adoption program for cats and dogs at the EHS shelter. I am grateful to be part of this amazing team and animal shelter and this is a dream come true. I have always wanted to work at an animal shelter. EHS is a no-kill private volunteer shelter. Its mandate on EHS's website says,

> We (EHS) are completely dedicated to the well-being of our animals and take extra steps to ensure they receive the care they need. This includes veterinary care and special training for animals with behavioral issues. For dogs, this can include spending time at a training facility where they have access to one on one time with expert trainers.[69]

I have been spending time getting to know the individual dog's and cat's stories from EHS's website and seeing photos and videos of the longer-stay dogs at EHS. The definition of longer-stay dogs is self-descriptive. It refers to dogs that have been at the shelter or in foster care for longer periods as they wait to find loving homes. Older dogs and cats are not as popular as younger ones are, even though they can make wonderful companions, especially to seniors or families that want a calmer pet. Every shelter animal has a story of its own and arrives with a past and history that is sometimes unknown. The animal shelter takes a chance and gives that animal a second leash on life.

The real intent and purpose of animal shelters is supposed to be to shield and protect vulnerable homeless animals as they wait for a loving home, as stated above. Shelters such as EHS show us that they care and that there are solutions for shelter animals. Shelters can really overcome this

---

[69] Etobicoke Humane Society (2022), https://etobicokehumanesociety.com/about-us/.

shelter debacle. In addition to finding ways to improve the situation for these animals, such as providing basic needs including food, shelter, care, and medical needs, fostering and sanctuary programs save lives. Eventually, my hope is that all animal shelters can become safe places of tender care, love, and protection. In the future, we will see this happen more frequently (We delve deeper into this in the next two chapters). We will realize that there are sustainable and lifesaving solutions for every healthy and adoptable animal to remain safe.

This chapter has highlighted what happens to animals in some shelters. There are many animal shelters across North America doing their best to save shelter animals. I have demonstrated that unfortunately, some well-intended policies can result in unintended consequences. At the end of the day, the animals that are not adopted pay the hefty price and suffer. We can alleviate the suffering of homeless animals and the burden on shelters by adopting animals. It is the responsibility of individual humans and the collective responsibility of the entire community to care about the plight of shelter animals. The burden should not be left solely on the animal shelters. It is also the responsibility of humans to take care of their pets and not dump them at shelters. It requires commitment from individuals and the community to help save shelter animals. If you're looking to fill your life with joy and want to bring home an animal, please support your local animal shelter and adopt an animal that is waiting for a loving home. You will not regret it, and you will save a precious animal's life!

CHAPTER 4

Solitary Confinement for Dogs and Cats: Second Chances

The Question is Not, Can They Reason, nor
Can They Talk, but Can They Suffer?"
—JEREMY BENTHAM

As I often say, animals give so much and ask for little in return. Keeping them confined is cruel. Please speak up for chained dogs and confined cats.

Companion animals are social creatures bred to live with humans. They depend on humans to fulfill their basic needs, protect them, and provide emotional and psychological support. Dogs are pack animals and descendants of wolves. They crave close connection and the company of their pack members—other dogs, animals, or members of their human family.

To make dogs happy, humans need to provide them with food, water, and daily walks. They need to give them lots of attention, enrichment, and love. In return, dogs give a lot back to us. They can provide emotional support and enrich our lives with their unconditional love, friendship, and loyalty.

There is so much evidence for the mutually strong human-animal bond that exists in this unique relationship. In fact, numerous scientific studies have researched and documented this mutually beneficial relationship. They have shown positive effects to the health of animals that have formed bonds with their human caregivers. This demonstrates to us that it is a reciprocal relationship. In other words, it is not only humans that reap health benefits from spending time caressing and cuddling their pets but also animals benefit from this relationship. As stated in the article "People and Companion Animals: It Takes Two to Tango," "For instance, stroking an animal was found to reduce the animal's heart rate.[70]

Other work has shown that dogs with caregivers who consider them as social partners have lower levels of morning cortisol,[71] suggesting that the way dogs are integrated into their human families' lives impacts the dogs' levels of stress. "Positive human-animal interactions even have effects at the neurotransmitter level (increased levels of phenyl acetic acid and catabolite phenyl ethylamine) in humans and animals, suggesting that both gain benefits from this interaction."[72] It can be logically inferred from this scientific evidence that when our animal friends are left alone and abandoned, negative health effects can occur.

The touching real-life story of Bailey and the Windermans demonstrates how human-animal relationships can have positive health effects. Bailey is an eight year old Chihuahua mix. He was condemned to an animal shelter in Huntington Beach, California. Fortunately, Bailey was rescued and was adopted by Mr. and Mrs. Winderman in 2018. "They sense when you're not feeling good, and they're happy to see you every day," said Don Winderman, a six-year veteran of the United States Marine Corp.[73] This family opened their home to three rescue dogs, including Bailey, and counted on them for emotional support. This heartwarming story goes to show the big golden hearts that animals are willing to share with us—to make us happy.

---

[70] Catherine Amiot, Brock Bastian, Pim Martens, "People and Companion Animals: It Takes Two to Tango," *BioScience*, Volume 66, Issue 7 (01 July 2016), 552-560, https://doi.org/10.1093/biosci/biw051.

[71] Schoberl et al., "Effects of Owner-Dog Relationship and Owner Personality on Cortisol Modulation in Human-Dog Dyads," Anthrozoös, 25:2 (2012), 199–214, DOI 10.2752/175303712X13316289505422,.

[72] Odendaal and Lehmann, "The Role of Phenylethylamine During Positive Human-Dog Interaction," *Acta Vet*, (2000), 183-188, https://doi.org/10.2754/avb200069030183.

[73] Aliya Jasmine, "Clear the Shelters Dog Provides 'Emotional Support' for Veteran, Family," *NBC Connecticut* (2 July 2019), www.nbcconnecticut.com/news/national-international/veteran-adopts-dog-clear-the-shelters-512067011.html?_osource=mobilesharebar.

Chained Dogs

Chaining a dog outside one's home and leaving the dog alone for hours is not the right way to treat it or any other furry friend. Coincidentally, when I started writing this chapter, I turned on my computer, and there was an MSN animal news story that caught my attention. I was shocked when I opened the link to the story from The Dodo. The title of the story, "Dog Who Was Chained up His Whole Life Looks Completely Different Now," was right on point with the topic that I was contemplating for this book.

At first glance, the photo of the dog (Odin) was adorable. He was smiling, and he appeared to be in good health, but then I scrolled down the page and felt sick to my stomach. There were more photos of an earlier version of this beautiful Alaskan malamute, and he was unrecognizable. I cried when I saw these images. He was in horrendous physical condition, and he looked like a barely recognizable skeleton. He was either severely burned or suffered frost bite from being left outside on a chain and in the cold. It was obvious that this poor, innocent creature had been neglected. By the time he was found, he was barely alive, but thankfully, this story had a happy ending. Many innocent dogs are left chained up and do not survive.

Odin's former owners (I would not even dare to call them pet parents, guardians, or caregivers) were a couple of breeders who used this dog, among others, solely for breeding purposes. He was treated like a commodity, used for profit, and left to suffer outside. He was relieved of this horrible situation when in October 2018; he was picked up by animal-rescue workers from Southern Pines Animal Shelter and Southern Cross Animal Rescue of Mississippi.

Sydney initially fostered Odin and ended up adopting him and bringing him back to life. Odin's journey and transformation is truly incredible and gives us hope that there are caring humans who are willing to save animal lives.

This extreme form of animal neglect should have been punishable with severe criminal penalties. Sydney had stated that when Odin was first rescued, he did not know how to behave in her home. It was apparent that he had not been treated like a dog.

Odin's remarkable story provides a glimpse of hope that even after neglect, there can be a happy dog and justice for other poor animals in similar circumstances. He was able to forgive humans, and he has a promising future. In the last photo, Oden and Sydney are smiling. He has been transformed into an incredibly happy and well-cared-for dog.

Bylaws for chaining dogs vary across jurisdictions. It is an abhorrent practice, and it should be banned everywhere. Although it is legal to tether and/or chain a dog in some places, there are restrictions outlined in legislation: tethering length, allowing the dog the freedom to move around unhindered, and of course, water and food, which are the dog's basic needs for survival. However, I hold the view that leaving dogs chained in solitude goes against the principle of social justice and that it is animal cruelty. Chaining up dogs is a cruel and barbaric practice. Dogs are domesticated and social animals, which should live with their human families. They need physical and emotional affection and tender care.

The promising news is that most people share the view of no longer tolerating this type of animal cruelty, including chaining up dogs. More people report incidents to the community. In the US, two Senators introduced the first ever animal abuse law, which makes the abuse of an animal a felony crime. The Preventing Animal Cruelty and Torture Act (PACT) outlaws and prosecutes animal abusers and killers. PACT amends the criminal code to no longer allow people to intentionally harm animals or cause serious bodily harm. Animal abusers convicted of such crimes will face felony charges and stiff fines. A prosecutor can sentence them up to seven years in prison. This is an important development and a societal shift. It holds people accountable for their actions against animals. In cases of neglect, it is more difficult to prove that someone willfully harmed their companion animal.

How You Can Help

You can contact your local animal authorities to gain a better understanding of the actions you can take if you see a chained dog. The Humane Society of the United States (HSUS) has online resources and information on dog chaining laws throughout the US and provides help regarding what you can do about it. Please do not ignore a dog that is being neglected. Encourage others to do the same. So much can be done when you want to make a difference: contacting local animal authorities at the municipal level, getting involved in advocacy efforts, and political campaigning so that we can end this cruelty.

Confined Cats in Cages

If you have ever visited an animal shelter and entered the area where homeless cats are kept, you might be sad and surprised to see that most of the time they are confined in small cages. It was quite stressful for me to witness cats in these cages, all alone, with barely any space to move. I cannot imagine how stressful those poor creatures feel being left in cages. I enjoyed letting out some of the cats when I was allowed to as a volunteer cat groomer. In other cases, I could see the other cats scratching at the cages, obviously crying for help to be let outside.

It is almost unthinkable how uncomfortable confined cats can be while locked inside alone. I strongly urge people to please consider adopting cats from shelters. Although there are many shelters nowadays that provide more space for them to roam, it is still the norm in some types of shelters—especially municipal and government-run facilities—to keep cats confined. If you cannot adopt a cat, consider fostering for a while to help relieve the shelters from being at overcapacity and allowing those cats to have temporary care and comfort in a loving home.

Solitary Shelter Animals

In 2016 when former US President Barack Obama was still in the Oval Office, he banned solitary confinement for juveniles who were locked up in prison, citing the damaging psychological effects of being isolated for extended periods of time. Similarly, locking up or chaining animals for extended periods of isolation can cause psychological trauma. Animals left in these sad situations are not criminals serving jail time, and they should not be treated this way. We can do better than sentencing our canine and feline friends to solitary confinement, and this can be achieved when we change the laws and impose hefty penalties and jail time for those convicted of these heinous crimes.

Dogs that suffer from the traumatic experience of being chained and isolated often become less trusting of humans and other animals. As a result of their extreme suffering and neglect, it may come as no surprise that they can become aggressive and unfriendly. Consequently, they are less likely to be adopted into a new home. I would even go as far as saying that locking up dogs in animal shelters and leaving them isolated without proper socialization can have damaging long-term consequences that are counterintuitive to the mandate of an animal shelter's purpose: to provide animals with shelter and protection, to ensure that they are cared for, and to increase their chances of being adopted.

I am fortunate to have many friends on social media who support and share my passion and love for animals. Through sharing uplifting and positive animal news stories and pictures, I have learned that there are many people like me, who care deeply about the well-being of animals. This platform provides an opportunity to engage with others in the animal caring community, who are directly involved in taking care of homeless animals, shelter animals, and rescues and who are promoting the adoption of shelter animals. To give you a shelter dog's perspective, here's a touching shelter dog story called "Do I Go Home Today?" It was written by Sandi Thompson, who portrayed it through the eyes of an animal.

> The family brought me home, all cradled in their arms. They cuddled me and smiled at me and said I was full of charm. They played with me and laughed at me and showered me with toys. I sure did love my family, especially the little girls and boys. The children loved to feed me; they gave me special treats. They even let me sleep with them—all snuggled in their sheets. I used to go for walks, often several times a day. They even fought to hold the leash, I'm very proud to say. These are the things I'll not forget—a cherished memory. Now that I'm in the shelter, I am without my family ... They said that I was out of control and would have to live outside. This I didn't understand, although I tried and tried. The walks stopped, one by one, they said they hadn't the time. I wish I could change things; I wish I knew my crime. My life

became so lonely in the backyard, on a chain. I barked and barked all day long to keep from going insane. They brought me to the shelter but were embarrassed to say why. They said I caused an allergy, and then they each kissed me goodbye. If I'd only had some training when I was a little pup, I wouldn't have been so hard to handle when I was all grown up. You only have one day left, I heard the worker say. Does that mean I have a second chance? Do I go home today?[74]

Hopefully, this story shows us how to relate to this situation and sense the world from a shelter animal's perspective. It seems difficult to be abandoned at an animal shelter after experiencing life with a home and a family. When I first read this touching story, I immediately thought about my beloved companions sitting in comfort. I sense them sitting by my side as I write this book or waiting for us to arrive home from work and the kids from school so that we can spend time together. I cannot imagine how horrible they would feel if they were abandoned. I imagine that you can sense the fear in this dog's tragedy and unthinkable fate.

I sensed that this dog from "Do I Go Home Today" had eagerly awaited and hoped that every time someone walked by his cage, he might get walked, or even better, he might find a loving human willing to take a chance on him and take him home.

Tools such as social media provide a plethora of information on animal rights, and a larger platform. It is an excellent way to share stories about homeless animals and information to save animal lives and give them voices. On one of my social media networks, an animal advocate posted a video of a pit bull-Staffordshire dog mix as he was crying, clawing, and trying to escape the confines of his lonely shelter cage. I felt heartbroken to read the post about an innocent dog locked up in jail. What was this dog's crime? He was born the wrong breed in a society that labels it as dangerous. This was a plea for someone to open his or her heart and adopt or foster this poor soul, as death was near in this so-called shelter if he overstayed his welcome.

It is estimated that thousands of innocent dogs and cats are killed

---

[74] Sandi Thompson, "Do I Go Home Today?" Rescue Every Dog Stories (2001), http://rescueeverydog.org/poetry.html.

in shelters every day. This is a sad reality, which we cannot continue to ignore. Even in this darkness, there is a glimmer of hope for a much happier future when this situation will improve, and this practice is no longer tolerated anywhere. The good news is that animal-shelter euthanasia rates have decreased over the years, thanks to the massive success of the No Kill Movement. As people take a stand for shelter animals and give them a voice, shelters have more accountability for transparency. They need to be committed to providing homeless animals in their care with protection, socialization, and affection, so they are ready to be adopted. It really is a two-way relationship, where both the shelters and the community need to be equally committed to ending the unnecessary killing of homeless pets in shelters.

Break the Shelter Stigma for Homeless Pets

There are many ways to get involved and to help shelter animals leave these institutions alive and make a fresh start. I think the most important strategy is to educate and bring awareness to this issue and to encourage others, including your friends and family, to adopt rather than purchase animals from breeders or pet stores. If more people choose to adopt animals from shelters, the result could be remarkable and break the shelter-adoption stigma. As well, the live-release rates would improve, and fewer animals would be confined to lonely cages. I want to reiterate this point, as I genuinely believe that the key to improving the situation for abandoned companion animals is to break the cycle of overrun shelters and needless killing by encouraging adoption. Intention and action play a big part in saving shelter animals' lives.

Thankfully, prominent animal welfare organizations such as Best Friends Animal Society (BFAS) are totally committed to eliminating homeless pets. Their mission is as follows:

> Every day, more than four thousand dogs and cats are killed in America's shelters, just because they don't have safe places to call home. But every day, there's something each of us can do to help save those lives. The mission of

Best Friends Animal Society is to bring about a time when there are No More Homeless Pets. We do this by helping end the killing in America's animal shelters through building community programs and partnerships across the nation. We believe that by working together we can Save Them All.[75]

I am very inspired by this organization's commitment to end shelter killing nationwide. As stated on their website, "We will reach no-kill in this country by 2025."[76]

The shared commitment of the community and the shelters working together to ensure that every cat and dog lives his or her natural life span can help save more lives nationwide. In other words, it takes a village. Helping shelter animals is a community-wide responsibility, which should not be left solely in the hands of the shelters. So many people in the community want to help, but they do not know how. This helpless attitude may lead some animal-loving and well-intentioned people in the community to turn a blind eye to an animal's suffering. I do not blame them. Knowledge is power.

The time is ripe for change and educating others. Many achievements have been accomplished recently in the animal sheltering world, including community-wide efforts. As a result, there have been many successes for the sanctity of our animal friends. The future of animal shelters still has much room for improvement. This goal can be achieved with the social acceptance of new ideas like socially conscious sheltering.

As well, breaking the stigma includes not labeling dogs based on their particular dog breed. In fact, there are no bad dogs, but rather, there are irresponsible guardians who do not train their dogs to behave. There are also unfortunate circumstances that contribute to a dog's behavior, such as an unstable beginning or being surrendered to a shelter or rescue. As well, other circumstances can lead to a dog behaving in an aggressive way, which we may never completely understand. It is worthwhile to try to rehabilitate the dog with a trainer and implement a program. Dogs want to please their

[75] Best friends Animal Society. "We are our Mission." (2022). https://bestfriends.org/who-we-are/our-mission.
[76] Ibid.

human families (guardians), and they will not bite or behave in an aggressive manner unless they are provoked.

Here is an example of a dog that was given a second chance at life. Before I begin to share the facts of this real-life story, it is estimated that up to half of the dogs deemed aggressive and exhibiting behavioral issues are killed before they reach the age of two.[77] Here's Jake's story. A five-year-old, larger rescue dog (the article does not disclose the breed) had bitten a family member. But it wasn't a minor incident. This bite resulted in over two hundred stitches. Dog trainer Kerry Vinson was contacted by Jason Taillier, who was Jake's human guardian—for a consultation. At that time, Kerry shares in the article that this was the worst dog-bite incident that he had been involved with, but nonetheless, he agreed to meet with Jason and Jake.

When meeting the dog, Kerry thought he could work with the dog safely, so he did. He provided Jason with a program, which he followed.[78] Thankfully, Jake had a loving family that gave him a second chance, and he went on to live for ten more years without any further dog-biting incidents or exhibiting aggressive behavior. He passed away at the ripe old age of fifteen years. Here's Jason's comment, which is heartwarming and a true story of commitment and love.

> The incident of biting a family member would lead most individuals to put a dog down but I knew we wanted to investigate every option before considering that, as we took this dog, from a rescue and promised him a life, and that is what he got. The incident happened when he was 5 and he was 15 when he passed on. He lived an amazing life those past 10 years; swimming, hiking, chasing balls, and just being a family member. There was not one incident after that (original) one; he was a loving, kind dog. So happy I never gave up on him; he taught me and added to my life, and he had a great life and I thank you for that.[79]

---

[77] Kerry Vinson, "Jake's Story," *The Scalpel Newsletter of the Toronto Academy of Veterinary Medicine*, Volume 32, #3 (August 2016) 4.

[78] Ibid.

[79] Ibid, 16.

CHAPTER 5

A Better Future for Shelter Animals and Ways of Sheltering

Saving one dog will not change the world, but surely
for that one dog, the world will change forever.
—KAREN DEVISON

As I often say, please adopt animals from shelters and give them a second chance; you will not be disappointed. You will gain a grateful best furry friend and find unconditional love.

Thankfully, there is much hope on the horizon and a promising outlook for the future of animal sheltering. People care about companion animals, and pet adoptions are on the rise. Animal shelters do not only help animals in need to find forever homes but also the personal experience of adopting can make humans happier and feel good about their decision. Anyone that I have met who has adopted a pet from an animal shelter can attest to this fact. I have had the pleasure of seeing people's faces light up when they share their adoption stories. It seems that shelter animals might even sense that they have been rescued and saved, and in return, they offer their human parents so much support, comfort, and unconditional love.

The positive steps and actions taken now can determine the future of animal shelters. It takes cooperation and collaboration between shelters, rescues, and the community to save shelter animal lives and find good, loving homes. With respect to community efforts, the shelters that are dedicated to saving and rehoming homeless animals have a more positive outlook and work with fosters, rescue groups, and the community to ensure that the animals are saved.

Animal shelters across North America are doing amazing work for shelter animals. Sheltering models are proving to be successful and are worth consideration and discussion. They offer sustainable solutions and much hope for a better future to overcome the shelter debacle.

THREE SHELTER MODELS

Socially Conscious Shelters

Socially Conscious Animal Sheltering (SCS) is an innovative approach to animal sheltering, which deserves consideration. It involves a humane approach for animal shelters to fulfill their mandates for homeless pets through transparency, accountability, and compassionate care. SCS is a set of principles that facilitates best outcomes for homeless cats and dogs in animal shelters.

SCS facilitates cooperation with the animal-welfare community to collaborate within all communities and support people and their pets. The SCS model includes collaboration with animal shelters, rescue groups, policy makers, law enforcement, veterinarians, behavior professionals, human-animal service providers, and members of the community.[80] In some ways, the SCS model is similar to the no-kill model discussed in more detail below. What is unique and somewhat different from the no-kill model of sheltering is that SCS places more responsibility on the community to work together so that homeless shelter animals will receive nurturing care and gain the respect that they deserve in communities.

Here are the eight tenets of the SCS model, briefly outlined below for reference. I suggest that further information and detail can be found on the scshelerting.org website.

---

[80] "Creating Best Outcomes for All Animals," Socially Conscious Animal Community (2022), http://scsheltering.org.

1. Place every healthy and safe animal. Healthy is defined as either having no signs of clinical disease or evidence of disease and a veterinarian has determined that it has a good or excellent prognosis for a comfortable life. Safe means that the animal has not exhibited behavior that is likely to result in severe injury or death to another animal or person.

2. Ensure every unwanted or homeless pet has a safe place to go for shelter and care.

3. Assess the medical and behavioral needs of homeless animals and ensure these needs are thoughtfully addressed.

4. Align shelter policy with the needs of the community.

5. Alleviate suffering and make appropriate euthanasia decisions.

6. Enhance the human-animal bond through safe placements and post adoption support.

7. Consider the health, wellness, and safety of animals for each community when transferring animals. Moving dogs and cats from communities that do not have homes available for them to communities where people are actively seeking pets' saves lives.

8. Foster a culture of transparency, ethical decision-making, mutual respect, continual learning, and collaboration. SCS is committed to transparency. This can include reporting accurate statistics, sharing policies, and fully and quickly admitting when mistakes are made. Integrity must be the foundation of all decisions. Every shelter can learn something from every other shelter. It is important to be curious and to share innovative solutions to common problems. Only by working together can we ensure the best outcomes for all animals. This is the view of the SCS Community Movement, which strongly advocates the position that all animals should be treated respectfully and in a manner that minimizes their suffering.[81]

Further, SCS suggests that we should strive to ensure that all healthy homeless animals have a safe place to go for care.[82] As well, it is essential to align the policies of animal shelters to that of their respective community

---

[81] Ibid.
[82] Ibid.

needs. In addition, they must ensure that euthanasia decisions are made appropriately and that they take into consideration all health concerns of animals that are being transferred, to minimize the spread of diseases and to improve "the human-animal bond through thoughtful placements and post-adoption support."[83] Lastly, the SCS model strives to foster transparency, "ethical decision-making, mutual respect, continual learning, and collaboration."[84] Animal sheltering should not be based solely on a fixed number but rather on a variety of applicable factors.

The main criticism of the SCS model is tenet five with respect to animal euthanasia. This tenet suggests that shelters are not allowed to place animals with behavioral issues into the community. In theory and at first glance, this tenet makes sense. We should not be permitting dangerous dogs to be adopted without careful training and rehabilitation. The troubling part is that the SCS model proposes to euthanize the dogs that are a grave moral concern to society. Although there are some types of animals, such as aggressive dogs that simply cannot be rehabilitated and should not be placed with families or out in the community, most animals with minor behavioral issues can be trained and can go on to enjoy long and happy lives. As for the aggressive animals, there are animal rescues that are willing to take them and dog behaviorists who can train them. In that respect, the no-kill philosophy that no animal is euthanized unless the animal is irremediably suffering is more humane.

In the animal-welfare community, cooperation with the community and individual responsibility can lead to a more sustainable future for animal sheltering. I suggest that both models deserve merit for standing up for homeless animals and giving them second chances to find loving homes. I understand that the No Kill Movement has been around for a long time and has been a successful leader for shelter animal lives. It has led to accountability and transparency in animal shelters. It has saved many innocent animals, but it also received criticism from the animal-welfare community.

Despite some of these concerns, the No Kill Movement has made tremendous progress and has led the way for the respectful and humane treatment of shelter animals. I suggest that the SCS model be viewed as complementary to the no-kill model in shelters and their communities. For

83 Ibid.
84 Ibid.

example, in some US cities like Colorado, the SCS model has seen success. When I first came across the words "Socially Conscious Sheltering," I was interested and keen to learn more. Although I greatly respect the No Kill Movement, and its overall success is very impressive, I personally think that the words *no kill* are harsh. I think *socially conscious sheltering* has a more uplifting and positive tone for animal shelters.

Although SCS is a new model in animal sheltering, it is proving to be successful with shelters across America that adopts its eight tenets. It will likely garner support from more shelters in the future and gain attention from the mainstream community of animal lovers. One key issue with the SCS model is that it lacks concrete and measurable standards. With more time and application, it is likely that the eight tenets noted above can be adjusted, improved, and tailored to fit individual shelters and their communities. Regardless of their shortcomings, both the SCS and no-kill models deserve credit, as they share a common goal to improve the shelter system and save the lives of vulnerable shelter animals. We can applaud these strategies for their success and keep an open mind as we strive for cooperation between shelter communities and the future of no-kill and SCS models.

It takes widespread support from the community and increased public awareness. At the moment in the animal sheltering world, some terms are familiar to those on the front lines but might be confusing to the public. For instance, some people might not relate to harsh words such as *no kill* or heard of these words. I suggest *socially conscious sheltering* for some communities. I propose positive uplifting terms, easier language, and definitions for the future of the animal sheltering world, which keep the community aware and part of the solution. As we look to a brighter future for animal sheltering, we should seek general public support and community-wide efforts and involvement for it to succeed in the long run. In other words, we want to include the community. It is important to realize that animal sheltering is a community-wide problem and that including the public's opinion, feedback, and responsibility is part of the solution. After all, animal shelters rely on their communities to adopt the animals in their care and promote responsible pet parenting, which includes providing opportunities for adoption.

It is impressive to witness the advances and the success stories of animal shelters that have committed to the no-kill model. There is no doubt that to date, this strategy for reducing shelter euthanasia and saving animals' lives has been remarkable. However, a more aligned and unified approach to animal shelters is required for the future if they are to continue to move in the right direction. For that reason, I am leaning toward the SCS model being integrated with the no-kill model across North America. They must work together for the future to succeed. Here's a brief overview of the No Kill model of animal sheltering and its strong components, including proposed model legislation, which deserves thoughtful consideration and integration.

The No-Kill Model

The term *no-kill* was introduced to end the practice of euthanasia in the animal-shelter system. It is defined as "ending the killing of all but those irremediably suffering animals."[85] This concept has been widely accepted, and it is part of a revolution in the United States, with animal shelter reform, proactive lifesaving programs, and political advocacy campaigns.

No-kill is an all-encompassing model that relies on shelter commitment, flexibility, open and accountable processes, and the resources to save animal lives. Here is a brief outline of the major components of the no-kill equation. It involves commitment and accountability—commitment to reject kill-oriented ways of doing business and accountability to provide clear definitions, a lifesaving plan, protocols and procedures that are oriented toward preserving life.[86]

The specific components of the no-kill model are ten principles that a shelter must adhere to.

> A comprehensive trap-neuter-and-release program
> High-volume, low-cost spays and neuters
> Transfers to rescue groups
> Volunteer foster care programs
> A comprehensive adoption program
> Pet-retention programs that seek advice and assistance
> from shelters

---

[85] https://www.nokilladvocacycenter.org/uploads/4/8/6/2/48624081/def_no_kill.pdf.
[86] https://www.nokilladvocacycenter.org/no-kill-equation.html.

Medical and behavioral programs
Community development, marketing, and public relations
Volunteer program
Proactive redemptions
A compassionate director in an animal shelter is important.

As mentioned earlier, the no-kill model has made significant progress for shelter animals and has saved countless companion animals' lives.[87] Despite some of the controversy surrounding this model, it is used in many shelters across North America.

There is an additional component: the legal protection and rights of companion animals. In other words, companion animal rights are to be legally codified in legislation. An important first step is to pass city ordinances or municipal animal-shelter reform laws that focus on encoding their protection. The Companion Animal Protection Act (CAPA) is the interim model legislation. CAPA is based on the premise that no shelter animal should be killed if the animal can be placed in a suitable home, a private sheltering agency or rescue group is willing to take care and custody of the animal for purposes of adoption, or in the case of feral cats, they can be sterilized and released to their habitats. Other provisions include the maintenance of a registry system of support organizations, compliance with checklists before resorting to euthanasia, and accessible adoption programs.[88]

Organizational transparency and accountability are paramount under CAPA. For instance, a shelter is required to notify rescue groups and the public at large by posting the kill notification on the shelter's website, as well as on the animal's cage. Animals that may be euthanized without delay under CAPA are those who are irremediably suffering. CAPA outlines requirements for checking the identification and licensing of animals that enter a shelter.[89]

Further, an animal shelter is required to maintain an updated list of all animals reported as lost. Honesty and transparency are central. Members of the public, especially those who wish to relinquish their pets for unjustifiable

---

[87] https://humaneloudoun.org/hslc-about-us/no-kill-philosophy/no-kill-equation/.

[88] http://www.rabbitadvocacy.com/companion_animal_protection_act.htm.

[89] Ibid.

reasons, will hopefully rethink when they are made aware that their animals may be killed. Human guardians who are relinquishing their family companion animals must be notified about the likelihood that their animals may be killed and sign a statement that says they understand that the shelter may kill their pet.[90] That is a powerful tool. It is a transparent and an honest approach to animal sheltering, which deserves praise, as it puts the responsibility on the pet's human caregivers to consider the consequences.

Humane Animal Sheltering (HAS) with Compassionate Animal Care

It is time for a progressive and comprehensive new model for animal sheltering, which integrates the main philosophies of the no-kill and SCS models. Both models deserve praise, and they should be considered by shelters. However, neither approach needs to be all-encompassing, as animal sheltering is not a one-size-fits-all approach. Therefore, some shelters can tailor and adapt their sheltering programs to suit their needs more individually based on their practices. We are considering compassionate care for vulnerable creatures with individual stories and needs. Careful consideration for each animal should be at the forefront of sheltering practices.

The future for animal sheltering looks bright with both models, using an open, mindful approach, getting cooperation from shelters, rescues, and the community, and everyone working together to save shelter animals' lives. The key here is commitment to compassionate animal shelter care. Taking in animals that need a safe haven, protection and individual attention, and providing them with basic needs to survive is not simply enough. It requires proper care and individual attention, with enrichment programs to help these animals transition and adapt and to set them up for success so that they are placed with loving families and in safe homes.

I propose a new animal sheltering model that integrates the no-kill model with the SCS model: Humane Animal Sheltering (HAS), which is a holistic, mindful, and conscious approach to animal sheltering. HAS proposes compassionate care at its core and awareness that every single

---

[90] Ibid.

animal's life is worthy and that it matters. Each animal is viewed as special and unique, with an individual story and a past that it can overcome with patience, safety, and protection, which includes nurturing, loving, and tender care.

HAS allows for second chances and promotes adoption, fostering, transferring, rehabilitation, and collaboration between shelters, rescue groups, sanctuaries, behavior specialists, veterinarians, and the community. It is the next step in sheltering and a humane approach. It includes compassionate care with committed leadership and staff. There is a strong commitment and intention to save every one of them. Therefore, humane euthanasia is only offered as a last resort. It is reserved only for animals that are irremediably suffering.

It takes *no-kill* off the table because this vocabulary is no longer needed in humane sheltering. It is widely understood and accepted among the animal-welfare community and even government-run municipal shelters that killing homeless animals is not tolerated and that humane sheltering is the next frontier for shelters. Positive collaborative relationships are the keys to a successful strategy, which ensures that animals are placed in safe facilities and receive care.

I have seen animal rescues in my community that rescue and rehabilitate shelter dogs. They take the dogs from municipal shelters to foster them for adoption or place them in rescues or sanctuaries. Success in saving shelter dogs involves commitment, strong social networks (positive relationships), ongoing communication, and rescues working collaboratively with animal shelters and their staff. These are key factors for successful outcomes and comprehensive lifesaving strategies. With compassionate committed care and collaboration with the community, shelter animals are seen as part of the community and are not left behind or allowed to be killed.

The most important component of a successful HAS sheltering model is cooperation between shelters and the community, which includes rescues, fosters, veterinary clinics, and volunteers rallying together for animals. Robust social networks committed to save shelter animals are essential for the strategy's ongoing success. I am pleased to share with you that in my community, there are positive collaborative social networks, cohesion, and cooperation between animal shelters and rescues, which work together to save more animals.

Alongside these collaborative efforts between the shelters and rescues, the HAS model goes one step further than the no-kill and SCS models. It places onus on human guardians to take adoption seriously, to take greater responsibility to keep their pets with them (especially dogs), and to keep their animals out of the shelter system in the first place. That involves offering helpful resources and outreach for those adopters who might encounter challenges and behavioral issues, which can be overcome with individual attention such as training manuals and lessons. For those pet parents who want to give up their pet for whatever reason, solutions are offered. It is understood that dropping off an unwanted pet carries responsibility. Every effort is made to help the pet parent overcome their issues; however, if these solutions are not possible, the shelter takes their pets and places them for adoption or fostering.

Again, the key component of HAS is positive relationships, with a progressive approach to sheltering, and compassionate care. The goal is to be proactive with successful strategies and solutions in place that anticipate common problems that new adopters might face and help them overcome these challenges the beginning. There is an interview and screening process during the initial adoption application to anticipate common mistakes whenever possible. As well, since the HAS model relies on responsible pet parents to adopt animals from shelters, it places heavier burden on this initial adoption exchange to ensure that they are serious.

Successful stories with shelter animals involves patience, and guidance, being provided with tools to overcome issues that could be easily overcome such as dog training. The transition from shelter to the home is no easy task or from one home to another and support to help ease the stress and make the transition smoother to the new pet parent and animal is essential.

Animals have had a stressful experience that led them to the shelter. Sometimes the situations that present problems such as having a home with small children, other pets, moving, or families that have never shared their home with an animal can be stressful. HAS proposes that ongoing support is offered to set them up for success. HAS wants to empower new pet parents with tools and education which is similar to tenet two of the CSC model however it elaborates on the initial adoption encounter to ensure that families are placed with the right fit. For instance, I have met pet behaviorists and dog trainers that work with animal shelters and rescues and offer reduced rates or free lessons to families to help them move forward in a positive way.

HAS focuses on a commitment to save every shelter animal and re-home them by using a robust social network with experts, like-minded individuals, and the community at large, all working together. In other words, shelters are bridges of communication and places of protection and possible transport of homeless pets. The more public exposure an animal has to prospective adopters, the greater the chance to place that animal in a loving home. For those animals that don't do well in shelters, they are placed in fosters or rescues. The goal is not only to succeed and save every precious animal's life but also to find the right home. CAS and the no-kill models are integral and complimentary to the HAS model. They include an animal's individual care, history (if it has been disclosed), proper placement, post adoption checks, and ongoing support.

Although it is vital to find suitable, loving homes, it is equally important for animal shelters to ensure that the adoption process goes as smoothly as possible for the long haul. That is a key component in a positive outcome for shelter animals, which are integral members of communities. The words *no kill* are gone, as we enter a new era and a positive approach to animal sheltering, which places all animals in care and offers them safety, nurturing, individual attention, and most of all, guaranteed protection.

Responsible Animal Guardian

It is a privilege to share one's life with a companion animal, but it comes with great responsibility. This is particularly true for canine caregivers. Let's face it; dogs crave companionship, love, and sometimes a lot of attention. For instance, bigger dogs need to be trained because they can get into trouble, so investing in a dog trainer for better behavior can be a positive and worthwhile experience. In return, dogs give so much back to us. They are loyal, brave protectors and loving companions to their human families. If they are strong, there is a risk that they can also bite and hurt people (including children) and other animals. In other words, taking care of a big dog is a serious commitment, and the laws treat it accordingly. With this responsibility comes a need for reasonable and proactive efforts to prevent mishaps and a corresponding punishment for a breach of this responsibility from occurring.

It's also a human's responsibility to control the breeding potential of the dog, either by spaying or neutering or ensuring that the breeding process is done in a controlled and legitimate environment. Since companion animals such as cats, dogs, and rabbits can reproduce in a short amount of time, if guardians do not control their breeding, animal shelters face deep burdens in just a few short years. This cannot continue to be overlooked. Recall that in less than seven years, tens of thousands of unwanted offspring can over-populate the streets and shelters with just one un-spayed and uncontrolled female dog or cat. In essence, it takes only one irresponsible guardian to devastate the lives of thousands of animals and contribute to pet overpop-ulation in our animal shelters. Responsible dog guardianship is a critical factor in progressive sheltering.

Taking care of a domestic cat also carries a responsibility. They should be kept indoors. Our dearly departed family cat, Jackson, was born from a feral cat mother, but since we adopted him, Jackson learned to prefer to stay indoors. We did not allow him to go outside. When he was a kitten, someone left the door open, and he disappeared for a few days. It was a devastating time for our family as we frantically searched for our cat for many days. Eventually, he came back to us and was an indoor cat for the rest of his life. Occasionally, he sat in the backyard with us.

There are cats that spend time outdoors. I knew of two cats in my neighborhood that got hit by cars and passed away. There is another friendly cat that roams free. He's a beautiful beige Bengal, which spends most of his time outdoors. We named him Tomcat. I have witnessed two occasions when he was almost hit by a car. I tried to speak with the neighbors to con-vince them that they should keep their cat indoors, but it did not work. He continues to visit us, and although I must admit that I am fond of Tomcat, I would encourage cat caregivers to keep their feline friends inside for their safety and for the preservation of wildlife. Cats are sophisticated hunt-ers that kill birds and other small creatures. Sadly, my mother witnessed Tomcat with a dead chipmunk in his mouth. I am glad that I did not see this scenario. It makes me sad. It is also the law in most municipalities and jurisdictions not to permit cats to roam freely outside.

The Future for Our Best Friends

As noted earlier, The Best Friends Animal Society (BFAS) is an American not-for-profit organization. It strives to "end the killing in shelters and to bring about a time when there are no more homeless pets … by 2025."[91] By implementing a national strategy to reach all parts of the United States, BFAS believes they can achieve this goal.[92]

Although there are thousands of no-kill animal shelters and communities nationwide throughout the US and Canada, there is still a long way to go if we are to achieve the ultimate goal of eliminating the word *kill* from our animal-sheltering vocabulary and replacing it with CSC and softer words. New sheltering approaches that focus on compassionate care, such as CSC and HAS, is the next frontier, which includes humane sheltering.

Meanwhile, we can look to BFAS, which believes that with a community-wide animal resource center to "prioritize allocation of workspace from impoundment and toward community services … it will help Americans keep their pets in their homes and keep transitioning homeless pets out of the shelters and into foster care."[93] In other words, a collaborative effort is needed.

BFAS maintains that to reach the goal of a no-kill community standard among all shelters nationwide, love and care for each animal is needed every single day.[94] Further, shelters must provide a means of rehabilitation for animals whenever it is possible. With this in place, unwanted behavior may be successfully treated.[95] This is what the BFAS hopes for the future of animal sheltering. Julie Castle, the CEO of BFAS, said, "I'm very confident … it's going to be a lot of work, but it's definitely doable."[96]

The future of animal sheltering appears to be more organized, as mentioned by Dr. Jed Rogers, DVM, and CEO of Firehouse Animal Health

---

[91] Julie Castle, "The Future of Animal Shelters: The Best Friends Blog," Best Friends Animal Society (6 December 2018), bestfriends.org/blogs/2018/11/21/the-future-of-animal-shelters.

[92] Ibid.

[93] Ibid.

[94] "2025 Goal," Best Friends Animal Society (28 May 2019), bestfriends.org/2025-goal.

[95] Ibid.

[96] Julie Castle, "The Future of Animal Shelters," Best Friends Animal Society (6 December 2018), bestfriends.org/blogs/2018/11/21/the-future-of-animal-shelters.

Center in Austin, Texas.[97] As such, with greater organization, adequate care is provided to animals that are in need in a timelier manner. "You can have a better chance of doing a good job if you're sharing best practices and adhering to standards," said Dr. Rogers.[98] Clearly, the underlying principle behind a more organized and stronger animal-sheltering system is unity, collaboration, and teamwork. By building positive relationships between animal professionals and the public, a bright future with better care for shelter animals can become a reality.

There is a conscious effort on the part of humane societies to save animal lives. For instance, the Cocheco Valley Humane Society (CVHS) in New Hampshire reported that in modern times, more and more seemingly unadoptable animals found on the streets were no longer being euthanized but were kept for rehabilitation purposes.[99] In essence, animal shelters are conditioning unadoptable animals with behavioral problems into house-friendly, adoptable, furry friends.[100]

In the past, the solution to these types of issues found in unadoptable animals would have simply been to put them down, but this is no longer the only solution. Additionally, overpopulated animal shelters are transporting dogs, cats, and rabbits to rescues and shelters that have space so that every animal receives proper care. In fact, the CVHS reported a significant decline in overpopulation in their jurisdiction, which means that their efforts to address the animal shelter debacle is working![101] Further, the CVHS reported that due to these changes being implemented, there has been a significant decrease in the euthanasia rates across New Hampshire. Between 1980 and 1993, the average number of dogs and cats that were euthanized in the state annually was around 11,300.[102] By 2003, the average number of euthanized animals dropped significantly to about 2,575. By 2013, it was around 1,153.[103]

---

[97] Portia Stewart, "DVM360 Investigative Report: For the Love of Dog: The Future of Animal Sheltering," (2018), veterinarynews.dvm360.com/dvm360-investigative-report-love-dog-future-animal-sheltering.

[98] Ibid.

[99] "The Future of Animal Shelters," Pope Memorial Humane Society (2018), popememorialcvhs.org/the-future-of-animal-shelters.

[100] Ibid.

[101] Ibid.

[102] Ibid.

[103] Ibid.

Although it appears that the US does not have comprehensive data regarding animal shelters nationwide, the CVHS suggests that their overall numbers indicate a reduction in overpopulation and the euthanasia rate.[104] As well, the CVHS is adamant about removing space-based euthanasia shelters and supporting cost-friendly spaying and neutering procedures and progressive policies that assist with spay and neuter programs. Taking on more responsibility individually and within the community, adopting pets into loving homes with follow-up, shutting down puppy mills, and closing unethical breeding operations mean that animal sheltering is improving. This is the promising future, and we are moving toward a more humane sheltering with integration of the tenets of the socially conscious sheltering model and no kill sheltering.

Adopt Don't Shop: Don't Breed or Buy While Shelter Animals Die

In addition to the previously mentioned call to action, there are many things that you can do individually to help reduce the number of animals that enter the shelter system in the first place and limit the number of adoptable, treatable, and healthy animals from losing their lives. For instance, the most obvious way is by adopting a shelter animal, and raising awareness, including educating your friends and family. Remind people to adopt and not to purchase their pets.

Adoption is the key to saving animals' lives. By choosing to adopt, you are making a positive contribution and saving a life while providing a loving home to a neglected and unappreciated animal. In addition, by taking an animal out of the shelter system, it frees up more space for others. Sadly, animal shelters across North America are overrun with strays and surrendered animals. By adopting animals and encouraging others to do the same, more space is made available for other incoming animals in need of shelter, protection, and tender, loving care.

---

[104] Ibid.

Dogs Are Amazing Creatures, and Their Lives Are Not Disposable

Another way to help is to take a step back when you have made the decision to adopt. Too many animals are adopted without sufficient research done on their breeds and lifestyles. They are often surrendered back to shelters. Instead of presuming an animal's demeanor based on your first impression in the shelter, there are several things you can do to understand what the animal is like and how it will respond to you. Remember to try to educate yourself about the animal's breed and predicament, without judgment, before meeting for the first time.

Many shelters have open areas where you can walk the dog around. For instance, freeing the dog from the sensory overload experience inside the enclosure may give you better insight into the dog's true personality. Once that dog has had a chance to adjust to you and calm down, you may find a loving and well-behaved canine companion for your family to take home and love.

Remember, a frightened shelter dog may show signs of aggression, but by nature, it may not be aggressive at all. By stepping back and taking some time to genuinely appreciate and understand the nature and real personality of the shelter animal, you can discover a wonderful animal and save a precious life. When you choose to bring home a pet for your family, you open space in the shelter for other furry friends that are in need of loving homes.

Please stop shopping for pets online or from breeders. If you insist on purchasing your next puppy from a breeder—even if it is an ethical breeder—remain aware that shelter dogs and cats are being killed every day. If the stigma of not wanting to adopt a shelter animal continues, the needless killing of animals, which for whatever reason find their fate in this broken system, will continue as well.

Adoption Is a Serious Commitment

Animals are complex creatures with special needs and individual personalities, tastes, peculiarities, and preferences. Although adopting an animal from a shelter can save a life, it should not be done spontaneously, unless you are willing to commit to that animal for the rest of its life. Anyone who has shared his or her life with an animal knows how unique and special this experience can be.

My beloved animal friends have touched my heart in special ways. I learned that each one had its own personality and displayed preferences for toys, people, other animals, food, and attention. For instance, our dog Freddie is not friendly to strangers, is a picky eater, and has separation anxiety. He has a hard time staying home alone, and he has had to sleep next to our bed since he was a puppy. He would not do well in a shelter. But he's very loyal to his family. He so loves that it makes my heart melt each time I see the excitement in his eyes.

We almost adopted a new puppy recently named Luna. Unfortunately, a family friend had to give away his puppy when he moved to a rental building that did not allow dogs. When he signed the lease, he was heartbroken, as he had bonded with this new puppy. He was proactive, and he tried to find her a loving home. He looked everywhere, and no one was willing to adopt her. It was during the COVID-19 pandemic, when it seemed as if so many people adopted a pandemic pet. Luna is a lovely looking one-year-old mutt with a fun personality. She is strong and likes to pull on her leash. We agreed that she would not do well in a shelter environment. We agreed to adopt her. We did a few meet and greets outside with Lily and Luna, and to my surprise, they got along very well. She was submissive to Lily, which was good. I read dog behavior manuals and watched videos on introducing a puppy to a senior dog.

The next step was to introduce her to Freddie, which I thought would be easy. He gets along well with other dogs, but for some reason, he was not happy. To my surprise, Luna lunged at Freddie when he showed that he was fearful. It was not a friendly encounter. We made the difficult decision not to adopt her. Thankfully, there was another family that was searching for a dog, so it was a happy ending. The adoption process is not easy and needs to be well thought out for pets and families. Bringing home a pet is a serious responsibility and commitment for the rest of that animal's life. Here's an example of what could've ended badly. It is better to do due diligence at the onset to avoid heartbreak and ensure that there is a lasting relationship.

Each Animal Is Special and Unique

If you have shared your life with any type of companion animal, whether dog, cat, horse, turtle, parrot, or rabbit—you have noticed that each pet is a unique creature. Our family dog Lily is a big German shepherd breed. She commands presence, but her personality is different from other dogs. She cries for attention and lies on her back for belly rubs. She loves cats more than dogs. She has taken the role of the protector of the house. When we come home, we find our shoes and laundry downstairs. It is safe to say that she missed us. When we enter the house, her joy and excitement is heart-melting. On the other hand, Freddie is a shy, scared dog. He wants to be held and taken everywhere. Each one has a distinct personality.

Our bunny Zoey was shy, timid, and slow to show us affection when we first brought her home. I do not know what happened in Zoey's past, but I do know that she was surrendered at an animal shelter when she was two years old. It took almost six months of patience, tenderness, love, and a few carrots to gain her trust. Now Zoey craves human affection and social interaction and thrives on a lot of attention. She recognizes her name and comes over when she is called. She loves to play chase and hide-and-go-seek. She is loveable, but she doesn't like everyone. Gaining the trust of a shelter animal can take time and patience but is a real joy and such a gratifying and transformative experience for both animal and human.

If it is possible to know the animal's story and personal history that knowledge might help mitigate future mishaps with new adopters and adoption placements. It involves a mindful, caring, and holistic approach to animal sheltering. I can say from my personal experience, as a volunteer of many years, interacting with shelter animals has taught me that each one is special and deserves a second chance. They thrive on stability and trust. Despite their past experiences, they are willing to give second chances. Luckily for us, they seem to forgive their past humans for failing them, move forward positively, and even thrive in their new surroundings.

There are many inspiring and uplifting stories of shelter and rescued animals, which have endured and overcome hard lives and gone on to have happy endings and long lives. Some shelter animals have experienced horrendous abuse, but thankfully, they have overcome their personal circumstances to become loving companions to their human families. It does take effort, long-term commitment, and dedication on the part of the human to help them. After all, it is an animal's life and well-being that we are talking about. For their part, animal shelters and rescues need to be careful during the adoption process in order to ensure that the human and animal are a good fit. My final thoughts are these: Adoption is serious a commitment. You need to be ready to take on the responsibility of bringing home an animal and remain patient while you both adapt to this new lifestyle. It's worth the effort to save a shelter animal's life!

Companion animals are here *with* us and not for us.

CHAPTER 6

Debate for Furry Friends and Defense for Nonhuman Animals

What dogs? These are my children, little people with
fur who make my heart open a little wider.
—OPRAH WINFREY

Pets Are Part of Our Families and Furry Friends and the Law

Although most people can agree that our fur friends are members of our family, they might be surprised to learn that they are regarded as personal property under the law in some places. Those who share their homes with companion animals would disagree that their family dogs or cats are objects akin to chairs, but the laws state just that. Historically, the legal system has defined the human relationship to animals in terms of property and ownership.

Most people that share their lives with pets agree that companion animals are not things but are regarded as loved family members. They have inherent worth and value, and most importantly, they are loved. They are not a piece of furniture (as stated in some laws). People's pets are living, breathing beings with big personalities. Therefore, they should not be classified as personal property. These laws are outdated and not aligned with mainstream social values and sentiments toward companion animals. Broader social awareness for progressive legal change is a vital next step in updating the laws and awakening humans to the fact that animals need protection. It is time to modernize the legal system to reflect these sentiments and elevate the status of animals.

Companion animals deserve better. The human-animal bond should be reflected in our laws as special and unique. In fact, understanding the real emotions and feelings of animals is often easier than understanding a human's feelings because animals do not try to filter or hide what they are feeling.[105] Animals are capable of expressing empathy, and they have their own means of communicating. For example, dogs bow to one another throughout play, signaling their playful intentions.[106] Without the bow, another dog might misinterpret a playful bite as an attack.[107] Certain animals can even express behaviors akin to human ones, such as dolphins swimming together as a family and calling each other by name.[108]

Companion animals can form deep, strong, and lasting bonds with other animals and humans. There is a connection and friendship between them as they play and sleep on the couch next to each other. When our beloved dog Charlie passed away, we noticed that Lily missed him. She displayed grief, sadness, and sorrow by refusing to eat her food for a few days and crying (moaning) as if she knew he was gone. As well, when our beloved cat Jackson passed away, it was apparent that Lily missed him. After all, they were together since they were fur babies. We found Lily looking for Jackson where he would spend a lot of time and she was crying for him. When my husband recently returned from the hospital after an injury, Lily gently approached him and sniffed the area of his injury, started to cry, and lay her head next to him on the floor.

---

[105] Marc Bekoff, *The Emotional Lives of Animals* (California: New World Library, 2007), 45.
[106] Ibid., 97.
[107] Ibid.
[108] Kate Good, "10 Important Life Lessons We Can Learn from Animals," One Green Planet (March 2019), https://www.onegreenplanet.org/animalsandnature/important-life-lessons-we-can-learn-from-animals.

Moving Away from Animals as Commodities

Classifying animals as personal property in the laws and categorizing animals as owned objectifies their status and diminishes their worth. Ownership has several negative impacts on our relationships with them. It suggests that an animal's interests are not worth consideration because it is an inanimate object solely there for people rather than viewing them as a living, creature. This notion contradicts the view that an animal is more than an inanimate object. It suggests that it lacks inherent value. As author Craig Brestrup suggests, "She (a cat) becomes an object alongside other consumable objects for keeping and tending only so long as convenient and useful. The separated one fails to notice the animal as a creature of needs, feelings, and attachments."[109]

Our relationship to companion animals is beneficial to both human and animal. It is based on mutual benefits (as outlined in the first chapter). It is filled with unconditional love and companionship, which is the essence of the human-animal bond. As such, I prefer more updated terminology and suggest that we replace the word *owner* with *guardian* when referring to this human-animal relationship. As Craig Brestrup eloquently states,

> In the relation of one life to another, ownership is not a beneficial framework, for something owned lacks an autonomous center of value. While that fits for an automobile, it does not for a life. An entity owned can only serve the wants of the owner and not claim its own priorities. An owned animal becomes a consumer item, disposable and replaceable as all such items are, and not a locus for commitment. The notion of companionship, rather than ownership, offers a more promising ideal for the mutuality of one life with another. [110]

In pet custody disputes, the notion of legal ownership is problematic because it continues to treat animals as objects and likens them to things

---

[109] Craig Brestrup, *Disposable Animals: Ending the Tragedy of Throwaway Pets* (Camino Bay Books, 2002).
[110] Ibid., 17.

such as property. This notion becomes even more problematic and amplified when couples can be ordered to sell the pet in question and have to split the proceeds. In my personal experience when a couple's relationship ends and there's a legal battle, most of the time, it becomes clear that they both love their dog or cat and consider them a member of the family. A custody battle that ensues and results in a monetary outcome is not usually what they want. I have found that most couples are happier when they have shared custody and do what's best for their beloved pet. As such, the current legal system that treats family pets as owned is outdated. It does not end well for the pet in question or have the desired outcome. I propose mediation of pet custody disputes whenever it is possible, rather than court.

Canada, It's Time to Catch Up with Animals Rights

It might come as a surprise that Canada has some of the worst animal-protection laws and not only for companion animals. It does not have enough proper policies in place to protect wildlife in captivity, farm animals, or companion animals used in research. Even with mainstream views prevailing, the Canadian justice system remains hesitant to make changes to laws that govern animals. On a boiling-hot day in 2015, animal rights activist Anita Krajnc fed water to one of many thirsty pigs trapped in a truck on its way to slaughter. Krajnc was then charged with mischief to property for her actions.[111] Her council argued that the pigs were persons and not property.[112] An expert in neuroscience and animal behavior testified that pigs form social groups, have complex methods of communication, empathize, are sentient, and have a high level of intelligence.[113]

Despite her opinion that pigs are persons, which is supported by ample evidence, the court did not accept that finding. It classified the pigs as property.[114] However, the ruling was that compassion is not a crime, and there were no further actions against Krajnc.[115] The judge in this decision noted

---

[111] R. V. Krajnc, ONCJ (2017) 281.
[112] Ibid.
[113] Ibid.
[114] Ibid.
[115] Ibid.

that this case experienced rare public attention.[116] The public's unusual attendance and support for Krajnc are evidence of a change in mainstream society's attitude and growing interest in animal rights.

Legal Personhood of Nonhuman Animals

> Animal Rights are not a gift we give animals ... they are a birthright we have taken from them.
>
> —Ryan Phillips

The shift to recognizing animals as persons under the law would not be a far stretch because personhood does not equate to human beings under the law. Corporations are considered persons under the law. If animals were granted personhood as well, they could experience benefits such as court-appointed guardians to represent their legal rights.[117]

There is hope on the horizon for courts to grant legal personhood to nonhuman animals. Recently, a United States court recognized animals as legal persons. In an unprecedented case, the Animal League Defense Fund (ALDF) filed an application supporting a Colombian lawsuit to stop a cull of Pablo Escobar's hippopotamuses long after his death.

What is the Nonhuman Rights Project (NhRP)

The Nonhuman Rights Project (NhRP) is an American nonprofit animal rights organization that is seeking to change the legal status of nonhuman animals from that of property to that of persons. They have fought for the rights of nonhuman animals through litigation, legislation, awareness, and education.[118] NhRP focuses primarily on those species of animals that have been scientifically proven to demonstrate self-awareness and

---

[116] Ibid.

[117] Ibid.

[118] "Humans Are Not the Only Animals Entitled to Recognition and Protection of Their Fundamental Rights," Non-Human Rights Project (2022), https://www.nonhuman-rights.org.

autonomy, such as chimpanzees and elephants.[119] While they have noted that they care about all animals, their legal strategy seems focused on those animals that they feel are most likely to break through the legal wall due to their similar characteristics to humans.[120] For example, a baby chimpanzee demonstrated human characteristics when she was rescued from poachers in the Congo. The chimp named Mussa demonstrated joy while in the rescue airplane and helped the pilot with the flight controls.[121] Throughout the flight, Mussa and the pilot shared tender moments together, and she happily jumped into another rescuer's arms upon landing.[122]

The NhRP's first client was a chimpanzee named Tommy, who was a chimp actor in movies. Here's the background provided by NhRP on their website:

> When we found Tommy, a male chimpanzee, he was living alone in a cage in a shed on a used trailer lot along Route 30 in Gloversville, New York. Believed to have been born in the early 1980s, Tommy was raised from infancy by Dave Sabo, former proprietor of "Sabo's Chimps." Tommy appeared as "Goliath" in the 1987 film Project X, according to Sabo. Animal activist and TV icon Bob Barker and others alleged that trainers beat the chimpanzees used in the film with blackjacks and clubs. After Sabo died in 2008, "ownership" of at least some of the chimpanzees passed to the Laverys. The status of these other chimpanzees—including whether or not they're still alive—is unknown."[123]

---

[119] Ibid.

[120] Ibid.

[121] "Adorable Chimpanzee Rescued from Poachers, Helps Pilot Fly to New Home," NBC (2 March 2018), https://www.nbc26.com/news/national/adorable-chimpanzee-rescued-from-poachers-helps-pilot-fly-helicopter-to-new-home.

[122] Ibid.

[123] Non-Human Rights Project online, https://www.nonhumanrights.org/client-tommy/.

Steven Wise, the founder and president of the NhRP visited the place where Tommy was kept. He described his cage as "a dungeon."[124] While the NhRP was unable to free Tommy because they were denied leave to appeal and this was an unfavorable judgement, it paved the path for future cases.

In 2018, they were successful in bringing a habeas corpus hearing for an elephant named Happy.[125] This elephant's story is monumental in the legal fights for animals and their freedom. It has been called the most important case for animal rights. Unfortunately, Happy was not granted legal status, and the New York high court ruled she was not a person. She is an Asian female elephant from Thailand, which was born in the wild. She was captured, locked alone in a cage, shipped to America, and sent to a Bronx Zoo in 1972. She was torn from her family and taken to a foreign land where she was used by humans for entertainment and amusement. She used to give rides to New York schoolchildren and perform tricks. Happy has been living in the Bronx Zoo since that time. Now she is fifty years old and retired, but she remains alone and confined. This is unnatural to an elephant's nature because these majestic animals usually seek family and exploration. The legal outcome of Happy's case is yet to be determined.[126] The NhRP is fighting for her release from the Bronx Zoo, with the goal of transferring her to a sanctuary where she can live the remainder of her life with other elephants.[127]

Hopefully, the NhRP's persistent and wide-reaching public support can help win this fight, and they will succeed in the case to relocate this deserving senior elephant for the remainder of her life. She should not be kept isolated in the zoo and used as human entertainment. It is shocking to read about Happy's story and almost unbelievable that, in this day and age, with climate change and the real threat of ecosystems collapsing, an elephant's battle for freedom in her later years not being granted is disappointing. Although the Bronx Zoo insists that she is not lonely, as there is another

---

[124] Charles Siebert, "Should a Chimp Be Able to Sue It's Owner?" *New York Times* (23 April 2014), https://www.nytimes.com/2014/04/27/magazine/the-rights-of-man-and-beast.html.

[125] Ibid.

[126] Ibid.

[127] Lauren Choplin, "New York Elephant Rights Case Moves Forward with World's First Habeas Corpus Order Issued on Behalf of an Elephant," Nonhuman Rights (19 November 2018), https://www.nonhumanrights.org/blog/first-habeas-corpus-order-happy.

elephant there named Patty, the two elephants are not kept together, but they can sometimes smell each other.[128]

Elephants are the largest land mammals and are extremely intelligent. They are known to be empathetic, compassionate, and sympathetic creatures.[129] They live in families, and they are known to be protective of them, grieve when they lose loved ones, and form social bonds. I am not alone in my sadness for Happy. This case has received public attention, with over 1.5 million people who have signed a petition to free this elephant, celebrities speaking out, and a public campaign that is shared on social media (#FreeHappy). Public protests of activists standing in front of the zoo with statements that say, "Happy is not Happy," continue to be held for her release.[130]

Although Happy's case remains to be determined, and the US judicial system desperately needs updating, another animal-right's case in Ecuador has received worldwide attention. Ecuador became the first country in the world to recognize the legal right of nonhuman animals! A headline in *Euronews* reads, "Wild animals in Ecuador now have legal rights thanks to a monkey named Estrellita."[131] The groundbreaking legal case centered on a woolly monkey named Estrellita that lived in her home. She was taken from the wild when she was one month old and was kept as a pet for eighteen years. Owning wild animals is illegal in Ecuador, so Ecuador's officials forcibly seized her from her home on the grounds that keeping wild animals was illegal in Ecuador, and she was put in a zoo. Her legal guardian, Ana Beatriz Burbano Proano, filed a habeas corpus petition to determine if detaining her was valid; however, unbeknownst to Ana, a week after Estrellita was locked away in the zoo, she died.[132] Although this was a sad ending, it was an important legal case. This landmark ruling will certainly open the doors for other animal cases and jurisdictions to make similar rulings.

---

[128] Jill Lepore, "The Elephant Who Could Be a Person," *The Atlantic* (16 November 2021), https://www.theatlantic.com/ideas/archive/2021/11/happy-elephant-bronx-zoo-nhrp-lawsuit/620672/.

[129] Ibid.

[130] Ibid.

[131] Rosie Frost, "Wild Animals in Ecuador Now Have Legal Rights Thanks to a Monkey Named Estrellita," *Euronews* (4 January 2022), https://www.euronews.com/green/2022/04/01/wild-animals-in-ecuador-now-have-legal-rights-thanks-to-a-monkey-named-estrellita.

[132] Ibid.

Animals Are Sentient Creatures

Animals are complex, living, breathing, and sentient creatures. They can feel and experience a whole range of emotions: happiness, sadness, loneliness, and joy and even display personalities and preferences. The concept of animals as sentient creatures was adopted in several countries, and this will be discussed in more detail later. Some countries have passed animal sentience laws. Some of the countries having codified animal sentience include: Spain, Switzerland, France, Argentina, New Zealand, Australia, Tanzania, the United Kingdom, the Netherlands, and Sweden. Some other places include Alaska and California, and Quebec, in my country Canada.

New Zealand took this first crucial step when the Animal Welfare Amendment Bill passed in 2018.[133] The bill amends the act "to recognize that animals are sentient" and "to require owners of animals, and persons in charge of animals, to attend properly to the welfare of those animals."[134] Essentially, the bill bans using animals for testing and research and makes it easier to prosecute animal-cruelty offences.[135] New Zealand has taken a large step forward, and hopefully, it is setting a unique precedent for others to follow.

Australia began the journey to recognize animals as sentient beings when they introduced the Animal Welfare Legislation Amendment Bill in 2019.[136] The bill passed, meaning there is now stronger protection for animals. For example, new offences include kicking, abandoning, or acting in a way likely to cause an animal stress or injury.[137] Traveling in a moving vehicle without properly restraining the animal could result in a fine or one-year imprisonment, and failing to exercise an animal for more than a

[133] Sophie McAdam, "New Zealand Now Recognizes All Animals as Sentient Beings," Auxx (24 June 2018), https://auxx.me/new-zealand-now-recognizes-all-animals-as-sentient-beings.
[134] Ibid.
[135] *Animal Welfare Amendment Bill*, (NZ), 3A.
[136] Mr. Steel, Minister for City Services, Austl, Murrumbidgee, Legislative Assembly, Parliamentary Debates (16 May 2019) 1,806.
[137] Gavin Butler, "New Laws in the ACT Aim to Acknowledge that Animals Have Feelings," Vice (14 May 2019), https://www.vice.com/en_au/article/bj9vxa/new-laws-the-act-canberra-australia-acknowledge-animals-have-feelings-sentient-beings.

day could result in a $4,000 fine.[138] Hopefully, the passage of these laws can push for more precedents in other jurisdictions.

Many places in North America have not taken these steps to recognize animals as sentient. The only Canadian exception is Quebec, which redefined the status of animals in the province's civil code in 2015. The code now states, "Animals are not things. They are sentient beings and have biological needs."[139] The change allows the recognition of pain and suffering endured by animals when handling abuse cases.[140]

Additionally, in the US, California passed a law that considers the best interest of pets in divorce proceedings. The courts can grant sole or joint custody of a pet by considering factors like who purchased the animal, who is the primary caretaker, and who will provide the dog or cat with the best quality of life.[141] While this is a progressive step forward, the legislative wording may hinder the application of the law to pets in shared residences apart from marriage, such as other family members, common-law relationships, or roommates.

Slowly, the Canadian legal system is acknowledging a need for change. In a 2018 case out of the Newfoundland Court of Appeal, Justice Lois Hoegg wrote a powerful dissent on the topic. She articulated that animals are not akin to property and that legal ownership should not be determined solely on who purchased the animal.[142] The majority judges decided the dog in this case should belong to the person who purchased her, rather than the person who took care of her.[143] In many of these cases, steps for incremental changes for farmed animals, research animals, and wildlife are excluded. Following New Zealand's example, the recognition of domestic animals as sentient can be a stepping stone toward legal protection for all animals.

---

[138] Ibid.

[139] Art 898.1 CCQ.

[140] "Quebec to Change Status of Animals from 'Property' to 'Sentient' Being," Canadians for Ethical Treatment of Farmed Animals (12 August 2014), https://cetfa.org/quebec-to-change-status-of-animals-from-property-to-sentient-being/.

[141] Suzana Gartner, "Who Gets the Dog or Cat in a Divorce?" Suzana Gartner Animal Lawyer and Advocate (30 November 2018), https://www.suzanagartner.com/who-gets-the-dog-or-cat-in-a-divorce.

[142] Baker v Harmina, NLCA (2018), 15.

[143] Ibid.

Animal Sentience for Animals

Updating the laws to classify animals as sentient beings rather than property is possible and happening. As we can see from other examples, some
countries have started to update their animal-protection laws to reflect this
sentiment while other places are slower.

Changing the legal status of companion animals to recognize their
sentience can be easier as people are attached to their beloved pets. It can
open the doorway for much-needed change for other species along the way.
But thankfully, places that are recognizing animals as sentient are also realizing that companions and other species deserve this recognition. Just as
the NhRP has chosen those animals that express self-awareness as the best
legal angle for change, slower countries such as Canada can present its own
approach to gaining legal rights for animals.

We can build meaningful relationships and share intimate moments
with our animal friends, as they are integral members of the family. When
we look at family photos of gatherings and celebrations, we can see that
our dog or cat is part of the event, poses for the photo, and even partakes
in the family's festivities. While companion animals may not have as much
self-awareness as chimpanzees, elephants, or dolphins do, they display emotions because they are unique and impressive in their own way. They enrich
and give meaning to our lives.

In times of struggle, we turn to our animal friends for comfort, love,
and support. This has become evident with the surge in adoptions during
the pandemic. For example, dogs are often great for therapy. They can
provide comfort to those going through a difficult time. They seem in tune
with human emotions, and they can sense when we need soothing.

Like humans, dogs are capable of learning and moving on from their
pasts. Hector's story is a testament to a dog's ability to learn and change.
Hector the pit bull had been forced to participate for two years in a dog-
fighting ring. Luckily, Hector was rescued by a couple, who trained him to
become a therapy dog. Hector disproves the poor stereotypical representation of pit bulls. Despite starting his life in violence, he took on a loving and
supportive role in hospitals, nursing homes, and schools. From his rescuers,
it took patience, a little love, and redirection onto the right path

Humans turn to dogs for service support too. Support dogs are highly intelligent. They can be trained to answer the door, retrieve items for their caregivers, help them get around, and assist during emergencies by bringing them the phone and barking to signal for help. Support dogs can also lead emergency responders to where their guardians may be in distress.[144] When Marine veteran Chris Galliher talked about his German shepherd service dog named Raider, he said, "He can tell when I get anxious and when I get irritable, so he comes up and nuzzles me to remind me that everything is going to be OK."[145]

Conclusion

Our unique and special bond with our beloved companion animals speaks to their abilities to connect with our emotions and sense our feelings. Their ability to experience emotions can be used as proof that they are sentient creatures that deserve strong legal protection. Animal sentience for companion animals is vital and necessary, especially as more legal cases come forward concerning people's pets. These legal decisions can open the doors for other species. This cements changes that are needed to push and encourage lawmakers to consider the best interests of pets in court cases and to make decisions that factor in the individual companion animal's well-being rather than objectifying them and awarding monetary judgements.

The legal system needs to recognize animals as sentient beings and regard people's pets as special, inherently worthy, unique individuals with personalities and individual needs. It's not a one-size-fits-all approach. Animals are complex, and they have feelings. Their best interests should be considered. They can form special bonds and attachments with their human families, and they have special needs. They are worthy of love and respect, and they deserve better.

It is clear that today's mainstream society shares this view. There is a growing desire for updating these laws as jurisdictions around the world are changing their animal-protection laws to reflect the public's sentiment that

---

[144] "What Services Do Dogs Provide?" Service Dog Certifications (2 June 2016), https://www.servicedogcertifications.org/services-service-dogs-provide.

[145] Melissa Smith, "4 Service Dog Stories that Will Warm Your Heart," Petful (8 December 2016), https://www.petful.com/service-animal/heartwarming-service-dog-stories.

animals are sentient creatures; they are not property. What's fascinating is that there has been more progress as animal sentience laws are finally recognizing not only companion animals but also other animal species. That is a major step forward for animal rights. As sentiment grows for animals in our society, it is a victory for animals.

It is impressive that organizations such as the Nonhuman Rights Project have made it their mission to grant legal status to certain species of wildlife animals and to free confined wild animals to sanctuaries. As they work to achieve and advance the legal rights for members of certain animal species other than humans, a positive and changing sentiment is happening all over the world. If we keep this momentum going, ideally, the rest of Canada and the United States will stand with Quebec, Alaska, and California to recognize animal's best interests in divorce cases and to see them as sentient beings. They have needs, intelligence, and a whole range of abilities. They have the capacity to give and receive love.

CHAPTER 7

Have a Heart for Horses: End the Abuse and Slaughter of Horses

A Great Horse will change your life.
The truly special ones define it.
-AUTHOR UNKNOWN

Horses Are Heroes and Noble Creatures

There is another domesticated animal that deserves special status—horses. They are majestic and soulful creatures, which have been intricately connected to humans for thousands of years. Horses consistently impress us with their grand stature, intelligence, gentle demeanor, intuitive nature, and their emotional abilities, which help humans to heal.

My first up-close-and-personal encounter with a horse was an extraordinary experience. I had been pleading with my mother for years to learn how to ride horses at a nearby horse stable; however, my mother was worried that I might injure myself and that I was not old enough.

When I finally turned sixteen, my mother agreed to allow me to take horse-riding lessons. I was excited, but I had to wait until the summer. When school had finished, I eagerly signed up. I had never had the privilege of being that close to a real, live horse, so when I finally did, it was a very memorable experience. I was mesmerized at the large, imposing stature, strength, beauty, and nobility of the black horse that I met that day. Her name was Savannah. I vividly recall the feeling of awe and glory. I realized that this black beauty had a unique personality and that she was a shy horse.

I was instructed to be brave and not to show fear, as the horse would sense my feelings. It took some time to feel at ease with Savannah and to get to know each other. I was told that I needed to build her trust. The instructor showed me how to groom her, and I went to the barn whenever I could. I sensed that she recognized me. We started to communicate, and I built her trust. Eventually, I found the courage to ride Savannah, and stepping into the saddle was a special experience. Unfortunately, I reinjured my back after a few weeks of riding, so it was only a momentary experience.

Horse Advocate

Years later as a horse advocate, I came to understand the criticisms around riding horses. Through my advocacy work, I learned that horses are highly social animals that thrive on companionship. Horses can have rich and varied social lives, where they play and groom each other. Domestic horses need room to exercise and run. They require regular veterinary, dental, and hoof care. The sad fact is that most domestic horses in Canada and the United States (and all over the world) do not receive the care that they need. Often as horses get older, their medical needs grow, and the vet bills increase. Instead of caring for horses into their old age and providing them with a safe place after years of riding, breeding, showing, racing, pulling carriages, or working on farms, some horses are shipped over the border to be slaughtered.

Horses Deserve Better

Although horses play a distinct and unique role in society, their classification is not clearly defined. As mentioned, horses can be used for a variety of reasons to serve humankind. Yet other people keep horses as pets or companions, forming a special human-horse bond.

Due to this complexity in keeping and sharing our individual lives with horses, their role in society can be somewhat confusing. On the one hand, horses are regarded as domesticated animals that are kept by human handlers for riding or companionship. As such, these horses' statuses can be distinguished from working and wild horses. In other words, horses that are viewed as domesticated animals and are kept as companions (pets) are regarded as companion animals and family members, somewhat similar to cats and dogs. If you meet a human handler or caregiver of a horse, you quickly realize that his or her horse is a closely trusted friend, companion, and beloved member of the family.

On the other hand, there is a much different role and darker reality to the human relationship with other types of horses. Horses that are used for profit and entertainment are treated like objects and commodities in the horse-sporting industry. For many years, horse racing and betting were considered socially acceptable—an elegant sport available to the wealthy and privileged members of society. However, as this chapter highlights, using horses for human entertainment and profit has caused immense pain and suffering to these innocent creatures. It is a major setback for these innocent creatures and the animal-rights movement.

The Healing Power of Horses: Horses Are Intuitive Creatures

Horses and humans have enjoyed a long-standing and special bond throughout history. Like dogs, horses are loyal, and they can be therapeutic to humans. Through the use of equine therapy, horses can provide humans comfort and help with improving one's self-esteem, as they are natural therapists. They have been known to mirror people's body languages, and they are in tune with human emotions.

In an interesting article on animals that bond with humans, it may come as no surprise that horses are discussed.

"Research shows that horses have a strong capacity to recognize human emotions and positive and negative facial expressions," Tedeschi says. "They are particularly sensitive to anxiety and stress." And they can pick up on our emotions, as a result. People can have long, loving and very special relationships if they can build trust and affinity with a horse, this is most often accomplished by understanding horse psychology and communication and offering horses choices within this connection, [giving] trust instead of coercion.[146]

Healing with Horses

Horses are herd animals. They are known for attuning themselves to human emotion. As very intelligent and emotional animals, they can often reflect the behaviors of those around them. Learning to care for a horse can be rewarding, and it can help a human to improve his or her self-esteem and build confidence.

As we can see, horses are intuitive, they can sense humans' emotions, and they are accepting and nonjudgmental. Perhaps this is the reason that equine-assisted therapy has gained popularity. It has become a good experience for children and youth with self-confidence issues and those experiencing anxiety, stress, ADHD, autism spectrum disorder, depression, and PTSD. These gentle giants can provide the comfort, emotional support, and calmness to help humans who are dealing with all kinds of difficulties to heal. They teach us to be more patient and loving and also to overcome fear and set boundaries. As motivational speaker Tony Robbins noted, "Horses change lives. They give our young people confidence and self-esteem. They provide peace and tranquility to troubled souls—they give us hope."[147]

While researching horse therapy, I found this helpful information on Badge of Life, a Canadian website, which says,

"Equine Assisted Therapy is an innovative, evidence-based therapy practice which builds on the human-horse connection to help people learn more about themselves and to use that learning to change their lives. Equine Assisted Therapy involves no riding or horsemanship, making it both safe and effective. Clients work directly with horses face-to-face on

---

[146] Carolyn Steber, "9 Animals Capable of Bonding with Humans," Bustle (January 22, 2019), https://www.bustle.com/p/9-animals-that-can-connect-with-humans-15831321.

[147] Tony Robbins, "Horses Change Lives. They Give Our Young People Confidence and Self-Esteem. They Provide Peace and Tranquility to Troubled Souls—They Give Us Hope" (2020), https://twobeartrc.org/.

the same footing. This ground level work enables clients to better perceive the horses' actions and reactions as they work to process and solve their life challenges."[148]

I can understand the point of view of some animal rights activists who strongly oppose horse riding. I believe that horse therapy is different. I watched a television episode on Oprah Winfrey's show, which featured a clip of an activity that helped women heal with horses. Oprah and Gayle King were on a retreat with a selected group of sixty women who suffered from stressful life experiences. They went to Marival Spa, which was located in Arizona, for a spa treatment and to learn life balance through mindfulness.

In that episode, women encountered horses, and they could sense when the women were afraid. It showed a women's seemingly simple exercise of putting hoofs on the horses, which turned into a transformational experience. As stated on Oprah.com, "The Equine Experience,"

> One emotionally revealing activity at Miraval is the Equine Experience. With the help of best-selling author and psychotherapist Wyatt Webb, the women get to interact with horses on an emotional level. The goal is to get the horse to lift its leg so they can clean its hoof—but it is harder than it sounds. The horse senses how a person is feeling, and will only raise its leg when it feels comfortable.[149]

The horses were in tune with the women's emotions. They could sense their fear, and they would not cooperate when one of the women approached the horse. It was interesting that the horse actually sensed her fear. Finally, when the woman joined forces with another woman in the group, and they were no longer afraid, the horse cooperated and allowed them to put the hoof on. That experience helped them to gain confidence and to heal.

This television episode reminded me of when my husband and I signed up for a healing-with-horse's meditation experience through mindfulness, at a retreat in the countryside. We were open to the experience, but neither of

---

[148] https://badgeoflifecanada.org/self-care/equine-therapy/.
[149] "Girls Getaway: Arriving at Marival Spa, The Equine Experience," Oprah.com (May 14, 2007), https://www.oprah.com/health/Girls-Getaway.

us knew much about mindfulness or interacting with horses before we went. It was an amazing experience to be in nature (We live in the downtown area of a city) and out in the countryside and to encounter horses. I recall being intimidated by the horse's stature (standing at six feet tall). I seemed so much smaller, and I couldn't help but notice that the horse was very strong. Nonetheless, I realized quickly that this creature was not intending to harm me but was there to help me. The horse and I bonded during the meditation exercises, and by the end of the retreat, I was able to feed him carrots from my hand.

My husband later revealed that he enjoyed this experience. Being the only man at the retreat (He's a trooper), he had no idea that horses were so gentle and that they had the capability of sensing his emotions. The horse he was working with was the largest of the herd, and it took courage to connect with the horse, but he did it well. By the end of the retreat, the horse and my husband were buddies. Overall, it was an enjoyable and gratifying experience. I learned from this wonderful experience that horses are therapeutic. They can help humans practice patience and mindfulness through interactions with them. They can help us calm down and heal.

This personal experience taught me that horses are emotionally and intelligently deep animals. They are wise teachers, they can form bonds with humans, and they help them navigate through stressful situations with calmness and ease. Although horses are much larger and physically stronger than humans are, they can relate to us on our level of comfort and use their strength for goodness.

As well, during this mindfulness experience (which I recommend), I learned that each horse has its own individual personality, which is similar to other animals and humans. For instance, the horse that I bonded with at the retreat was shy and timid. It took some time, but once I became comfortable with this horse, I could sense a mutual affection and bond between us. In fact, every horse there was a unique creature. Earning a horse's trust can take some time, but it can be rewarding and empowering. It's a unique opportunity to form a connection with a horse and find inner strength, resilience, calmness, self-confidence, and self-esteem, through this kind of experience bonding with horses.

It was hard to imagine that any horse was being mistreated after having experienced those personal encounters with them. When you meet a horse firsthand, it's a memorable experience, but when you interact with them on an individual basis, something very special can happen. You begin to realize how horses' calm demeanors and kind natures help humans heal from stressful conditions, as they are therapeutic animals. You can see how remarkable horses are and that our connection to them deepens. It makes us more aware of how intuitive and emotional these majestic creatures really are. I simply cannot fathom that horses are used as objects and commodities for human entertainment or sport (racing horses). Even more horrifying is horses sent for slaughter. It is wrong and animal cruelty at its worst, but this is the sad reality for so many horses. Horses are treated differently in our society, which is dependent on their roles. They can be beloved family members, healers, therapists, loyal companions, and friends.

Here's a story of one horse's life. It was used as a racehorse, it became a family member, and then it was sent to slaughter to face an unthinkable and untimely death. Sargon's story can serve as a reminder that horses deserve stronger legal protection and that horse slaughter must end.

Sargon's Sad Story

Horses are betrayed by the current state of the laws in Canada and the United States. Horse racing is another inhumane activity. Humans who engage in horse racing use whips and electric prods to force horses to sprint at speeds so fast that they often sustain injuries like hemorrhages in their lungs.[150] Every week on average, twenty-four horses experience fatal break-downs and injuries at racetracks across the United States.[151] This does not include the horses that are discarded by the racing industry when they are no longer profitable. Horses are viewed as commodities. Their wants, needs, feelings, and health are not considered. What many do not know is that when horses are no longer making their owners a profit, many are discarded and sent to slaughter.

In Canada, selling horses to be slaughtered and consumed for meat is still legal. The shocking story of a family horse named Sargon is an example

---

[150] "Horse Racing," PETA, https://www.peta.org/issues/animals-in-entertainment/horse-racing-2.
[151] Ibid.

of the pain and betrayal that is caused by a lack of protections for horses. Sargon was a thoroughbred that later became a therapy horse. He lived with his caregiver, Kim Wilson, and her son, in Lindsey, Ontario. As a former racehorse, Sargon was bought and cared for by Kim for six years. He was her therapy horse. She lovingly took him in when he was no longer able to be used for racing purposes. She taught him tricks and provided him with comfort, love, and a loving home.[152]

In August 2016, a woman whom Kim was in contact with asked for Sargon to be temporarily rehomed to her farm, supposedly to be a therapy horse and companion for an elderly man with cancer. Kim agreed, but she had no intention of transferring legal ownership of Sargon and planned to visit him while he was on the farm. Kim made considerable efforts to ensure that the new home would be suitable for Sargon before transferring him. Unbeknownst to Kim, it turned out that these new caregivers had no intention of caring for Sargon. He was suddenly and quietly sent to a horse-boarding facility and sold for meat. Sargon was never seen alive again.[153]

Sargon's Legacy Lives On

I had no idea this horrific horse tragedy was happening in my country! This shocking sad story of Sargon being sent to a slaughterhouse in Quebec without his guardian's consent and without any warning or opportunity to save his life was unthinkable. It was apparent that Kim and Sargon formed a special human-horse bond during their six years together. This would be the only period in his life where he was accepted and loved as a beloved family member rather than viewed as an object and commodity.

The news clipping of this innocent horse remains etched in my mind forever. To make matters even more concerning, when he was being used as a commodity and racehorse, Sargon was allegedly injected with various drugs to enhance his performance. This sad reality brought up concerns about public safety, given that he was slaughtered for human consumption.

---

[152] https://radiowaterloo.ca/justice-for-sargon-kim-wilson-stolen-therapy-horse-retired-racehorse-sold-to-slaughter/.
[153] Ibid.

He was a loved companion animal, and Kim cared about and loved her horse and in return he loved Kim too. Unfortunately, this situation is more common than people can imagine. Thousands of innocent horses are sent to slaughter each year. Raising public awareness and education about the tragedy of horse slaughter can bring more attention and sympathy to their plights.

Kim's story was featured on the front cover of newspapers. She was pictured with her beloved horse. I was surprised to learn about the large number of horses that are sold and slaughtered for meat each day. I cannot imagine that in Canada, horse slaughter is happening in front of our eyes. This is the ultimate betrayal to our trusted friends. They have so loyally served humans. My hope for Sargon is that his unthinkable fate and story live on in our hearts and that they are motivations for serious efforts to end the horrible horse-slaughter industry in the future.

Horse Slaughter and an Urge for Change

Thousands of horses in Canada are exported each year from Canadian cities. It is a profitable business. Horsemeat is seen as a delicacy for human consumption when the horse is no longer of economic value to their human handler. These poor horses often spend over twenty-four hours in transport, without water, food, or rest. They endure an unthinkable fate when they are slaughtered in inhumane ways for Japanese delicacy horsemeat called *basashi*. There are groups taking action. Horse activists hold protests, seek to ban this horrific practice, and show their dismay, but unfortunately, this transport is legal in Canada. As stated in *The Guardian*'s article, "Canadian law allows them to be exported without food, rest or even water for up to 28 hours." [154]

It may be hard to learn that this practice happens in many parts of the world, including Mexico and France, but when I heard it was happening in my home country, it became more personal and horrifying. These horses that are shipped abroad for slaughter are later processed and consumed by

---

[154] "Protests at Inhumane Export of Live Horses to Japan for Food" *The Guardian* (2021), https://www.theguardian.com/environment/2021/mar/27/protests-at-inhumane-export-of-live-horses-to-japan-for-food.

humans. These horses are typically sent in live shipments to Japan and South Korea. Imagine your family dog or cat sitting in a dark and cold shipping container for weeks of transport, confined, scared, unable to move, and not provided with food or water. It's a fate worse than one can imagine.

Although it is illegal to sell a horse for human consumption in the United States, horses are shipped to countries like Canada, France, and Mexico, where they are slaughtered for their meat. When horses are shipped alive, they are crammed together in very tight cold cages, and they are unable to even lie down or rest. Legislation permits horses to be transported for up to thirty-six hours without access to food or water, but it is sometimes much longer because of flight delays.[155] In many instances, horses acquire injuries during transport.[156] In Canada, the Health of Animals Regulation stipulates that there must be sufficient headroom for the horses to stand in a natural position, but this is consistently violated by the Canadian Food Inspection Agency (CFIA). There are also many cases of horses dying or being injured during transport.[157]

Once at the slaughterhouse, the suffering continues. The problem is exacerbated by the methods used to incapacitate the horses to prepare them for slaughter. Horses are stunned with captive bolt guns prior to slaughter. However, many horses cannot be stunned effectively, which means they are sometimes conscious when killed.[158] Furthermore, horses endure psychological and emotional trauma, as they are flight animals, and killing them in an assembly-line environment makes them panic even more.[159]

---

[155] Canadian Horse Defence Coalition, "Ask Air Atlas to End the Shipment of Live Horses for Slaughter," Change.org (2015), https://www.change.org/p/richard-broekman-staff-vice-president-commercial-development-and-charter-sales-email-richard-broekm-peter-beckett-senior-director-charter-sales-and-marketing-email-peter-beckett-atlasair-com-jo-ask-atlas-air-to-end-the-shipment-of-live-horses-f.

[156] Sara Amundson and Kitty Block, "Bipartisan Bill Introduced in Congress to End Slaughter of American Equines," A Humane World (5 February 2019), blog.humanesociety.org/2019/01/bipartisan-bill-introduced-in-congress-to-end-slaughter-of-american-equines.html.

[157] "CHDC Sues CFIA for Overcrowding of Horses Exported for Slaughter," Canadian Horse Defence Coalition (2018), https://defendhorsescanada.org/chdc-sues-cfia-for-overcrowding-of-horses-exported-for-slaughter.

[158] "The Status of Horse Slaughter in Canada," Animal Justice (2013), https://www.animaljustice.ca/blog/the-status-of-horse-slaughter-in-canada.

[159] "Why End Horse Slaughter," Canadian Horse Defence Coalition (2018), https://canadianhorsedefencecoalition.org/why-end-horse-slaughter.

This extremely inhumane procedure in which the horses are transported and killed is only part of the problem. Horses that are transported out of the United States are most often retired racehorses or have been treated as family/companion animals. They have not been raised specifically for human consumption. They ingest many drugs that traditionally regulated food animals would not be permitted to consume. This includes a frequently administered painkiller dubbed bute, which is a US Food and Drug Administration and CFIA-banned carcinogen.[160] Not only does the law allow horses to be moved to other jurisdictions where it is legal to slaughter them, but the horsemeat being consumed may be laden with prohibited and dangerous drugs.

In response to these issues and in an effort to ban this horrible practice, US federal legislation called the Save America's Forgotten Equines Act (SAFE) Act was introduced. The SAFE Act would have permanently banned the transport of American horses out of the United States to countries where they could be legally slaughtered.[161] There is no federal law preventing individuals from shipping horses out of the United States to be slaughtered for meat. There is also promise that individual cities and states will enact this legislation. For instance, the city of Colorado has introduced legislation to ban horse slaughter.

Several factors can influence the purchase of horses for slaughter. Horses that are vulnerable to purchase and slaughter are ones that may lack training, have medical or genetic conditions that render them useless to humans, or be considered too old.[162] A horse may also become unwanted if a human caregiver suffers economic challenges and simply cannot care for the horse any longer. Horses can be given to seemingly caring and well-meaning individuals, who end up selling them for slaughter, just like Sargon. Tragic stories like this one happen, every single year, to horses that are transitioning into new homes.

Thankfully, there are many horse lovers, enthusiasts, advocates, and

---

[160] "The Status of Horse Slaughter in Canada," Animal Justice (2013), https://www.animaljustice.ca/blog/the-status-of-horse-slaughter-in-canada.

[161] Ibid.

[162] Michelle N. Anderson, "Homeless Horses: An Update on Unwanted Horses in the United States," The Horse (9 Oct. 2018), thehorse.com/160071/homeless-horses-an-update-on-unwanted-horses-in-the-united-states.

activists and caring groups working toward bringing inhumane practices against horses to an end. For instance, the Canadian Horse Defense Coalition (CHDC) is an incredible organization that strives to shed light on the horrific practices imposed on horses. The CHDC has called upon the House of Commons to make changes and to prohibit the exportation and slaughter of horses for meat, specifically by amending the Health of Animals Act.[163]

HORSES USED FOR RIDING
Stella's Story: From Heartbreak to Happiness

As I continue to advocate for animals, I get approached by animal rescues from time to time. Recently, I was contacted by a rescue regarding a couple who wanted to give up their majestic, young mare named Stella, a four-year-old purchased solely as a riding horse. I was told that she was a wedding gift, which a husband John had bought his wife Tracy. They were newly married. John bought Stella for a lot of money from a horse breeder, who guaranteed her to be in good health. Unbeknownst to John, Stella had a genetic disease that caused her to drag her hooves and stumble. It interfered with her ability to be ridden. His wife no longer wanted her when she found out that Stella could not be ridden, leaving this creature with no place to go.

They tried to return the horse to the breeder, but he did not want her back. Sadly, both parties involved—the breeder and the human handlers (John and Tracy)—did not want to keep Stella as a companion. Instead, they saw her as nothing more than a commodity and just another unwanted horse destined for an unthinkable fate. I found out that if Stella did not find a home, their veterinarian was willing to put her down, which was terrifying. The rescue organization that contacted me was full. They did not have space for Stela. When I learned about this sad story, I tried to find her a home or at the very least, another rescue organization that was willing to provide temporary shelter, comfort, and care. I wanted to ensure

---

[163] "New E-Petition Calling on the House of Commons to Prohibit Horse Slaughter," Canadian Horse Defence Coalition (2016), https://canadianhorsedefencecoalition. wordpress.com/2016/08/27/new-e-petition-calling-on-the-house-of-commons-to-prohibit-horse-slaughter/.

that she found a home with a new family that loved her or find a place at an animal sanctuary.

This horse's journey to find a home was not a simple one. I was given a one-week deadline to find her a suitable home; otherwise, she would be euthanized. The couple was still paying for boarding fees, so they were not happy. Thankfully, through collaboration (working with rescues) and sheer determination, I found another animal rescue that had space for Stella to stay temporarily. They were keen to help and join in the search to relocate Stella safely.

With only a few days left until she was to be euthanized, I reassured the couple that we would find her a safe place. We were hit by a stroke of luck. The couple was pressuring me, as they wouldn't continue to pay for her boarding. A rescue wrote back and agreed to take Stella into its care. It promised to help find Stella a loving family that would open its heart and home to this horse. This animal rescue recognized the value of her life, despite her medical condition. She was finally saved when she was adopted by a human family that was looking for another horse.

Stella is showered with love from her new human family. I received a kind note from the lady who adopted Stella. It turned out that the woman has several other rescue horses but told me that Stella was the most magical horse that she's had, due to her sensitivity and gentle demeanor. Stella even has a goofy personality. The lady that adopted Stella thanked me for helping to save her life. Thankfully, Stella is free to enjoy the rest of her life on her own terms, with a loving family, on a farm with other rescue horses. I am grateful to have played a small part in Stella's story and to share in this happy ending. I was overjoyed when I received photos and updates from her human family, which showed Stella living her remaining days freely, in open country pastures on a farm with other horses and a loving family who cares about her, as she deserves it.

The Ugly Truth of Horse Racing

Most horses are not as lucky as Stella. Racehorses are pushed to their physical and mental limits. They are forced to perform for human entertainment and profit. These animals are the heart of the horse-racing industry, yet so many die sad and lonely deaths. Although horse racing has been an immensely popular sport in the US and a lucrative industry that generates billions of dollars in revenue, it takes a heavy toll on the health and well-being of the horses. In essence, horses in the industry become commodities that are utilized for racing and then discarded when they are no longer physically capable of performing as well as they did at the peak of their career.

Recently, a news headline flashed on my news page, revealing that thirty thoroughbred horses had died at the Santa Anita racetrack in California during one year. Two of these horses, Formal Duke and Truffalino, suffered and died from injuries related to racing and to race-day injuries. Truffalino had a fatal heart attack, and Formal Duke had to be euthanized due to the extent of his injuries. Deaths such as these are common in the horse-racing industry. The unnecessary and preventable deaths of these horses are far more common than we think, and until recently, they seem to have gone largely unnoticed.

Fortunately, the governor of California, Gavin Newsom, reacted positively to public outrage over these recent deaths in Santa Anita and signed legislation allowing state officials to intervene by suspending or shutting down racetracks with little notice to the owners. This is a positive step forward in the fight to abolish an outdated and cruel sport, which has little regard for the horses' lives.

Horse racing is one of the most horrific examples of animal abuse and exploitation. It features two frighteningly juxtaposed versions of reality— one of an elegant and highly regarded sport that is catering to wealthy people, and another that uses these innocent creatures as a means of profit and human entertainment. Support for the horrible horse-racing industry is slowly dwindling, and more people are voicing their opposition to the mistreatment of horses in this cruel sport.

Perhaps the deaths at the Santa Anita racetrack have sparked this recent outrage and concern, which have been compounded with a greater societal awareness about this horrific industry and the animal exploitation that ensues. Many US states are passing laws to punish those convicted of animal cruelty crimes. This public sentiment, along with updated laws, is leading to a shift away from horse racing as a socially acceptable form of entertainment.

Horse racing as a sport should be outlawed. Horse racing as an industry cannot survive in the long term without public support. As sad as these recent deaths are, they have brought to the forefront of the public's eyes, the much-needed public attention to this horrific and ugly truth. It has been revealed that thoroughbred horses are drugged; hit, abused, and forced to race when they are lame (suffering physically and in pain). They are too often neglected and abused.

Horses are at the heart of this sport, but their well-being is the last priority. We can hope that as people realize animal cruelty and horse abuse are the names of this game, this barbaric sport will lose its popularity, and horse racing will not survive. I think it's safe to say that the horse-racing industry is losing and on its way out. Thanks to animal advocates, activists, horse lovers, caring citizens, and animal-welfare organizations vocalizing for horse protection this sport will not last. Horses will be valued and regarded as worthy and noble creatures and no longer used for riding, racing, or working when these types of industries are shut down.

Remembering Ryder the New York City Carriage Horse

Media attention was drawn to the New York City (NYC) horse carriage industry in August 2022 when Ryder, an elderly, beautiful brown horse collapsed on the streets. Ryder was a 26 year old Standardbred NYC carriage horse who fell down on a sweltering hot and humid day on the summer streets of Manhattan. Thankfully, there was a bystander who recorded a video that went viral on social media, which helped bring public attention. At that time of his collapse, Ryder was losing weight, looked frail and emancipated and a veterinarian suspected lymphoma, according to a spokeswoman for the carriage industry. This heartbreaking video of Ryder's horrible fall was shared on social media and it sparked a call to action with activists taking a stand against this cruel and inhumane industry calling for a ban to horse carriages. After this tragedy, Ryder was allowed to live out his remaining days in peace at a farm sanctuary but collapsed on the farm and suffered a seizure so the decision was made to euthanize him. Sadly, Ryder died where he had been retired after his accident. Allie Taylor, the president of Voters for Animal Rights, said in a statement "Ryder's death is yet another tragic reminder that horse carriages do not belong on the streets of New York City."[164]

A CALL TO ACTION TO END CRUEL HORSE INDUSTRIES

How You Can Help Horses and Become a Horse Advocate

Action is needed to ensure that cruel carriage horse industries are banned and lawmakers pass the SAFE Act. If you live in the United States, you can help horses by writing to your local politicians and encouraging them to support this legislation. You can share details about SAFE's legislation on social media and educate others. By doing so, you bring attention to this important cause, and you can gain broader support from the community.

There are groups working to pass SAFE. This initiative shows the power of groups working together—the collaboration of the equine industry and animal welfare organizations—which formed the Final Stretch Alliance to End Horse Slaughter, to permanently ban the slaughter of American horses. This strong alliance urges US federal lawmakers to permanently ban horse slaughter in the US and end the export of American horses for slaughter in other countries.[165] This is promising news for the future of horses. It will end this horrific industry. Finally, horses have a strong voice.

Canadians need to push for similar legislation to be passed in Canada. Not only should Canada ban the sale of horses for meat slaughter on a federal level but also ban the exportation of horses for the purposes of slaughter. Simply banning the slaughter of horses in Canada may only

---

164 Sarah Maslin Mir, "The Horse Who Reignited New York's Carriage Ride Controversy Has Died," The New York Times (October 2022), https://www.nytimes.com/2022/10/17/nyregion/carriage-ride-horse-dead.html.

165 "Equine Industry and Animal Welfare Organizations Announce Collaborative Effort to Pass Horse Ban Slaughter," The Humane Society of the United States (May 2022), https://www.humanesociety.org/news/equine-industry-and-animal-welfare-organizations-announce-collaborative-effort-ban-horse.

exacerbate the problem, as horses would continue to be shipped to Mexico, where it is still legal.

If you live in Canada, check out the Humane Society International's website. You can become informed, learn how they are pushing for a federal ban on horse slaughter by raising public awareness, actively campaigning for legislative change in Canada, and read about Animal Justice's joint efforts with the Manitoba Humane Society, as they work to ban this cruel practice. You can also join forces and collaborate with the United States and other countries in Europe to help put an end to this tragedy. These silenced horses need our strong voices. You can become a horse advocate and join the Canadian Horse Defence Coalition. On social media, you can even follow organizations such as Horses in our Hands that focus on advocacy efforts to help horses.

Further, banning the slaughter of horses in Canada without banning exportation may add to the number of horses killed in Japan. According to Statistics Canada, although in recent years, there has been a decline in demand, over 1,300 horses were exported to Japan between January and March of 2017, "A batch valued at more than $3.5 million."[166] These horses are typically raised for meat on remote farms in Alberta. Once they are ready to be shipped, they are taken to the Calgary International Airport and loaded into crates, sometimes with four horses crowded into one crate.[167] They remain in the crates for up to twenty-six hours, without food or water until they land in Japan for slaughter.[168]

There are several resources and avenues that one can take to help horses avoid tragic fates. For instance, Michelle Anderson, digital managing editor for TheHorse.com has provided several ideas for ways that people can get involved. Horse caregivers can draft retirement plans for their horses as a contingency, should they have a sudden change of circumstances. On an individual basis, horse lovers can volunteer at animal rescues to help train, adopt, and handle horses. By volunteering or donating to horse

---

[166] Anna Brooks, "Tracking Canada's Horse Slaughtering Trade from Alberta to Japan," Vice (15 June 2017), www.vice.com/en_ca/article/zmegw4/tracking-canadas-horse-slaughtering-trade-from-alberta-to-japan.
[167] Ibid.
[168] Ibid.

organizations that care for them in transition, you can make a real difference to their quality of life.[169]

In the United States, there is hope on the horizon as SAFE gains momentum: The horrific horse slaughter for the meat industry will lose its support. I know most of us that care about horses and their fates look forward to the day this federal law is passed. We know that most people are vehemently opposed to the slaughter of horses for human consumption. This public sentiment is reflected in the laws of numerous US states, including California, Texas, New Jersey, and Illinois, all of which passed laws against the cruel practice of horse slaughter. Let's keep the hope that SAFE passes as a federal ban on horse slaughter in the US. In the meantime, we must keep advocating for horses.

Conclusion

We can work together to improve the plight of these majestic creatures. Horses have a long-standing history of serving humans. They've loyally fought in battle with our soldiers. They've provided human transportation, entertainment, and emotional, psychological, and developmental therapy and been companions to humans. It is time to give back to horses and to recognize them as trusted, brave, and loyal friends, unique individuals, family members, and emotionally intelligent creatures, which deserve to be loved and treated with dignity and respect.

Stronger laws that protect horses such as SAFE need to be passed for these deserving creatures. Politicians are crucial for this initiative to succeed with legislative changes. However, it's up to the people who care about horse issues to become vocal advocates and to inform the public masses and society of what is happening. The formation of the alliance for SAFE is an example of collaboration between various organizations. Individuals that are interested in advocacy need to speak up for silenced horses. As an animal advocate and horse defender, you can contact your local municipalities and start political lobbying campaigns with community building to rescue horses headed for slaughter. You can check websites such as Animal

---

[169] Michelle Anderson, "Six Ways to Help Horses," TheHorse.Com (26 April 2015), https://thehorse.com/111923/six-ways-to-help-horses/.

League Defense Fund (ALDF) and the Humane Society in the United Sates (HSUS) for helpful guidelines on helping horses. You can contact the Horse Defense Coalition of Canada (HDCC) if you are located in Canada.

Small changes can make a big difference. Every single one of us can help horses. You can volunteer at an animal sanctuary that rescues horses. You can post stories of horses that have been sent to slaughter on social media to wake up and educate others, bring attention, and expose horse slaughters. If mainstream support becomes as strong in Canada as it is in the US, this industry will eventually lose ground. You can inform others that riding in horse-drawn carriages or purchasing horses from a horse breeder condones animal mistreatment. There are many ways to make a difference for horses that need to be saved.

Many horse rescues and sanctuaries hold fundraising events, and these can be great opportunities to learn more, get involved, become educated, and raise awareness on horse's plight. You can advocate for abused and neglected horses. Remember, horses require special care that can be costly, and these rescues and sanctuaries rely on people's donations and volunteer efforts to continue to help horses in need of special care.

You can become a horse advocate, contact your local animal organizations, and find out how to adopt or sponsor a rescue horse. You can help find a temporary placement, foster, or search for a home by raising funds for horses in need. You can work with a local animal rescue organization that is willing to raise funds for horses. I encourage you to make a difference by getting involved and helping to save a horse's life. Horses are so magical and offer so much to humans that they can literally change people's lives. They are intuitive and intelligent creatures that deserve to be loved and treated with dignity and respect. Horses are here *with* us not for us.

CHAPTER 8

Sentience: Animals Experience Emotions and Why It Matters

There is no fundamental difference between man and animals in their ability to feel pleasure and pain, happiness and misery.

—CHARLES DARWIN

As I often say, the way we treat animals –companion, farm, and wildlife –is a reflection of our moral progress. As highlighted in chapter 6, the common law system in many places still regards animals as personal property—treated the same way as inanimate objects like chairs or cars. Under the common-law legal system, the legal status of animals as property has existed this way for hundreds of years. However, it is very problematic when judges make decisions based on an animal's status using this definition. It is an antiquated view, which does not provide adequate legal protection for animals or consider their best interests, as the law is limiting and outdated.

Although likening an animal to an inanimate object such as a piece of furniture or a person's vehicle, which has no feelings or emotions, is the law, it is inconceivable to most of us, and this view is unpopular among mainstream society. As well, scientific research that proves otherwise is convincing the public that this is not the case. Animals are *not* inanimate objects, and they should not be regarded as personal property. The legal system that regards them as such doesn't recognize that animals are complex, living, breathing, individual creatures.

> The question is not can they reason, nor can they talk, but can they suffer?

This quote was written in the eighteenth century by Jeremy Bethan, a famous English philosopher and social reformist. It fits well. In fact, animals can experience a wide range of emotions: happiness, sadness, fear, and pain. They can certainly suffer, so the notion of animals as property does not fit or conform to scientific data. Also, anyone who has shared his or her life with an animal companion can attest to the fact that the pet is a beloved member of the family. Based on these views, animals deserve stronger legal protection under the law. It is our moral obligation to protect vulnerable animals from unnecessary pain, suffering, and harm.

Looking into Lily's warm brown eyes, which are so full of love and expression, or hearing Freddie's squeals of excitement whenever I enter the room (even if I've left for only a few moments) are evidence that Lily and Freddie experience a wide range of emotions. I cannot imagine them being treated as inanimate objects. My companion animals are family members.

Laws that suggest that animals are akin to objects and personal possessions that belong to us, that they do not have feelings and emotions, or that they do not experience suffering are outdated. Thankfully, this view is losing ground, as the tables are turning in favor of granting stronger protection to animals. We can see laws around the world changing to reflect modern-day society's public sentiment that animals have feelings, and they deserve legal protection.

Animals are amazing creatures with the capacity for happiness, sadness, pleasure, and pain. As more scientific data is brought forward that proves their abilities to feel much in this world, more people are speaking up for them. As more people seek legal protection for their furry family members in the judicial system, animal's best interests are going to be considered, and I believe the laws will change to reflect the mainstream views of animals.

Hope is on the Horizon

Progressive animal laws from countries all over the world are beginning to shift in a positive direction and to recognize that animals are sentient creatures with feelings and emotions; therefore, they should not be considered personal property. When the laws are updated to recognize companion animals as sentient creatures, I believe this change will open the doors for other animal species. In other words, when the legal system codifies that companion animals have the right to protection, the laws can consider their best interests in divorce cases and provide adequate protection against animal abusers. The criminal justice system can align itself by increasing penalties when sentencing criminals who are convicted of abusing animals.

Currently, companion animals—in particular dogs and cats—have the strongest legal protections. For example, companion animals are protected by cruelty laws in every US state. Unfortunately, other animal species, such as farm animals and wild animals, are offered minimal protection. A study from *The New York Times* revealed that the sights and smells of familiar humans can activate a part of a dog's brain that is called the caudate, which is associated with positive emotions.[170] These sensory experiences are not limited to dogs. Other studies have shown that several species (rats, whales, and elephants) feel and exhibit emotions just as humans do. For example, in studies, rats have shown empathy for their fellow species, opting to save other rats instead of getting a treat for themselves. Elephants, whales, and chimpanzees are known to show grief-like behaviors in the wake of loss.[171] Bereaved mother monkeys that have lost a child turn to their communities for help, expanding their social networks.[172]

These studies confirm what animal lovers already know: All animal species are sentient. They can experience a full range of feelings and emotions: happiness, sadness, pain, suffering, loneliness, and fear. Animals have

---

[170] Gregory Berns, "Dogs Are People, Too," *New York Times* (5 Oct 2013), nytimes.com/2013/10/06/opinion/sunday/dogs-are-people-too.html.

[171] Jessica Pierce, "Do Animals Experience Grief?" The Conversation (24 Aug 2018), https://www.smithsonianmag.com/science-nature/do-animals-experience-grief-180970124.

[172] Jonathan Balcombe, "Yes, Animals Have Feelings," *LiveScience* (11 Dec 2014), https://www.livescience.com/49093-animals-have-feelings.html.

a desire to be loved, and they express love for one another. This awareness of other nonhuman animals' abilities to feel the same way as a dog or cat does can bring about change and open the door for other species.

Animal Sentience and Why It Matters

It is promising that there has been a shift in recognizing that other animals are capable of experiencing a wide range of emotions and that they are sentient. For instance, Marc Bekoff, a well-known professor of ecology and evolutionary biology, has worked extensively with nonhuman animals, and he actively researches animal sentience. I have read many of his articles. One of his most remarkable stories came from a trip to Kenya. While watching a group of wild elephants, he noticed that one of the elephants, Babyl, was crippled, and she could not travel as fast as the rest of the herd. From a pure survivalist perspective, one would think that the other elephants would leave her behind to fend for herself, but they waited for her. Bekoff's guide confirmed that they had been doing this for years. The other elephants were waiting for Babyl because they cared for her.[173]

Carl Safina, another animal researcher, tells a story of an old and almost blind woman getting lost. She was found the next day surrounded by elephants, which were guarding her.[174] They saw another creature in distress and chose to help. Not only do they have their own emotions, but they can also feel and respond to the pain and suffering of others. These real-life animal stories show us the complexity of their emotions, especially considering the way that some wildlife animals, such as majestic, compassionate, social, and intelligent elephants, are treated when they are held in captivity and the lack of legal protection that is offered to them.

---

[173] Marc Bekoff, "The Emotional Lives of Animals," *PBS Nature* (31 October 2012), https://www.pbs.org/wnet/nature/animal-odd-couples-excerpt-the-emotional-lives-of-animals/8005.

[174] Simon Worrall, "Yes, Animals Think and Feel. Here's How We Know," *National Geographic* (15 July 2015), https://www.nationalgeographic.com/news/2015/07/150714-animal-dog-thinking-feelings-brain-science/#close.

The Science on Sentience

Over 2,500 research studies confirm that animals do experience emotions just like humans.[175] This innate ability in animals to experience emotions (animal sentience) has long been discussed by philosophers and scientists alike; however, it has only recently begun to be acknowledged and finally recognized by political thinkers, the scientific community, and legal authorities. In 2009, the European Union recognized animal sentience in its Treaty of Lisbon. Cambridge University proclaimed animal sentence in 2012 with its Cambridge Declaration on Consciousness.[176]

Some may say that animal sentience is virtually undeniable; however, laws are many steps behind mainstream society's views in some countries. For instance, one might be surprised to learn that the laws in place to protect animals in Canada are minimal. There are criminal laws, which forbid "unnecessary pain, suffering or injury to an animal" and "causing … injury by willful neglect."[177] This is a low bar of legal protection. On a promising note, there are countries and states that are starting to legally consider animals as sentient, which can create a positive ripple effect for the rights of animals and their legal statuses as individuals with feelings.

In Quebec, Canada, animal sentience was codified in the laws in 2015, and this change made it more difficult for their citizens to mistreat animals, thus offering them protection.[178] By classifying animals as sentient in some countries like New Zealand, they have made more progress and banned cosmetic testing on animals.[179]

---

[175] Emily Birch, "Crying Elephants and Giggling—Animals Have Feelings, Too," The Conservation (10 January 2018), https://theconversation.com/crying-elephants-and-giggling-rats-animals-have-feelings-too-87977.

[176] Suzanne Monyak, "When the Law Recognizes Animals as People," The New Republic (2 February 2018), https://newrepublic.com/article/146870/law-recognizes-animals-people; European Union, *Treaty of Lisbon Amending the Treaty on European Union and the Treaty Establishing the European Community*, 13 December 2007, 2007/C 306/01, available at: https://www.refworld.org/docid/476258d32.html.

[177] Criminal Code, RSC, c C-46, (1985), 444-447.

[178] "Quebec Defines Animals as 'Sentient Beings' in New Legislation," *CTV News* (4 December 2015), https://www.ctvnews.ca/politics/quebec-defines-animals-as-sentient-beings-in-new-legislation-1.2687500.

[179] Monyak, *Supra,* note 144.

While the United States does not recognize animal sentience federally, states such as California, Alaska, and Illinois that are paving the way. They require judges in divorce cases to consider the best interests of the companion animal when deciding pet-custody disputes.[180] In some ways, this is similar to human family law cases when couples are separating and the best interest of the child is applied. This acknowledges that an animal has physical and emotional needs beyond those of an inanimate object.

These positive, progressive steps offer promise for the future of animal rights. They flow from the recognition of animals as sentient and more than property. These states in America are just a few examples of changes that are happening worldwide. For instance in Europe, a separating couple in Spain was granted joint custody of their pet dog, Panda. He was a Border collie that both parties wanted to keep, after their split from a twenty-month relationship. They went to court and allowed a judge to decide if the man or woman in this case could have ownership of Panda. In a rare ruling, the judge decided that both parties had joint responsibility and that they could be co-caretakers of the dog. This decision to regard the best interests of the dog and to recognize the relationship of the couple to the dog more as guardianship rather than property opens the doors to more favorable judgements in other countries. According to an article in *People* magazine, "The judge's ruling takes a clear stance that pets should be considered living beings under the law, as opposed to property."[181]

Punky the Dog Goes to the Supreme Court of Canada

Not recognizing that animals are sentient and are able to experience a range of emotions can have disastrous consequences in many other types of cases, including a dog bite. Punky, the cattle dog, suffered a tragic end at the hands of the law. This four-year-old dog was deemed dangerous and was put down following a biting incident at a local dog park in 2017.

---

[180] Ibid.

[181] Katie Campione, "Judge in Spain Grants Couple Joint Custody of Their Dog Panda in Rare Ruling," People 21 October 2021), https://people.com/pets/judge-in-spain-grants-couple-joint-custody-of-their-dog-panda-in-rare-ruling/.

For two years, Punky was separated from his human guardian, Susan Santics, who was in a legal limbo while fighting vehemently to save his precious life. He was kept confined in an animal shelter, isolated, and away from his family. The public rallied behind Punky, creating online petitions to save him from being killed. Santics was heartbroken and requested to see her beloved dog so that she could say a final goodbye and give him some treats and love before losing him forever. But there was no empathy or opportunity that was offered to Susan in the cruel Canadian justice system and her request was denied.

The Supreme Court of Canada denied hearing Punky's case, and he was put down with no chance of redemption.[182] The fact is that Punky misbehavior proves that he was a sentient being, which felt emotions. He had the capacity to make mistakes, as humans do. The love that he gave to Susan and the rest of his family and the anxiety and sadness that he must have felt in his final days are heartbreaking. This sad story showed that the Canadian public believed that Punky's life was worth fighting for and that he was a sentient being, which was capable of redemption. He deserved a second chance. However, the Canadian legal system failed him. It is time to take a stand for dogs like Punky so that similar cases are not lost in a legal battle. Punky's precious life was taken because he was regarded as no more than an inanimate object.

I cannot imagine the pain and agony of losing one of my furry babies to the legal system. While I read Punky's story and followed the case, the dog reminded me of Lily, a large-breed dog. Being a German shepherd with guarding instincts, she can be territorial and intimidating. We were almost in a similar circumstance when she was younger. We when we took her outside; another large dog in a dog park attacked her. After that incident, something changed, and Lily became fearful of other large dogs. She was not friendly to other dogs anymore. She was fine with the family but not with strangers. That being said, when our children were younger, they were left somewhat unattended with Lily from an early age. They played dress up, fetch, and her favorite game—being chased with a tennis ball in her

---

[182] Jason Proctor, "Dead Dog Walking: Can Punky Ever Be a 'Good Canine Citizen' Again?" *CBC News* (13 Apr 2019), https://www.cbc.ca/news/canada/british-columbia/dangerous-dogs-punky-court-1.5096502.

mouth. She was always kind to them. But looking back now, I realize that dogs can be unpredictable, so it's important to be vigilant.

We are aware that she's a large dog and that she could pose a threat to public safety. I cannot help but wonder what would have happened if she had bitten someone. I would probably have defended her legal right to live and have fought for a chance at rehabilitation with dog training. Through my experience as a former dog defender, I know the laws are strict regarding dog bites; in Punky's case, the judge's insistence on conviction with the death penalty was too severe and another example of an outdated legal system. This case had a disappointing outcome, and it was a wake-up call that it could happen to any other dog. The law system is lagging.

Law reform is needed. Every time a dangerous dog case ends as Punky's did (dog losing its life with a death sentence), it becomes easier to justify the killing of dogs, which under the right conditions, could have had a good chance of rehabilitation. The allowance for courts to make conditional orders and give chances would balance the public's need for safety and the responsibilities of guardians. Humans have a moral and ethical obligation to protect animals, and Punky's legacy can live on to continue to advocate for changes to the legal system.

CHAPTER 9

Social Justice: Animal Abuse as a Precursor to Human Violence

> You can judge a man's true character by the way he treats his fellow animals.
> **—SIR PAUL MCCARTNEY**

I often say the way that we treat the most vulnerable members of society, including children, the elderly, and animals, reflects back on ourselves. Please be kind and show compassion.

In criminal animal-abuse cases, whether negligent or intentional, the convicted perpetrator rarely gets punished appropriately. Animal abuse and cruelty raise serious questions about our society at a deeper level. It asks us to examine our values and our moral and social progress as we move toward a more just and peaceful humanity.

Violence toward animals was proven to be linked to other crimes toward humans, particularly domestic violence and other social crimes connected to aggressive behavior. There have been numerous studies conducted indicating that animal abuse is a social-justice concern and drawing connections between companion animal abuse with other human violent and criminal behavior. As such, crimes against companion animals, including neglect of an animal, raise serious concerns for society's well-being.

Forms of animal abuse and cruelty may include violence toward one's individual pet, but it is broadly construed to include situations in which dogs are found chained outside or trained to be involved in dog fighting. Additionally, while dogs may be the most frequently abused animals, there are other rampant forms of abuse toward other companion animals like keeping an animal in poor conditions without water, food, adequate shelter, and medical care.

Justice, the Neglected and Hurt Horse

You may recall the story of Justice the horse, who was mentioned previously, who was left without the necessities of life. He was three hundred pounds underweight, very weak, and suffering from rain rot. He was infested with lice, and he had a difficult time walking.

His former human handler, Gwendolyn Vercher, pled guilty to neglect when she was charged with animal cruelty. Vercher received a lenient sentence for this horrific crime. She served three years of probation and paid restitution for only a partial of the costs of caring for Justice. In my opinion and in that of many others, this was a mere slap on the hand and an inadequate way to punish her for this criminal act. Harsher penalties can also deter others from thinking that they do not need to provide the necessities of life to the animals in their care.

Abuse against animals does not result in harsh punishments, and convictions do not lead to adequate compensation to cover medical expenses, which result from the abuse. In seeking compensation for the abuse that Justice went through, ALDF, filed a lawsuit on Justice's behalf seeking monetary compensation to cover his ongoing and future medical expenses. Vercher was convicted of first-degree neglect and was ordered to pay restitution in the amount of $3,700, which was nowhere close to covering the expenses for Justice's care.[183]

Filing the lawsuit gave a glimmer of hope to those wanting to see a more compassionate shift for animals in the legal system. However, the judge dismissed the lawsuit, claiming that Justice did not have legal standing

---

[183] https://aldf.org/case/justice-the-horse-sues-abuser/.

and that if this decision were allowed; there would be a flood of lawsuits to come. Because animals do not have the status of persons under the law, they do not have legal standing to bring claims against owners who abuse them. Legal standing applies to human beings and legal entities, such as corporations.

As a result of Justice's plight, a public campaign was launched to draw attention to his story. He became the representative for 2019's ALDF's National Justice for Animals Week. It is an annual event created by ALDF to raise social awareness about animal abuse and cruelty through public campaigns. Most importantly, they provide tools and an action plan, which show people how to report animal cruelty to authorities and work with their community to pass stronger animal-protection laws. ALDF appealed the judge's decision that Justice does not have legal standing to sue his abuser. There is hope that Justice's story can bring awareness to the severity of animal-abuse crimes and give animal's standing to sue their abusers in court.

Desmond's Legacy Lives On

Desmond's story is another heartbreaking case and a reminder of the need for stronger animal protections. Desmond was a brown pit bull-boxer mix. He had lived with a young couple, Wullaert and his girlfriend, for over six years. After years of an unhealthy relationship, the couple split up. The girlfriend surrendered Desmond to an animal shelter called The Robin I in New Haven, and he was immediately loved by all. He was described by the shelter as a docile, gentle, and lovable dog. Wullaert reclaimed Desmond from the shelter and brought him to his new home. The shelter staff had high hopes for Desmond, but Wullaert fell on hard times and barely fed Desmond. He would leave Desmond alone for up to twelve hours per day, which meant Desmond had no choice but to urinate in the home. Wullaert tragically murdered Desmond by lifting him off the ground and twisting his collar tightly around his neck until he died. Instead of receiving jail time for this brutal crime, Wullaert was enrolled in an accelerated rehabilitation program. People were outraged when they heard about this lenient sentence, and the news sparked protests in the community for justice for Desmond.

After hearing his sad story, one individual, Christine Kiernan, worked to mobilize a group that she called Desmond's Army. A new animal protection law dubbed Desmond's Law was enacted because animal activists spoke up for this innocent dog, gave him a voice, and stood against the judge's order for Wullaert's sentence to be served at an accelerated rehabilitation program. This demonstrates the need to speak up for the voiceless and vulnerable members of our society. Being a strong front for animals has shown that we, as a collective, have the power to change the system. It is not just about animal rights. It's about ending the vicious cycle of violence, which starts with people's pets and companion animals as the victims.

The Birth of Desmond's Law

Desmond's Law was passed in Connecticut on October 1st, 2016. This groundbreaking law for animal rights gives a voice to abused animals. It is the first state in the US to allow judges to appoint lawyers and law students as legal representatives for abused animals in criminal cases of cruelty, abuse, and neglect. Violence against animals often has close ties to violence against humans, either coming as a precursor to escalating crimes or indicating a home environment where there might be domestic abuse.

Michael Vick's Dogs

Many people remember the horrific and highly publicized 2017 case of former football player Michael Vick, who pleaded guilty to illegal dog fighting and related criminal charges. He was charged with animal cruelty after it was revealed that Vick and others operated a business in Virginia named Bad Newz Kennels, which had in its possession fifty pit-bull-type dogs that were trained to fight and kill each other in the name of entertainment. Bad Newz Kennels also ran a high-stakes' gambling ring, taking in thousands of dollars.[184]

The scariest part of this brutality and violence toward these animals was that Vick became a registered dog breeder. Only later, it was revealed

---

[184] "Case Study: Animal Fighting—Michael Vick," Animal League Defence Fund, https://aldf.org/case/case-study-animal-fighting-michael-vick/.

that the dogs that did not perform well were murdered by being hung, shot, electrocuted, or slammed to the ground. For the remaining dogs, Vick and his associates allowed the dogs to fight other people's pet dogs.

Vick's Dogs: Light at the End of the Tunnel

Perhaps the light at the end of the tunnel was that some of these poor dogs were rescued. In 2009, Vick had served eighteen months in jail and agreed to speak to various community groups as part of an anti-dogfighting campaign by the Humane Society of the United States (HSUS).

It was a turning point in animal-abuse cases. Through public awareness of these pit bull type dogs that were being exploited, tortured, and abused, this highly publicized dog-fighting operation ended up being a catalyst for change. The light of this tragic story comes from the resilience of the dogs that were the victims of these horrific and disturbing crimes. Best Friends Animal Society (BFAS), which was given custody of the most traumatized dogs, helped. John Garcia, who took the sanctuary's dogs, flew from Virginia to Utah with the dogs so that they would be familiar with him when they arrived at the sanctuary. As of 2010, it was reported that many of the dogs were adopted into loving homes and that they were living out their days with children and other dogs. Others worked as therapy dogs in hospitals and children's programs. However, some of the dogs had ongoing medical and emotional trauma from their experiences and remained in the care of BFAS for the rest of their lives.

The story is important for many reasons. It highlights the horror of dog fighting and the dogs' rescue, hope, and new lease on life. These dogs suffered and remained resilient and loving. They are heroes in my eyes, and they have touched so many people. This story has been turned into a movie called *The Champions*, which is a "documentary that follows five of Vick's dogs from rescue to adoption, as well as six pit bulls with BFAS. It's an uplifting reminder of how our discussion of dogfighting—from the rescued dogs to the people who put them in danger—has evolved into a story about second chances."[185]

---

[185] Laura Moss, "The Ongoing Rehabilitation of Michael Vick," Treehugger, (5 December 2019), https://www.treehugger.com/ongoing-rehabilitation-michael-vick-4864117.

Handsome Hudson

Let's teach others to view Pitbull breed dogs in a favorable light and not label them or attach the negative stigma of these dog breeds as inherently dangerous. One of my favorite dogs in the neighborhood is a rescue dog named Hudson. He is a handsome dog with a strong stature, muscular physique, and a white and shiny grey coat. He is friendly and affectionate. Whenever he sees me his tail happily wags with enthusiasm and he brightens my day. Hudson has a responsible, and loving pet parent. His story was not always a happy one. He is a rescue dog who was saved from a miserable fate; previously he was a fighting dog and there are scars on his head. He was the victim of abuse. Unfortunately, some people are afraid of dogs that look like Hudson due to stereotypes and unfavorable mentions in the media.

It is important to demystify these misconceptions of pit bull type dog breeds and raise public awareness on responsible dog guardianship and joy these dogs can bring into our lives. Sadly, some jurisdictions have banned this dog breed and many innocent pit bull type dogs have lost their lives. Pit bulls are the most discriminated dog breed. We can change these views and update laws by educating others to push politicians to repeal breed specific legislation. Sharing positive stories of pit bull dogs and signing petitions to ban these discriminatory laws can be helpful ways to show support. There are organizations that are dedicated to pit bulls. Society is slowly back to realize that pit bulls, like other dogs, can be loving companions as well.

Legal Standing for Animals

Thankfully, legal standing for animals and proposals granting animal's legal standing has been introduced in multiple jurisdictions across the US. For instance, Desmond's Law ended up giving abused animals their own legal representation. It is a win, and it provides a solution by giving companion animals another layer of legal protection. They have the ability to bring lawsuits against their abusers. Since this law's enactment, multiple representatives have been appointed in Connecticut for animals who were victims of cruelty.

In the case of Justice the horse, the lawyers representing him are appealing the decision to a higher court, in hopes of giving this horse better standing in the legal system, which would be necessary for him to receive the compensation that he deserves. Thankfully, Justice's story did not end in tragedy. Justice is still alive and doing far better in the hands of his current caregivers at Sound Equine Option, a nonprofit horse rescue and rehabilitation organization. However, due to the extent of his injuries and future expenses for his care, it has been challenging to find him a permanent home or family willing to care for him.

These real-life animal-abuse stories are intended to serve as reminders that the laws must be stronger and that there needs to be harsher penalties to protect animals from perpetrators. We must ask ourselves what this means for society and question whether people who hurt animals should be permitted to keep them in the future. Furthermore, mistreating those who are unable to defend themselves raises some serious questions about whether the way we treat animals is a reflection of our progress as a just and moral society.

Animal Advocacy

I want to leave this positive message with you: You can make a difference for animal-abuse victims. I want to empower you with some practical action tools that you can use to make this difference. These crimes are starting to get noticed, as states like Maine, Illinois, Michigan, and New York are enacting stronger animal-protection laws. These states have lengthened jail sentences in accordance with new legislation modeled after Connecticut's Desmond's Law.

This positive change for animals, which previously might have been forgotten in a legal system, signifies hope for a more just world. The times are changing, and we can rejoice in knowing that an innocent dog such as Desmond left a legacy. His untimely death has not been forgotten but has inspired advocates to stand up and give a voice to animals in need.

Desmond's Law resulted in the implementation of a program for dogs and cats to have legal representation in animal-abuse cases. This animal-protection legislation allows for legal advocates to testify on behalf of animals in abuse and neglect cases. This one dog's tragic fate at the hands of a murderer who faced no harsh punishment holds a deeper message for the future of animal law. It rejected the old system of weak animal-protection legislation to open the doors to a new legal system that stands up for innocent animals, which would otherwise have no one.

In Connecticut courtrooms, there are now groups of animal supporters who continue to speak up for Desmond and other innocent animals that fall victim to animal-abuse crimes. They are known to sit in on court cases, wearing bright purple attire to make their presence known and to remind the public justice system that crimes against animals should be taken seriously.

Crimes against Animals and Humans: The Link

Crimes against animals have also been strongly linked to crimes against humans who have already experienced violence or suffering. A connection has been observed between the harm historically caused toward vulnerable groups and the animalization of these groups. It is not difficult to think of degrading terms that have been affiliated with animal imagery. In his book *Politics*, Aristotle said he believed that enslaving certain groups of people who do not possess reason was justified, because it was the same as enslaving an animal.[186] This shows the connections between our disregard for the lives of animals and the violence toward humans.

Research Proves the Link

Numerous research studies have provided documented evidence on this link. I researched these connections in preparation for an animal-law presentation. I am convinced that people who hurt animals can go on to be dangerous members of society. Many killers started out hurting animals, and violence against animals is a glaring warning of potential future violence toward humans.

A 2018 study called *An Exploratory Study of Domestic Violence: Perpetrator's Reports of Violence against Animals* found that of the inmates

---

[186] Charles Patterson, *Eternal Treblinka: Our Treatment of Animals and the Holocaust* (New York: Lantern Books, 2002), 19.

who were incarcerated for domestic violence crimes, 81 percent reported hurting animals as well. In other studies, there have been links made between animal abuse and domestic violence, as well as other criminal behavior, including property and drug offences and violations and other forms of violence.[187]

Hurting and killing an animal has long been used as a demonstration of power and a warning to partners in violent relationships. A 2011 study found that those who committed acts of violence toward animals were more likely to engage in sexual violence. They exhibited more controlling and intimidating behaviors around their partners.[188] As such, animal abuse is a crime that is part of a broader justice issue for society, and it must be taken seriously by the courts.

Helping Protect Pets: SAF-T

There is growing recognition that the need to help vulnerable members of our society—both human and nonhuman animals—goes hand in hand. It has been proven that human abuse and animal abuse are clearly linked. When it comes to domestic violence, 70 percent of survivors report having pets that were injured, maimed, killed, or threatened during an incident. In addition, almost half of these victims reported these crimes and delayed leaving their situation out of concern for their beloved pets. Unfortunately, there are few domestic-violence women's shelters that allow pets. Thankfully, there are animal welfare organizations such as RedRover, which helps domestic-violence survivors overcome this barrier through various grant programs, an online directory, and outreach efforts that help victims and advocates find solutions.[189]

---

[187] Sarah Chiara Haden, Shelby E. McDonald, Lara J. Booth, Frank R. Ascione, and Harold Blakelock, "An Exploratory Study of Domestic Violence: Perpetrators' Reports of Violence Against Animals," Taylor & Francis (03 May 2018). 337–352, https://www.tandfonline.com/doi/abs/10.1080/08927936.2018.1455459.

[188] Clifton P. Flynn, "Examining the Links between Animal Abuse and Human Violence," Crime Law Soc Change (2011), 456.

[189] Nicole Y. Forsyth, "Session 3: Preserving the Critical Bond between Domestic Violence Survivors and Pets: Breaking the Barriers" Animals and Us: Research, Policy, and Practice (11 October 2018), https://scholar.uwindsor.ca/animalsandus/schedule/Thursday/6/.

There are other resources. *Sheltering Animals & Families Together* (SAF-T) is a manual that was written by animal and family advocate Allie Phillips, when she realized how many domestic violence victims end up returning to their abusers to protect their pets. Phillips draws on the correlation between domestic abuse and animal abuse in the household, clearly showing that when there is one form of violence in the home, everyone else in the home is at risk.[190]

The SAF-T manual explains how victims wanting to flee their homes may subject themselves to further violence or even become homeless, to avoid leaving their pets in dangerous situations. Phillips's manual sets out guidelines for how to protect victims of abuse. She gives shelters for domestic violence victims' options for assessing whether allowing pets on-site would help residents. If so, the shelter can assess options that would benefit residents, such as allowing pets to stay in rooms with the victims or safely housing pets in a kennel, either outdoors or in a separate room.[191] Programs such as SAF-T are vital for helping both animals and victims, but they also speak to a need for systemic change in the way vulnerable community members, be they pets or humans, are seen and treated.

Take Action against Animal Abuse

We can make a difference and help animals that are victims of abuse. Society can improve the lives of animals by speaking on their behalf. Many violent crimes against humans are treated with criminal sanctions, and punishments are ordered through the justice system. Similarly, crimes against animals should be treated no differently. In fact, animals are vulnerable members of society (akin to children and the elderly), with no ability to protect themselves from harm.

Animals deserve to be free from harm. As an animal defender, you can take action to help fight against animal abuse and ensure that justice is served. If you witness or know of an individual animal being abused, please do not hesitate to contact your local authorities. If your jurisdiction

---

[190] Allie Phillips, *Sheltering Animals & Families Together (SAFE-T)* (2015), http://alliephillips.com/wp-content/uploads/2015/08/SAF-T-Start-Up-Manual-2015.pdf.
[191] Ibid.

does not have strict regulations against animal cruelty, contact your political representatives and ask for changes to laws. For reference, you can use the model animal protection laws from other US states, such as Connecticut, which were discussed here.

It is promising to see that although they are slow moving, the laws are starting to change for the better as more states enact stronger animal-protection legislation. It is an exciting time for advocates who are motivated to enact real change because grassroots activism and standing up for the victims of horrific animal-abuse crimes can make a huge difference. We can see tangible evidence through Desmond's Law, where in a mere six-month time frame, representatives for animals were appointed by the court to represent animals that were victims of cruelty.

Although this chapter may have been difficult to read because it highlighted the challenges and some of the stories were heartbreaking, hopefully, the message that resonates with you is positive and meaningful. The time has come to acknowledge and wholeheartedly accept the notion that justice for animals is a legal right and part of the moral progress of society.

How You Can Help

You can share the story behind Desmond's Law in your state, become inspired by the group of animal advocates who stood up for this dog's rights or other laws in other states, and form your own army by building a coalition of like-minded individuals who want to see change. You can spread the word to your friends, write to lawmakers and politicians, and even run for office so that you can have a platform to make positive change. With every individual action, we get closer to enforcing stronger animal cruelty and protection laws.

Social media can be a powerful tool for educating others. Showing the connections between animal abuse and violence toward people can be effective. I hope that I inspire readers to take action in their own communities and to educate those around them about the progress that is happening and the changes that need to be made. You can take a personal stance against harm to animals by educating others to help vulnerable creatures.

The implications of allowing animal abuse to continue in our society go deeper than just harming individual animals. As the links between violence toward animals and aggressive behavior in humans becomes clearer, the human and animal rights movements further intersect. Our collective apathy toward the harm of animals, which is often reflected through our legal system, has dangerous impacts on some of the most vulnerable members of society. It perpetuates a culture of tolerance of violence. By enacting stronger legal protections for animals, we are sending a message that violence toward *anyone* is will not be tolerated.

CHAPTER 10

Exploring Animal's Best Interests to Understand Their Needs

I have often said that as the laws evolve, the legal system will consider animals' best interests. It will no longer interpret the law in terms of animals as people's personal property.

Animal Rights versus Animal Welfare

Animal rights acknowledge that nonhuman animals have their own interests and that they deserve protection and legal rights. Humans should not have the right to use them. As noted in an article from Treehugger, a good definition of animal rights is,

> Animals have a right to be free of human use and exploitation, but there is a great deal of confusion about what that means. Animal rights are not about putting animals above humans or giving animals the same rights as humans. Also, animal rights are very different from animal welfare. To most animal rights activists, animal rights are

grounded in a rejection of speciesism and the knowledge that animals have sentience (the ability to suffer).[192]

Animal welfare is about their well-being and humane treatment. It doesn't advocate for their rights.

Animal welfare is the belief that humans do have a right to use animals as long as the animals are treated humanely[193]

There is a divide amongst these two camps. I would suggest that most animal advocates and activists are more in line with the animal-rights philosophy rather than the animal-welfare philosophy, which seems outdated. I met companion-animal-loving people, including family and friends, who seem to think that their beloved pets deserve to be treated differently than other species. The woman who wears her fur coat and eats meat treats her beloved dog as her fur baby. Unfortunately, society for the most part seems more aligned with animal welfare, so there is more work to be done to convince the public to defend their rights.

Social media depicts animals in favorable ways, and the importance of their well-being. Despite these changing times, the division between proponents of animal rights and animal welfare thwarts efforts. The contention between these camps is frustrating, as to some extent, it prevents the animal-rights movement from advancing as a unified force.

This view extends to some people holding the opinion that animals should not be owned or kept as pets and condemning people who share their lives with companion animals. Some animal activists reject the use of dogs as service guides to help the blind, emotional support animals, or the use of police dogs. They argue that every animal has the same equal rights to existence as a human and that animals should not be used to serve humankind.

This high expectation to uphold keeps the mainstream away from participating in animal causes. They are more likely to agree on the need to remove companion animals from the property provisions of legislation

---

[192] Doris Lin, "What Are Animal Rights?" Treehugger (March 8, 2021), https://www.treehugger.com/what-are-animal-rights-127600.
[193] Ibid.

and recognize their sentience. There is broader support that companion animals should be granted the distinct status and that the relationship is one of family member and guardianship. Pet parenting is becoming a more preferred term.

Most animal-welfare proponents support the notion that animals should be well cared for. They advocate for the protection of some species of animals. For example, the founder of the US SPCA, Henry Berg, used the term *animal welfare* when he referred to homeless companion animals and the need for society to protect them by providing shelter and food and finding them loving homes when possible. Berg was one of the early proponents.

Some animal-welfare proponents do not oppose hunting and eating animals, but they do seem to abhor the cruelty, mistreatment, and killing of companion animals. They advocate for the humane treatment of animals used by humans for experiments or even other uses.

We can convince the public that animal rights are aligned with mainstream societal views, which requires efforts as we consider the well-beings, and best interests of animals.

The Conundrum of the Animal Rights Debate: Let's Talk about Rabbits

The debate about animals and their legal rights gets murky when we consider certain species and their statuses in our society. I cannot think of another animal that deserves more attention on this topic than the rabbit. It was not until I developed an intimate relationship with our beloved rabbit Zoey that I realized that she had an interest in her quality of life. Even more than that, she was unique, displayed preferences, has a personality of her own and showed a range of emotions.

Similar to other species, rabbits have distinct personalities. As stated in *Stories Rabbits Tell*, rabbits become autonomous creatures, which display as many moods, preferences, and communication styles as more familiar and beloved pets like cats and dogs do. They may not leap into our laps or beg to play ball (although rabbits have been known to do both), but they interact with humans as effectively, profoundly, and affectionately as their other pet brethren."[194] Zoey has a distinct personality that makes her a unique creature different from other rabbits. She's feisty, smart, stubborn, loving, and playful (She knows how to play fetch and dance like a ballerina). She's sweet and cuddly, and she craves love and companionship. She is bonded to our older son, Andrew. She wasn't always that way. When we first brought her home, she was terrified of us. She ran away and hid from us. It took patience, and lots of love to gain her trust. I learned from Andrew to let her be. He is in tune with her needs and she likes to sit beside him. It is remarkable and rewarding to see her transformation from a timid, suspicious, and almost like a wild animal to a friendly, affectionate family member.

No animal on earth has a more complex relationship with humans than the rabbit. On the one hand, rabbits are loved and revered—think of the beloved bunny rabbit in children's stories. On the other hand, rabbits are exploited, abused, used in experiments, and treated as objects.

In in the wild, rabbits are hunted for their fur. Domestic rabbits descended from wild rabbits. They are used in cruel and barbaric animal testing experiments. They are bred in horrific conditions and pet rabbits get killed in shelters when they are surrendered if they are not adopted. Their gentle dispositions make them the prime targets of animal cruelty and exploitation.

The sad reality is that the rabbit's status in society is confusing in mainstream society. We do not seem to know where the rabbit stands on the spectrum of animal rights. We are confused about their species and classification. For instance, some people (like me) share their lives with rabbits, and they are regarded as beloved family members, so they can be classified as companion animals. But they are also found in the wild and are considered burdens to people's crops, so they are viewed by others as rodents.

Rabbits are also bred on farms and are killed for fur and even human consumption. I have seen menus in fancy restaurants that served rabbit meat. I found that disturbing as I had a rabbit sitting in comfort at home and she is surrounded by love. So many contradictions exist for rabbits' classification and their plight and that is an example of the urgent call to action to view all animals, regardless of their relationship to us, the same way. Since rabbits do not fit into any category, their needs and interests need to be reconsidered and respected.

---

[194] Susan E. Davis and Margo Demello, *Stories Rabbits Tell: A Natural and Cultural History of a Misunderstood Creature* (Lantern Books: New York, 2003), 127.

Recognizing Rabbits' Rights

Rabbits deserve unique status. Animal rights can progress when an animal's well-being and best interests are considered. For instance, rabbits' needs and natural inclinations should be considered for real and meaningful progress. The plight of rabbits goes largely unnoticed, but it is time for them to be noticed and treated with dignity and respect.

Rabbits have a soothing and calming energy, which in some ways makes them an ideal companion animal. They are quiet and cuddly creatures. As well, they require lower maintenance than dogs, and in some ways, their care is similar to cats. Although they are considered exotic pets, rabbits like parrots, birds, ferrets, tortoises, hamsters, etc. are seen by an exotic veterinarian.

Rabbits teach us that despite our individual and personal relationships with them, similar to other creature companions, such as farm animals, or wild animals, all animals deserve to be recognized as sentient beings, whether or not they are loved and cared for by humans. There is no difference in Zoey's desire to live free from suffering than the wild rabbit that I saw outside hopping in front of my house the other day or an innocent rabbit sitting in a laboratory.

Rabbits' status in society needs to change, and their rights need reconsideration. However, before that time comes, people's perceptions of rabbits need to change—from thinking that they are cute and cuddly creatures that all have the same personalities to realizing that they can be so much more. Rabbits, like other sentient animals, have individual, special, and unique personalities, preferences, and likes. They can be loving or aloof and cuddly or standoffish. They are complex creatures with a range of emotions, needs, and feelings. Their interests should be considered. Rabbits, should be granted status in our society and recognized as sentient beings. Unfortunately, the classification of some species of animals gets murky when the rights of certain species don't fit into one category, such as rabbits. Our contradictory view and relationship to rabbits and their confusing roles in society—regarded as wild animals, companion animals (pets), or farm animals—should have no determination on their rights to live freely and from pain and suffering. Every rabbit, regardless of their roles in society, should be granted the same legal protection, no matter how they are perceived by the public or how they live.

Although I have developed a personal and close relationship with Zoey, I realize that other rabbits that are not considered people's pets deserve protection. In other words, my pet rabbit's life is as equally important as an unowned, shelter rabbit, wild rabbit, or farm rabbit, as well as those helpless creatures that are sitting in labs having to endure cruel experimentation. Every rabbit, no matter what their status in society is, deserves to be treated the same. Furthermore, when we consider our relationships to rabbits, we realize that every single creature, despite its species or personal relationship to humans, should be afforded with legal protection. No distinction should be made.

As animal lovers, advocates, and activists, we can do more for these lovely creatures. Here's an interesting thought from *Stories Rabbits Tell*, which is worth mentioning,

With the exception of protesting eye experiments on rabbits, however, animal protection groups have not done much to improve the lots of rabbits. This is because rabbits play an odd role in this culture. As domesticated "farm" animals, bred to provide a variety of products, rabbits can seem less worthy than either the more "noble" wild animals or the more familiar "pets," like cats and dogs.[195]

Although this statement is accurate, this book was written almost two decades ago. Since that time, there has been more interest in speaking up for this species. Animal-protection groups such as House Rabbit Society and other rabbit rescues educate people on caring for them as pets and advocating for their rights. Progress is happening, but it has been slow, so more work needs to be done to raise public awareness on these complex creatures. Rabbits, like other animal species, deserve as many rights as other species do, including domesticated dogs and cats.

Exploring Animal's Best Interests and Well-Beings

There is a disparity in what we say we believe about animals and what we do. Historically, humans have not considered the impact of their mistreatment of animals. In fact, animal well-being has been disregarded, in the

---

[195] Ibid., xx.

interest of profit for humans. The rabbit is a strong symbol of a nonhuman animal that has been exploited. For animal rights to make real progress, an animal's best interests should be considered as we move toward updating animal-protection laws.

In the beginning of this chapter, I stated that as the laws slowly evolve, the interests of animals will be considered. Then they will not be regarded in terms of personal property. This becomes possible when we take into consideration the fact that animals are sentient beings. It might seem obvious to someone like you or me. For others, it might require some thought.

Beyond that, an animal's interest is to live a happy life in its natural habitat or a loving home. Animals can adapt to their circumstances. They have an interest in sharing their lives and forming special connections with their own and other species. For instance, a friend of mine has two small breed rescue dogs. She also has a pet tortoise named Joey who lives with the two dogs. Joey prefers to spend his time outside of his cage and to roam freely. He tends to behave more like a dog. Here's what my friend says about Joey the tortoise: "He thinks he is a dog and loves to be pet like a dog and run with the dogs; he greets us at the door and is responsive to play." Joey shows love and affection for the dogs and my friend. I'm delighted when she sends me photos of the tortoise interacting with and even kissing the two dogs.

Animal Liberation

The philosophy of animal rights and liberation goes back to the influential and classic book called *Animal Liberation: The Definitive Classic of the Animal Movement* by Australian philosopher and professor Peter Singer, whose argument is rather simple: Animals can suffer, and it is wrong to inflict suffering on them. He introduced the term *speciesism*, which says that humans feel superior to animals, which leads to their exploitation.[196]

Singer's work has contributed to the animal rights movement, and has awakened society to transform our views on animals and help alleviate their suffering. Additionally, his view is that the interests of humans and animals should be given equal consideration. The notion of animals as live creatures

---

[196] John Tamilio III, "Further Animal Liberation," Philosophy Now (2021), **https://philosophynow.org/issues/142/Further_Animal_Liberation**.

that are sentient was born when it was acknowledged that they could suffer and experience joy, pain, and pleasure.

His view is compelling because it has opened the doors for the consideration of other species. I have deep respect for Singer's argument, but this view has a long way to go. Since it was written in the 1970s, there have been changes, but we have not made enough progress. There is still hope, as Singer's work has gained momentum in mainstream society in recent years, and his views are highly respected and a major contribution to animal rights.

It's important to keep the conversation going and bring more people participate in animal rights in a meaningful way. As the laws for animals evolve, there is momentum for the rights of animals to be acknowledged.

In some countries around the world, changes are happening, and animals are no longer classified as property. Spain has announced that it will give pets the same legal status as humans in divorce cases, which means that family dogs and cats are regarded as sentient, living beings and are treated more like children in these cases. This positive sign shows that the interests of companion animals are being considered. As well, Spain joins other countries like France, Austria, Germany, and Portugal in granting family pets' legal recognition and rights. In North America, as noted previously, US states such as California and Alaska have passed similar laws, which consider the interests of companion animals in divorce cases.

We must continue to speak up and advocate for animal rights by sharing these victories and achievements. Our voices can propel the legal system to change for the better and to have strong legal protections for all animals. Sharing news on social media and in the mainstream media has positive effects. It can put pressure on politicians, judges, and lawmakers to act for laws to be updated, not only for companion animals but also for all animals.

Spearhead Social Media

Education of the social masses is required. It is the key to improving the situation and achieving social justice on behalf of animals. There are powerful tools and platforms, such as social media. They can act as an important messenger and connect others in this cause.

The broader segment of society is becoming more educated through awareness and informed of animal rights through engagement on social-media networks. This unification process can open the door to a new way of approaching and advancing animal interests, like increasing accountability for shelters, caregivers, and guardians. More active participation and communitywide effort are required so that politicians and governments will be pressured to make changes in their communities. These messages need to be strong, united, and clear: It is unacceptable to mistreat, abuse, and exploit animals. There are solutions to prevent the abuse, cruelty, neglect, and disposability of animals. As Craig Brestrup writes in *Disposable Animals*,

Animal advocates are the voices for animals. Not a single voice, certainly, they range from moderates who advocate kindliness in our relations with animals to liberationists and rightists who find it hard to discern much morally relevant difference between them and us. But in some measure nearly all affirm the intrinsic value of dogs and cats, and much other nonhuman life. These are not stones after all, mere objects who turn their eyes to ours. They live, experience, and feel—and they give every indication to prefer to continue these activities."[1]

Acceptable Companion Animal Philosophy (ACAP)

Previously, you may recall I was focused on companion-animal issues when I first sat down to write this book. In my master of law's thesis titled *Reducing Euthanasia in City Shelters,* I proposed a new animal-protection model, a balanced approach to shelter care for the animal-welfare community to embrace. It is called Acceptable Companion Animal Philosophy (ACAP). I chose the words *cap* to put a stop to the killing of shelter animals. In brief, this sheltering model recognizes companion animals as sentient beings that deserve protection. Since I wrote my thesis several years ago, my opinion has evolved. I believe that every creature deserves to be recognized as a sentient being (not only companion animals).

Nonetheless, I think that ACAP is still relevant today. ACAP encourages members of the animal community—animal welfare organizations, shelters, and rescues and other groups that speak on behalf of animals—to work together. Shelters and rescues work with the community.

It is time for newer terminology so that the word *kill* is removed, and compassionate care is the focus. ACAP relies on team effort. There must be collaboration between shelters, rescues, and communities. It seeks to pressure politicians and governments to pass animal protection laws that protect shelter animals from euthanasia and places more accountability on shelters.

Broader community support, with collaboration and consensus to change the status quo, for animals is needed. Many shelter animals' lives have been saved thanks to wider community support. Rescuing saves lives. However, wider public support is still needed to move forward in a positive and meaningful way. Involve the public so that they are aware. People need to be educated on the mandate of animal shelters so that they will protect homeless animals, and euthanasia will only be a last resort reserved for animals that are irremediably suffering.

ACAP introduces new terminology for everyday citizens and the community. For instance, antiquated words such as *owner* and *ownership* are replaced them with more humane terms like caregiver, companion, pet parent, or human guardian. This new terminology moves us away from dominance over companion animals to a mutual relationship. The previous chapters have outlined the significance that companion animals play in our lives, emotionally, spiritually, and biologically. This new approach to sheltering reflects this sentiment. There is a cap on the killing of shelter animals. It is prohibited unless it is used to relieve an animal from irremediable suffering. Misnomers such as *euthanasia* and *putting to sleep* should be removed from a shelter's practices, unless used for medical reasons.

An animal shelter's mandate is to be a safe haven for homeless animals and a place of shelter and protection, akin to a women's shelter or a homeless shelter. Homeless animals are housed there for safety and protection, with the hope that they can find good, loving homes, through adoption, rescue, or fostering. Their best interests and needs are carefully considered.

Let's Get Together for a United Front: It Takes a Village

It takes cooperation and working together. As the author of the book *Getting to Zero: A Roadmap to Ending Animal Shelter Overpopulation in the United States*, Peter Marsh noted, "There is no single group that can end the killing of homeless animals by itself. It takes a village. That's because prevention is the key to ending homelessness and preventative programs should be deeply rooted in the community to succeed."[197]

Another solution to the shelter problem includes lifesaving programs that target the root of the problem. Focusing on prevention and the community must be part of this effort. For instance, educating guardians on the benefits of spaying, neutering, and government-assisted spay/neuter programs for lower income households to reduce pet overpopulation should be made available to communities.

ACAP supports mutual respect between humans and animals. It proposes that companion animals, due to their scientifically documented sentience, close bond/connection to humans, and important roles in enhancing human quality of life, should be granted distinct legal status. This legal recognition can lead to positive changes for other animal species. In the end, the goal is to grant all animals' stronger legal protection. It is in response to a societal shift that has occurred, in which society agrees that companion animals should not be viewed as property. It is coming from divorces, as couples are willing to fight for their pets in court. Most people can agree that their beloved dogs, cats, other pets are members of their families. It's easier to convince people to change the laws for their pets first, as they share the closest connection to humans.

Social change precedes legislative change. New laws and policies based on ACAP can hold humans more accountable, not only for the lives of those animals they adopt but also for those that are killed in animal shelters. Advocating for stronger legal protection of companion animals in the courts is an important start and opens the door to laws for other animal species.

Open the Doors for Other Animal Species

With incremental shifts in attitudes and legislative improvements for our closest furry friends, we can open the door to improving the plight of other animal species too. I made that connection to farm animals during my visit to a local animal rescue and sanctuary. Like most people, I shared my life

---

[197] Peter Marsh, "Getting to Zero: A Roadmap to Ending Animal Shelter Overpopulation in the United States," *Shelter Overpopulation* (2012), http://www.shelteroverpopulation. org/Books/Getting_to_Zero.pdf.

with companion animals. I did not have that personal, close connection to other species, such as farmed animals, until I visited a rescue and sanctuary, Coveted Canines. That quickly changed as I formed a special bond with a pig, which was housed at the sanctuary.

Her name was Penelope and she was an owner-surrender pet purchased from a pet pig breeder. As a side, some people do not believe that pigs make good pets and that when this is discovered, they are abandoned. Since she grew up with chickens, she loved hanging out with them. Penelope was protective of one chicken in particular, which would sit on her back. This chicken was killed by a hawk, and when this happened, Penelope was devastated. She grieved for a long time. There is no difference in the pain, suffering, and feelings of this pig and any other animal. From that moment on, I would speak up on behalf of every animal to have the right to live their natural lives free of suffering, whatever the species.

Unfortunately, that is not the norm. Farm animals are viewed as objects that are bred and raised for food. It's socially acceptable to dismiss the notion that farm animals deserve to have legal protection. Violence toward farm animals is deeply engrained in our culture. It is tolerated, and in almost all cases of systemic violence—be it toward humans or other animals— a stronger group exercises power over a vulnerable group. In the case of farm animals, a hierarchy devalues the impact that these animals feel while they are raised and then killed for food.

By deconstructing hierarchies, dismantling ideas of dominion, and recognizing respect for all living creatures, we can move toward a more compassionate world. When children grow up feeling love toward their family pets while being fed farm animals like pigs, cows, turkeys, and chickens, ideas of hierarchy are instilled in them from a young age. Teaching younger generations to show empathy for all animal species is instrumental in advancing animal rights for future generations.

Animal Interests beyond Themselves

Animals are known to show interest in caring for other animals and humans. For example, elephants form strong bonds with their babies and take turns looking after one another's children. There are many heartwarming stories of animals showing interest in protecting humans. I saw a news clip of an African gray parrot named Bud, which was kept as a family pet. He was the key witness in a murder trial of a woman who was convicted of killing her husband. Bud was in the home at the time of the crime, and he helped solve the case by mimicking the violent scene to the police authorities. He seemed distraught and disturbed by the violence and murder.

There is further evidence that whales protect other species too. A whale guided a scientist back to the surface as a tiger shark was approaching. In another story, a pet goat named Abigail alerted her human family by jumping on them when there was a house fire. This chapter shows us that our exploration and consideration of animal's interests to understand their individual needs is crucial in moving animal rights forward. It is captivating to realize that animals have preferences and they have the capacity to care for others within and outside of their species. It's very exciting to learn how complex and varied animals are. We are only beginning to explore and uncover the depth of their emotions as we share stories about their personal life experiences.

CHAPTER 11

Farm Animals: From Disconnect to Making the Connection

Farm animals feel pleasure and sadness, excitement
and resentment, depression, fear and pain. They are far
more aware and intelligent than we ever imagined.
—JANE GOODALL

Making the Connection for Farm Animals:
Splendid Stories Farm Animals Tell

As I often say, if more people met and interacted with farm animals, they would love them.

Like most people, I enjoy watching uplifting, heartfelt stories featuring animals. For example, I viewed a touching video with the release of two beautiful pigs named Wilbur and Anastasia, giving viewers a firsthand glimpse of their newfound freedom. I could sense their happiness when they were released, as they were prancing around finally free. These two precious pigs were rescued from a California equine sanctuary, which had to cease its operations. After that, animal control intervened to take custody of Wilbur, Anastasia, the horses, and other animals.

Prior to that time, Wilbur had lived for five years in a twenty-by-thirty-foot dirt lot. He suffered from arthritis and poor muscle development due to lack of exercise from being confined. Anastasia spent ten years crammed in a ten-by-fifteen-foot pen, and she was unable to engage in many natural physical movements, which are necessary for pigs.

My favorite part of the video was witnessing that heartfelt moment of their first taste of freedom and trusting the humans who were part of the rescue team, which instantly revealed to me the pigs' kind, gentle natures. They trusted these humans despite years of neglect and confinement. We can learn so much from these stories featuring farm animals like Wilbur and Anastasia. Farm animals value their freedom just as much as any other animal.

Another heart-melting video depicted the happy moment of freedom for a mother pig named Hope Apple Blossom and her six piglets. They were rescued from slaughter by Viva Dean Farm Animal Sanctuary in the United Kingdom. The video showed the piglets happily enjoying themselves as they were let outside, able to explore the outdoors of their forever home, and experience this new world. I was overjoyed to see the little baby piglets running—even dancing—to express their joy while roaming free and feeling the grass on their hooves. Unfortunately, these types of stories are rare and not the norm for farm animals. Nonetheless, uplifting stories are necessary to show people the possibilities of living without suffering.

The Plight of Farm Animals

I hope these stories can uplift and inspire others to be kinder to farm animals. So many of us read classic children's stories depicting farm animals as individuals, but these stories seem to be forgotten when children grow into adults. Tragically, the plight of farm animals is not considered, and people don't seem to make the connection that they are living sentient beings. According to Animal Clock, it is estimated that in the United States alone, almost ten billion land animals are raised for human consumption each year—one sixth of the world's total livestock animals.[198] These alarming and shocking statistics provide a sobering overview of the enormous number of farm animals killed in the US, and the numbers are disturbing.

---

[198] "Animal Kill Clock," Animal Clock (2022), https://animalclock.org/.

According to World Animal Protection, the situation in Canada is not much better, with more than seven hundred million farm animals being slaughtered for food every year. "When it comes to eating meat, many people are not aware how the animals are raised on farms and the suffering they endure."[199] Farm animals that are raised for human use are viewed as inanimate objects and are treated terribly when they are alive and are considered economic commodities. They are often subjected to extreme cruelty and are slaughtered at an unthinkably young age.

To begin to describe the living conditions and tragic fate of farm animals is very difficult for me. These creatures include pigs, cows, chickens, turkeys, sheep, lambs, goats, and more. These are only some of the many farm animals that are regularly bred into existence only to be abused during their short lives and then slaughtered for food. Farm animals used for meat, dairy, and eggs are the most vulnerable to severe neglect and abuse. Undercover investigations have shown abuses on farms and in slaughterhouses that are so disturbing that most people cannot bear to view the footage. Although it is difficult to watch, it is necessary to show this footage to reveal what really happens to innocent farm animals in slaughterhouses and to awaken people to this unthinkable fate for billions of innocent lost lives.

In the United States and Canada, there are virtually no regulations stipulating how animals should be treated on farms while they are being raised. There are voluntary, industry-set guidelines. Once the animals leave the farm and are taken to slaughter, transportation laws allow animals to be transported for up to fifty-two hours without water, food, or rest. They are kept in tight, confined conditions, with no protection from the extreme heat or cold.[200]

Farm animals can feel emotions. They should be treated with respect, dignity, and compassion. They have their own distinct personalities, which are just as varied as our beloved dogs and cats. They deserve to be recognized as sentient, feeling beings. Sadly, the current state of laws for farm animals offers them inadequate legal protection. Much of the extreme cruelty

---

[199] "World Farm Animals Day Highlights Need for Better Animal Standards," World Animal Protection (2019), https://www.worldanimalprotection.ca/news/world-farm-animals-day-highlights-need-better-animal-welfare-standards.
[200] Humane Canada, "Realities of Farming in Canada," Humane Canada, https://humanecanada.ca/our-work/focus-areas/farmed-animals/realities-of-farming-in-canada/.

that they experience is permitted across most US states and in Canada.[201] Although the dire conditions that farm animals endure are heartbreaking, and it might even be challenging to comprehend, there is a desperate need for education, and awakening to their plight. The suffering of billions of land animals and trillions of marine animals is the result of human actions.

It is not enough to read about the horrific conditions and their plight. Action is necessary. Real change is possible with farm-animal advocacy and activism through participation, which includes increased awareness and making compassionate food choices.

On some level, the plight of farm animals is the most tragic of all animal species, due to that disconnect that humans have with them. They do not realize that farm animals are living, breathing, feeling and complex creatures. Instead, they easily disconnect from them. I am aware that the fight for farm animal protection can seem overwhelming. It might be easier to turn a blind eye and remain willfully unaware of the extreme neglect and suffering of animals on farms. This conditioning starts early in our childhoods, as our parents tell us that meat is a healthy and essential source of protein. There is no regard for farm animals that are killed. It is up to us to change that perception and help others make the connection to farm animals as worthy creatures.

The sad reality of animal agriculture is hidden behind colorful milk cartons with smiling cows and television commercials of happy farm animals grazing in large green meadows. While viewing video footage, research, and literature for this particular chapter, I spent time thinking of how to write it with hope and optimism. I have to admit that it was difficult from a psychological view, as the plight of farm animals can be overwhelming. This is typical of the industries that profit from meat would have you believe, but it's far from the reality.

Television commercials and media are powerful tools. Animal agriculture has deep pockets with profitable industries, which provide insights into the deeply rooted social conditioning and complexity of the problem—humans can easily disconnect from feeling emotions for farm animals. This inability to empathize with farm animals and their tragic situations perpetuates the idea of disposable animals—in particular, the notion that

[201] "Farmed Animals: Farmed Animals and the Law," Animal Legal Defense Fund, https://aldf.org/focus_area/farmed-animals.

a farm animal's life does not matter and these poor animals are born to serve the needs of humans.

This lack of empathy and compassion is fueled by the powerful factory-farming industry, which is large, lucrative, and motivated to generate mass production of animal products. This, in turn, causes farm animals to be viewed solely as a means of economic profit, without any regard for their lives. When there is an entire industry devoted to commoditizing farm animals, it becomes easier to disassociate with the notion that these animals want to live and have feelings. The horrific reality is that animals undergo terrible suffering. There is a dire need for change through action and realization that farm animals have a right to live free from suffering.

Farm animal lives are disregarded by mainstream society, due to social conditioning and unawareness. These animals are viewed as cheap commodities used for human consumption and profit. They are not seen by most people as living breathing and emotional beings. They are disposable, replaceable, and alive for the momentary enjoyment of human palates. That is the root of the problem. Farm animals are another example of profit, consumerism, and supply and demand. If we stop supporting the dairy industry and start to consume vegan foods, these lucrative industries will eventually cease to exist. Here is a powerful quote on PETA's website by comedian Ellen DeGeneres: "I personally chose to go vegan because I educated myself on factory farming and cruelty to animals, and I suddenly realized that what was on my plate were living things, with feelings. And I just couldn't disconnect myself from it any longer."[202]

When I am confronted about my food choices, I take comfort from knowing that I am not contributing to factory farming and there are so many other people that feel the same way—especially influential people—who choose to be vegan. I have courage to speak up now. Growing awareness of the negative impact that meat and dairy have on humans is surfacing.

I am no longer the odd one out at social gatherings, thanks to my husband joining me, so whenever I am questioned about my vegan food choices, I have an ally. I think it helps that he is a medical doctor and surgeon. I have prepared an eloquent comeback that makes me feel comfortable. I discuss

---

[202] Logan Scherer, "Why Ellen Went Vegan," PETA (November 9, 2009) https://www.peta.org/blog/ellen-went-vegan/.

the benefits of veganism and share. I explain that it is a way of living, and that this vegan lifestyle goes deeper than the minor social inconveniences of shopping for dairy-free and meat-free products. I have a strong sense of self and a conviction to inspire others to raise questions. I encourage them to share their opinions without judgement. I am an advocate for these silenced farm animals—to give them a voice.

It is obvious that farm animals, just like dogs, cats, other domesticated animals, and wildlife animals, are unique, special, and sentient creatures, which deserve better treatment.

Farm Animals Have Personalities Similar to Pets

It might come as a surprise to some that farm animals have unique personalities and that they are more like our companion animals than we think. Farm animals can feel emotions and form bonds with their human caregivers. They crave love and affection similar to companion animals. On the website One Green Planet, Hannah Sentenac says,

> For most people, dogs and pigs are wildly different animals. One is considered a family member, a bedfellow, a best friend—while the other is considered … well, bacon. But the truth is, these two animals are actually incredibly alike. Pigs can learn tricks, they love to snuggle, and they're highly social animals. And the same premise holds true for all farm animals: they're sentient, emotionally complex creatures deserving of just as much respect, compassion and love as any household companion animal.[203]

Farm animals deserve to be treated better. We must reconsider that their lives matter too. More education, social awareness, and sharing uplifting stories that depict farm animals as individuals with unique personalities

---

[203] Hannah Sentenac, "Ways Farm Animals Are Just Like Cats and Dogs," One Green Planet (2014), https://www.onegreenplanet.org/animalsandnature/ways-farm-animals-are-just-like-cats-and-dogs/.

need to happen. This is especially true for younger generations that are less entrenched in their views and more open to change. Thankfully, a slow awakening is changing people's perceptions of farm animals. Their role in society is evolving as more people see them as individuals rather than disposable commodities used for human consumption. We are beginning to understand that farm animals are amazing, sentient and complex creatures. Farm animals are worthy of love and affection, similar to other animal companions. When they are seen as individual creatures with emotions and personalities, perceptions begin to change. That view can help to elevate their status in society to understand they have a right to live. Rescues and sanctuaries are recognizing these individual farm animals.

The Reality of Factory Farming

Educating people about what happens on factory farms is the key for positive change. As noted, it is a lucrative agribusiness industry that treats farm animals as mere commodities for human use—to the extreme. They are kept in the dark and in the confined quarters of these farms for their short lives, due to the stark reality that factory farming is a profit-driven business. These animals are treated with no regard for their individual existences, emotions, feelings, abilities to feel pain, and psychological and physical needs. Rather, their existence is reduced to their capacity to produce meat, eggs, dairy, and other economic products for human consumption.

It is important for humans to realize that farm animals, like every other animal species on this planet, have a range of complex emotions. They feel pain, and when they are hurt they cry and when they are subjected to violence and abuse, they suffer. Farm animals can give and receive love, form bonds with other animals and humans, have social connections, and display a desire to live out their natural lives when they are given this opportunity. At the very least, all living beings should be given the freedom to move and freedom from pain and suffering.

Farm animals, while they are domesticated, are treated differently under the law from other species of companion animals. There is a clear and disturbing paradox when some people connect with domesticated farm animals. In the *Journal of Animal Ethics'* article called "Pets or Meat:

Ethics and Domestic Animals," Professor Grace Clements explains the discrepancy between our pets and farm animals as she states, "We treat companion animals according to one set of guidelines and so-called "meat" animals according to an opposing set of guidelines, despite the significant similarities between the animals in question."[204]

Animal Activists and Ag-Gag Laws

Farm animal activists give a voice to farm animals. They are desperately needed to expose cruelty to farm animals; otherwise, the dirty dairy industry will continue to operate and harm these innocent creatures without consequences.

Farm animals used as livestock have virtually no protection under federal laws in the United States. This lack of protection allows the abuse and neglect to continue, which is problematic for those seeking to improve living conditions for abused farm animals. Ag-gag laws have made it difficult for animal rights activists to engage in undercover investigations and bring to light the truth and horrible conditions for animals on factory farms. Investigative footage from farm-animal-advocacy organizations, such as Mercy for Animals (MFA), has revealed substantial evidence of farm animals being mistreated. Disturbing footage showed cows being kicked, punched, and dragged, piglets' tails being cut off with dull blades, and chickens being stabbed and then stomped to death.[205] If not for the undercover work of MFA and some of these organizations, this horrific treatment would not have been brought to light.

Free-Range Reality Check

The United States Department of Agriculture, which regulates free-range products for labeling purposes, relies upon the producer's word that the farm animals are free-range. A farmer could label a product free-range

---

[204] Grace Clement, "Pets or Meat? Ethics and Domestic Animals," *J of Animal Ethics* (2011), 46-57, https://www.jstor.org/stable/10.5406/janimalethics.1.1.0046.

[205] "The Problem," Mercy for Animals, https://mercyforanimals.org/the-problem.

according to their subjective definition of what it means. Because there are few requirements for labeling products as free-range, birds raised for meat may be classified as such if they have some sort of access to the outdoors, regardless of how much space each individual animal is provided. Free-range farm hens that are unable to lay enough eggs to be considered profitable are then typically sold to slaughterhouses or live-poultry markets.

As on factory farms, free-range male baby chicks are considered worthless to the egg industry, so they are dumped into trash cans and suffocated, ground up alive, or sold to laboratories shortly after they hatch. Like other factory-farm animals, when free-range animals are no longer productive, they are killed.[206] No matter how much the animal agriculture industry tries to paint a picture of the compassion that surrounds its operations, when animals are used for profit, the desire to make money triumphs over the well-being of the animal.

Those consuming products from the animal agriculture industry should be made aware of where their food comes from and the way the animals are treated and killed. Perhaps then, they will rethink whether their meal is worth the suffering that innocent animals have experienced.

Some Farm Animals are *Just* Babies

Farm animal mothers love their fur babies like we do. You can see these mothers cuddling and bonding with their babies, even as adults. We can help these maternal animals thrive and live naturally with their families in peace and love by not supporting animal agriculture.

The dairy industry depends on secrecy because few would support its rampant violence and cruelty. The reality of the dairy-producing agribusiness is there is no consideration given to the fact that cows are deeply maternal animals that want to be with their calves just as much as any other mammal, including human beings.

For instance, veal is a cruel product of a dairy industry that slaughters male baby animals, sometimes a mere forty-eight hours after their births so that they can be sold at a premium price to fancy restaurants, in meat

---

[206] "Watch LCA's Award-Winning PSA, *Casa de Carne*," Last Chance for Animals, https://www.lcanimal.org/index.php/campaigns/other-issues/veganism.

stores, and to calfskin industries. Perhaps the anger that is directed at the messenger, rather than at the cruel meat industry, is a defense mechanism that allows them to continue eating these cruel products without guilt. That's been my personal experience when I speak up about where baby farm animals, such as the veal that is on their dinner plates comes from. They are *just* babies that are taken cruelly from their mothers.

Oscar Speech Gives Farm Animals a Voice

While it is true that the dairy industry has benefited from many years of hiding behind false advertisements of happy cows living in beautiful pastures, the veil is rapidly beginning to lift. February 9, 2020, marks a groundbreaking victory for animals, especially dairy cows. Joaquin Phoenix, actor, director, and passionate vegan activist won an Academy Award for Best Actor for his lead role in the movie *The Joker*. The memorable speech he gave at the Oscars has left its mark on Hollywood for a long time. Phoenix said:

> We feel entitled to artificially inseminate a cow, and when she gives birth, we steal her baby, even though her cries of anguish are unmistakable. Then, we take her milk that's intended for her calf, and we put it in our coffee and our cereal, and I think we fear the idea of personal change because we think that we have to sacrifice something, to give something up. But human beings, at our best, are so inventive and creative and ingenious, and I think that when we use love and compassion as our guiding principles, we can create, develop, and implement systems of change that are beneficial to all sentient beings and to the environment.[207]

While it wasn't the first time that Phoenix talked about farm animals

---

[207] Kelsey Piper, "We Don't Talk Enough about Animal Suffering. That's Why Joaquin Phoenix's Oscars Speech Matters," Vox (10 February 2020), https://www.vox.com/future-perfect/2020/2/10/21131025/joaquin-phoenix-speech-animal-rights-oscars-2020.

on a major platform, it was the first time in the history of the Academy Awards that animal rights were brought to the forefront. A strong message of love and compassion for the very animals that humans so brutally exploit, profit from, and slaughter was on every television screen, in every major news article, and on the minds of every individual watching the awards show. The suffering of dairy cows went from being an issue steeped in secrecy to being blown wide open and exposed to the world. As advocates for animals, it is important to ensure that this topic stays relevant and that we continue this wave of education that Phoenix started.

Love for Farm Animals

As I said before, if more people met and interacted with farm animals, they would love them. They would realize that farm animals are capable of deeply experiencing the world around them and feeling pain, pleasure, fear, sadness, and joy. They form bonds with humans and other animals. I had the pleasure of experiencing this during my first visit to a farm sanctuary. I remember meeting the farm animals and learning that each one of them had a face, name, and personal story. There were sheep, horses, cows, chickens, turkeys, rabbits, lambs, and goats. I was mesmerized with all of them. I bonded with a beautiful rescue pig.

The founder of the farm sanctuary could identify every farm animal, and she was eager to introduce me to the residents. They were lovely farm animals that she had rescued. Now they are living peacefully at her sanctuary. She was so passionate, and I could tell that she cared about each one of them deeply. It was a memorable experience. While we were talking, I could feel the black pig rubbing against me. Her name was Betty (named after the late Betty White). When she lay on her back, the founder encouraged me to rub her belly.

I was delighted to meet Betty, with her tail wagging. She seemed happy, and it was a pure joy for both of us. This precious piggy trusted me and responded to me warmly. In return, I was happy to give her belly rubs. I realized that there was no difference from this precious pig's desire for love and affection through receiving belly rubs than from my dogs. I learned through this personal interaction with Betty that she craved human affection and love just like my dogs and cat. Many people don't know that pigs are social creatures.

The tides are slowly turning for the plight of farm animals like Betty. We are seeing that farm animals are special creatures that are worthy of love. As more people take the time to get to know individual farm animals, they will love them too. In other ways, the plight of farm animals is improving, as they are featured more frequently in movies and are seen favorably in videos and stories as unique sentient creatures with personalities. When farm animals are seen as cuddly and worthy of love and affection, people's perceptions of them begin to change.

I watched a movie that depicted a sheep that was spared from slaughter when a woman caring for the sheep developed a bond to her, and the sheep became attached to her. This sheep even recognized the woman that fought for her freedom. This creature was seen as special by this woman. As more farm animals are featured in a positive light they are recognized as individuals with names, and they are regarded as sentient beings, with personalities, people's perceptions of them change. Eventually, farm animals' statuses in society will evolve to be viewed as beautiful, special, lovely, and unique creatures that deserve to live naturally and in peace. They will be treated with kindness, love and compassion which are what they deserve to be.

Farm animals are here *with* us not for us.

CHAPTER 12

Ditch Dairy and Meat: Love and Compassion for Farm Animals

A poor animal, how jealously they guard their bodies, for to
us is merely an evening's meal, but to them is life itself.
—T. CASEY BRENNAN

I often say that people don't know the dirty secrets of the dairy industry. Babies are taken from their mothers and killed. Animals on dairy farms live miserable, and much shortened lives. Please show kindness and compassion for farm animals; choose dairy free and go vegan.

Educate others to ditch dairy and meat and to show compassion for farm animals. One way is to encourage people to connect with individual farm animals as outlined in the previous chapter. We can make the connection to farm animals as living, breathing, cuddly, and loving creatures that are worthy of life. Engaging in tactful, non-adversarial conversation and in a polite manner is a strategy that awakens others to the truth about the dirty secrets of the dairy industry. In other words, speak from the heart when you share information and share your passion. If they are receptive, share your knowledge of their plight and personal experiences. Mostly use these conversations as opportunities to start an open dialogue and give farm animals a voice.

I have learned over the years that preaching doesn't work to change people's minds. When I feel that I am making someone uncomfortable, I stop the conversation and try to listen to them and their points of view or walk away. Since I am trained as a mediator, I try to engage in a meaningful discussion to hopefully open their hearts to see my point of view with more empathy and compassion. Sometimes it works, and other times, it feels awkward, but thankfully, most of the time, people are nice, polite, curious, and open-minded to having discussions on this topic.

With friends, I have shared my personal encounters with farm animals in lighthearted conversations, to show them that these lovely, interesting creatures have personalities. I have even shared my personal experiences of visiting farm-animal sanctuaries or sharing photos. I love telling the stories of the individual farm animals. Other times, I share that I went dairy-free when I found out what happened on dairy farms and how terribly the animals were treated.

Start a Conversation

Some people seemed interested in my animal-law practice, which was a great segue into a conversation about animal issues and rights. It was often an easy start to the conversation in a nonthreatening way. People seemed to find it amusing to hear pet custody cases about couples in a legal battle over Fido, the family dog. We would usually laugh lightheartedly, as they would find it intriguing that I defended the dog's best interests when couples split up. They would ask a lot of questions and smile. That was an entry point to talk about broader animal rights issues and bring up other species of animals. I liked to share my efforts, such as lobbying work, helping animal rescues and sanctuaries, and even my personal journey from vegetarian to vegan.

I am more tactful with people than when I was younger. I thought I could convince people to stop eating dairy by telling them the truth—that the milk they were drinking came from cows that were forcibly penetrated and impregnated once a year to keep them lactating. Then they were separated from their babies and were sent to slaughter.

Over the years, I have realized that trying to convince people to change their daily habits is an uphill battle and a challenge. Now I find it helpful to share this kind of information with animal lovers to try to persuade them to ditch diary. I understood that we are dealing with brainwashing from childhood and generations of systemic social conditioning, false advertising, and a powerful, lucrative, and secretive industry, which not only hides but normalizes the use of farm animals for profit. In the end, I am making a difference. If I can inspire and convince one person at a dinner party to try vegan through conversation or by creating inspiring social media posts, more animals will be spared.

On a more promising note, the situation is improving, partially due to the number of people waking up and realizing how cruel the dairy industry is. More people are going vegan. This is apparent from the many healthy options of plant-based products in the grocery aisles, the numerous scholarly medical articles on the health benefits of plant-based diets, and daily news feeds on Google that suggest that the dairy industry is declining.

Pet Pigs

Pigs are gentle, playful, friendly, curious, and incredibly smart animals. In fact, they are thought to have intelligence beyond that of a three-year-old human child. Some people might be surprised to learn that they are smarter than dogs. Pigs are also social creatures that form strong bonds with their family members, as well as with their human handlers.

I remember meeting a pet pig from a friend. Her pet pig Alice was sleeping like a baby in her arms as she whispered and showed me that Alice was dreaming in her sleep. It was a very memorable experience that left an imprint in my mind, as I didn't know that pigs had dreams and that they can be loved so deeply. My friend cared about her pet pig Alice, and in that moment, I realized that they are much more like other domesticated animals than I had previously thought.

On many occasions, Freddie has slept in my arms. I could sense that he was dreaming, and it always made me smile, as it was a joyful and emotionally uplifting experience. Through this story of a fellow animal lover's bond with her pet pig, I have made the connection. It took one moment of awareness to understand that farm animals are not much different from other companion animals. They have similar physical and biological needs, yet the law and mainstream society drastically distinguish them from dogs and cats.

An interesting article, which touched my heart, was featured in *National Geographic,* titled, "Pet Pigs Can Communicate with Humans—Especially When Food Is Involved" by Liz Langley. She discussed the similarities between dogs and pigs and revealed the recent rise in popularity of pet pig ownership (guardianship) in Canada and the United States.

In this compelling article, Liz Langley suggests that from 1998 to the present day, there has been a significant increase in people adopting pigs, going from approximately two hundred thousand to over one million pet pigs. Liz states, "But due to some irresponsible breeders, many people get tricked into buying a pig without realizing there is no such thing as a mini-pig—all pigs, miniature or not, get big, and the majority of these animals ends up in shelters or is euthanized."[208] This leads us to the problem of breeding animals that are already overpopulated, not unlike the issue we face with dogs and cats. I reiterate that keeping pigs as pets is controversial and probably not a good idea.

There are many pigs in need of rescuing from animal shelters or farms, but turning pig-pet guardianship into an attractive business may mean that the well-being of the animal is once again, not accounted for. As if there were not enough issues with pet pigs, many who take baby piglets as pets do not know how to care for a full-sized pig or may not have proper facilities for taking care of such large animals. Therefore, while this section advocates for viewing pigs the way that other family pets are viewed, it is with the understanding that first and foremost, there needs to be education regarding the commitment required and their unique needs. This includes increased awareness of both caring for large and strong animals, seeking out reputable adoption programs when considering a pet pig, and a deep regard for the well-being of these animals.

Although companion animals and especially dogs are known to be in tune with human emotions and to detect even subtle emotions, little research has been done on other species of domesticated animals such as potbellied pigs. Pigs can be trained to follow a human hand to receive a

---

[208] Liz Langley, "Pet Pigs Can Communicate with Humans—Especially When Food Is Involved," *National Geographic* (2019), https://www.nationalgeographic.com/animals/2019/07/pigs-dogs-pets-communication/.

reward. They are smart. A pig named Picasso, which was rescued from the meat industry and now resides at Farm Sanctuary in South Africa, has a knack for painting. Amazing videos of her with a paint brush in her mouth, exploring the ways in which the paintbrush strokes blend, have gone viral, and expanded the way that people view a pig's capacity to comprehend, explore, experience, and enjoy life. Langley concludes from the findings published in the *Journal of Animal Cognition* that pigs "did a great job" showing similarities in the study of "human-orientation behaviors of human-reared pigs and dogs."[209]

Pigs are affectionate animals, so this true story may not come as a surprise to many readers. A woman named Lisa Englehardt from Virginia Beach tried to persuade city council members that pigs weighing less than 150 pounds should be classified as pets if they were vaccinated and had microchips. At the time I was writing this chapter, this ordinance was being considered at the town hall. Virginia Beach law leaves pigs classified as livestock, so human caregivers of pigs like Lisa must keep their pet pigs in different locations. She is forced to keep her pig, Mr. Humphries, in Norfolk, even though her residence is in Virginia Beach, to ensure that Animal Control won't take him away. As Lisa says, "They could take it and then put it in the shelter, it's almost like you're taking a child away from its family." She continues to say, "It is basically stating that pigs are not considered swine and agricultural animals, because people who have them as pets are not raising them for food." As a further initiative, she created an online pig petition and obtained five thousand signatures to legalize pigs as pets.[210]

Another heartfelt, real-life story was featured on Oprah Winfrey's television show *Super Soul Sunday* and was written about on the Little Things website. It is a remarkable, story and short film about farm animals. It stars a pig named Emma, who arrived at Apricot Lane Farms as a skinny, sickly, and pregnant pig. Farmer John Chester was told that Emma would be lucky if she had six piglets. When the big day came, Emma beat the odds, giving birth to seventeen piglets, thirteen of which survived. The intense labor

---

[209] Ibid.

[210] Meghan Puryear, "Virginia Beach Woman Battles to Make Her Pig a Legal Pet," News Now (2019), https://www.13newsnow.com/article/life/pets/virginia-beach-woman-battles-to-make-her-pig-a-legal-pet/291-bbf33f49-ccd3-4904-a34f-ca06360c5e57.

took a toll on Emma, and she was fighting for her life after giving birth. Along with several other farmers, Farmer John bottle-fed the piglets so that Emma could heal and recover. Miraculously, Emma regained her physical strength, and she was able to feed her piglets.[211]

This is another example of a true-life animal hero story of survival and compassion, which shows us how deep the bond between human and farm animal can be. It also gives us a look into the similarities of motherhood that many farm animals, including humans, share. Emma the pig was able to live a full life: giving birth, beating the odds, and being able to feed her babies and watch them grow up to live their own lives. She even found a best friend and companion, a red rooster, and she lived her days in comfort, happiness, and peace. Unfortunately, the story of a farm animal having a happy ending is rare, and most pigs raised for meat endure a horrible, miserable existence, suffer immensely, and live very short lives.

A Pig's Plight

Pigs raised for human consumption endure terrible abuse from an early age. For instance, male piglets are subjected to intense pain as their testicles are violently ripped out and their sensitive tails are cut off without painkillers. Mother pigs are crammed and confined into exceedingly small, dirty gestation crates. Constricted by metal bars on all sides, they cannot lie down comfortably or turn around for nearly their entire lives.

The thought of these animals suffering is unthinkable, but this is the truth and sad reality that we can share with others. We know that intelligent, loving farm animals deserve love and respect, and no food or taste is worth the pain and suffering that they endure. In fact, pigs are known to be as smart as dolphins. They can reach an IQ of a three-year-old child![212] They are also affectionate animals. They can easily form special bonds with their human caregivers and other animals, including dogs. As stated in the

[211] Scott Neumyer, "This Mama Pig Was Extremely Sick but What She Did? Beyond Comprehension," Little Things (February 16, 2015), https://littlethings.com/lifestyle/emma-pig-miracle.

[212] "Reasons to Love Farm Animals Like Crazy," Animal Equality (November 6, 2015), animalequality.org.

article by Animal Equality, "We would all be huge fans of farm animals if we got to know them a little better."[213]

Farm Animals Similar to Companion Animals

There are many more heartwarming stories about the bonds that humans have formed with other animal species, including farm animals, which we have been conditioned to think of as food. The view that farm animals are not worthy of love or that they don't deserve a forever home is simply not true. I have met farm animals that have developed bonds with other animals, such as dogs. For instance, when I visited animal rescue and sanctuary, Coveted Canines, I was delighted to see two pigs and a group of small dogs running together and chasing one another. They were playing together. I couldn't tell the difference between the behaviors of the dogs or pigs unless I looked very closely at each of them. These animals were engaging in fun activities, freely expressing themselves, and having a good time. As more people can witness these farm animals behaving similarly to companion animals, they begin to understand that pigs and other types of farm animals are no different from our beloved dogs and cats and can love.

Scientific research shows that farm animals can be classified in the same way as companion animals. For instance, in a touching article "Soulful Photos of Animals Saved from Slaughter or Neglect," Ellyn Kale writes an interesting tribute and shares photos and heart-stirring stories of farm animals that were saved from slaughter or situations of severe neglect. In this captivating article, Kale includes the troubling lives but happy endings of individual farm animals and the journeys they have gone through before being saved. The photographer Janet Holmes included a story of her special relationship with one farm animal, a sheep she named Scout. Scout was found starving in a backyard slaughterhouse, along with a group of other sheep. It was mesmerizing to read about the heartfelt bond that existed between Holmes and Scout. Nothing feels better than knowing Scout's days

---

[213] Ibid.

of suffering are behind him and that there is a future filled with compassion at Catskill Animal Sanctuary (CAS).[214]

Holmes explains that sheep can recognize human faces, and this sheep always seems to remember her. Every time she visits, Scout comes over to say hello and asks for a back scratch, just the way a dog would. Ellyn Kale goes on to say, "Holmes never takes a single funny, heartfelt moment with Scout for granted. She understands that for every rescued animal, countless others will not escape a system that profits from their suffering. Farm animals raised for consumption are cut off from society, and they do not have the freedom to explore, play, or form bonds with other beings. However, CAS offers a kind alternative to the cruel world of farm animals that are rescued from neglect and slaughter. In this special place located in New York, animals and humans live side-by-side, as confidants and companions. In the end, animals are often our gateway to rediscovering our humanity. As CAS's sanctuary founder Kathy Stevens told Janet Holmes, farmed animals can be our "teachers and friends, if we dare to listen."[215]

Documentaries to Watch

Although Kale's article offers us a unique and positive approach to farm-animal rights by viewing them as individuals, this perspective is not the norm. There have been great documentaries released to date that have blown the cover off hidden animal agriculture industries, often showing stomach-churning images of animal suffering, which were not until recently, available for viewing. These documentaries include *Cowspiracy*, an environmentally focused documentary about the ways in which meat eating is causing immense ecosystem damage, and *Dominion*, which speaks to the lives of animals on farms. While I am the first to admit that these farm animal documentaries are not easy to watch due to their dark and violent content, I am a strong believer that they are relevant and important.

Just as connecting with farm animals as individuals is important, it is

---

[214] Ellyn Kail, "Soulful Photos of Animals Saved from Slaughter or Neglect," FeatureShoot (27 August 2018), https://www.featureshoot.com/2018/08/soulful-photos-of-animals-saved-from-slaughter-or-neglect/.

[215] Ibid.

vital to be educated about the reality of what happens within farms and slaughterhouses. When we view the footage of the lives of farm animals, we begin to understand the misleading advertising and marketing tactics used to trick consumers into thinking that grass-fed, free-range; cows and chickens are treated well and killed ethically. The truth is that most farm animals face unimaginable pain and suffering during their short lives and suffer cruel and violent deaths. Above all, we must recognize that all animals that are bred within a corrupt consumerist system, which is built to exploit them, end up suffering because their needs will never come before the business and commercial profits that they can bring.

We can investigate the root of why society blindly permits innocent farm animals to suffer. Most people individually do not want to hurt animals. When I talk to people about my advocacy work, they genuinely seem impressed with my commitment and passion for helping animals. When I worked as a lawyer, as noted, pet custody disputes were a popular topic, and people wanted to know more about protecting their family pets and the laws surrounding their individual dogs and cats. Their faces lit up with smiles when they shared photos of their beloved dogs or cats (even other animals such as rabbits, parrots, and turtles), but the discussion became more uncomfortable when I spoke about farm animals, the dirty dairy industry, or veganism.

It is important to see this topic from the perspective of the public and mainstream society. Most kids are told that eating meat is good for their health and to gain protein or that milk is essential for health and stronger bones. It is engrained in their minds. I can remember seeing television commercials when I was younger, which depicted happy and strong people drinking milk. It was common those days and widely accepted in mainstream society that milk was essential to a child's diet. It is still a subconsciously normalized behavior, which is rooted and culturally engrained in our society. As such, a radical social awakening and shift in perception is needed to change the system for farm animals and to improve their plight.

Farm animals are removed from people's daily lives. Let's face it; people don't have to think about what happens to animals in slaughterhouses. As well, the billions of dollars spent on marketing for dairy, meat, and eggs do not help their plight. Farm animals that are used for food have no voice or choice in what happens to their bodies. Our choice is constrained from a young age because we are bombarded with false advertisements, which are thought-out marketing, and centuries of social conditioning meant to hide the reality that people are eating dead animals.

Beyond all the lies and social conditioning, the fact remains that a dead animal's corpse and lifeless body is sitting on their plates. But people don't have to think about it. These farm animals endured a miserable existence to be consumed in a few minutes of trivial pleasure, without consideration for the suffering and pain that they had to endure to become this meal. Janet Holmes, photographer and volunteer at Catskill Animal Sanctuary, states,

> To stop exploitation of animals, we need to challenge ourselves and the system that normalize the use of animals. Not everyone is going vegan overnight (I did not), and no one is perfect. But people can take time every day to reflect on the specific choices they make and try to be honest with themselves about whether their actions are aligned with their values."[216]

Compassion for Cows

A few years ago when I took my family to visit a local farm sanctuary called Farmhouse Garden Animal Home, it was the first time that we met farm animals, such as cows, up close and face-to-face. It was a memorable experience that transformed my husband into a vegan. When he met, touched, and looked into the cows' big, warm, brown eyes and learned how gentle they were, he said that he could not imagine eating another steak. We were taken on a tour and introduced to the cows individually, and they had names and hierarchies. Cows are maternal creatures, and they are affectionate. Few things are stronger than their desire to care for the young in their herd.

The story of Farmhouse Garden Home is an amazing one. As stated on their website, "It is a story of farmer Mike Lanigan who decided that he

---

[216] Ellyn Kail, "Soulful Photos of Animals Saved from Slaughter or Neglect," Featureshoot (2018), https://www.featureshoot.com/2018/08/soulful-photos-of-animals-saved-from-slaughter-or-neglect.

could no longer send the farm animals on his farm to slaughter. It has since been a place of refuge and compassion for animals, giving them a chance to live safe, happy lives."[217] This is a story of a man making the connection that farm animals are living beings. Instead of sending animals to slaughter, he started a sanctuary.

Cows are known to be brave. They are also kind, sensitive, and gentle giants. They are intelligent problem solvers, and they are known to do amazing things, such as walking for miles to be reunited with their calves after being sold at an auction, leaping over fences to escape a slaughterhouse, and swimming across rivers to their freedom. There are videos of cows jumping out of a truck that was headed for slaughter and escaping their cruel fate.

Those of us who have had close encounters with cows recognize that their ability to understand one another and the world around them. Cow's lives matter, as well as other farm animals' lives. When more people realize this, it can bring about a societal shift. It will no longer be considered an anomaly that cows and other farm animals respond to their names or recognize the faces of those who take care of them.

As we make progress for farm animals and gains in the animal-rights movement, the aim is for farm animals, such as cows to no longer be viewed as docile, uncaring, and unintelligent animals without personalities, which are often the stereotypes that are reinforced. The more individuals that take the time to learn about and interact with farm animals, the easier it is to make the decision to stop harming them. I have suggested that everyone visits a farm animal sanctuary and that schools provide excursions for children to gain exposure and awareness of the complex lives of farm animals.

It is interesting to compare the treatment of animals within different countries, especially where cows are recognized as sensitive, intelligent, gentle giants that are worthy of love, compassion, and respect. Another example of the discrepancy in the treatment of animals is the way they are regarded in different countries. For instance, in India, cows are treated very differently than they are in the United States. Cows are considered sacred and smart. They are treated with compassion and respect. You can see them walking freely and unharmed among people on the streets. The great Mahatma Gandhi was a known protector of cows. He said, "The cow to me means the entire sub-human world ... extending man's sympathies beyond

---

217 Farmhouse Garden Animal Home, https://www.farmhousegardenanimalhome.com/.

his own species. Man through the cow is enjoined to realize his identity with all lives ... one reads pity in the gentle animal. She is the second mother to millions of mankind."[218]

A cow's natural life span is twenty-to-twenty-five years, but cows used by the dairy industry are killed after about five years because their bodies wear out from being pregnant and lactating. A dairy-industry study found that by the time they are killed, nearly 50 percent of cows are lame because of standing in constant confinement on filthy concrete flooring.[219]

During my visit to another farm sanctuary GLO, I heard the story of a resident rescue cow named Coco Bean, who lived there until the ripe old age of twenty-two. Sadly, I did not get to meet Cocoa Bean, as she had just passed away a few days earlier. I could sense how much the sanctuary cared about her and that at the end; she was surrounded by her family when she passed away. I wish I had met this lovely creature. On GLO's website, Coco Bean's description says,

> "My humans refer to me as 'Boss Lady,' probably because I am the Boss. If I want something, I get it—especially for the other cows to move out of my way. My horns help motivate them to do it quickly. And why shouldn't they? I'm almost 20 years old, and thanks to Sick on Sin, I am a celebrity. Enjoy my big smile on their merchandise, because in real life I am always very serious." She will be missed.[220]

Plight of Farm Animals

While I admit it is disturbing to watch footage from whistleblowers, it is necessary to reveal the truth about this horrific industry. Education is the key to awakening society. As more and more consumers realize that this cruelty is not isolated and that violence is a pervasive part of the farm-animal agriculture industry, they will hopefully stop contributing to this suffering.

---

[218] Paramhansa Yogananda, *Autobiography of a Yogi* (Self-Realization Fellowship, 1971), 423.
[219] **"The Dairy Industry,"** **PETA,** https://www.peta.org/issues/animals-used-for-food/factory-farming/cows/dairy-industry.
[220] GLO Farm Sanctuary, https://www.glofarm.org/.

We must continue to awaken people to the dairy's dirty secrets. A viral video, created by vegan activist Erin Janus in 2015 called *Dairy Is Scary*, was viewed five million times.

Education and awareness also come from people within the industry who are speaking out against what they have seen. One former farmhouse, slaughterhouse worker stated,

> Cows do think and have emotions. I worked in the largest slaughterhouse on the planet, Iowa Beef, now Tyson Foods. We killed 200 cattle an hour. They would weep, crying with big tears, trembling with fear, scared to death. Cows have emotions, just like your dog or cat.[221]

He continues to share in the article,

> You can smell the blood when you're getting close, and I am sure they knew what's up. The unborn baby calf's had the blood sucked out of them before taking a breath, and then thrown into what would become dog food. I have stories that can make your hair stand on end. Cows have emotions, just like your dog or cat and farm kids would have them as pets until parents would sell them to make your hamburger.[222]

While it is sad and heart-wrenching to read this and to have to think of what cows go through, these true-life stories of personal experiences are necessary to reveal the truth. With people sharing animal stories, education, and awareness, there is hope and promise for a better future for farm animals. Newsprint media is helpful, such as this interview with the former slaughterhouse worker, to make people aware of the things that happen and farm animal's plight.

Forbes magazine had an article about the struggles of the dairy industry and how so many more plant-based alternatives are becoming available to

---

[221] Jeff Learch, "Directly from the Slaughterhouse," Newsroom24x7 Desk (7 August 2016), **https://newsroom24x7.com/2016/08/07/directly-from-the-slaughterhouse/**
[222] Ibid.

consumers.[223] It is obvious that dairy consumption in the United States is on the decline. Dairy farmers are starting to look to nondairy alternatives so that they can continue their operations. The World Economic Forum published that milk sales dropped by more than $1 billion due to plant-based alternatives. According to the Dairy Farmers of America (DFA), the sale of milk dropped over $1 billion in 2018.[224] This is good news. A societal shift is happening. More people are adhering to the plant-based approach, and it is becoming more widespread and socially accepted as a popular choice, especially amongst the younger generations, who are perhaps more open to incorporating healthy lifestyle changes and are more vocal about animal suffering.

Compassion for Chickens

During my visit to another local farm sanctuary, I met a hen named Russell Crowe, which sat patiently during a photo shoot as I stroked his chin. I forgot to ask the reason that he was named after the actor Russell Crowe, but he did have a lot of charisma, and he seemed to love the spotlight! He was cuddly, and he craved my affection. Most people don't know that hens are thought to be as intelligent as cats and dogs. They have knowledge that is passed down from generation to generation, and they learn by watching each other. Sadly, most hens do not get an opportunity to live freely. They are used for egg production and are crammed into windowless sheds with little to no ability to move freely. But most people don't know this, so we need to teach people more about chickens as individuals with feelings.

If more people knew that chickens were mistreated and injected with chemicals, perhaps they would consider plant-based food options. Chickens raised for meat are bred to grow so fast that they frequently cannot even walk without pain. Abuse from factory farm workers is common, as seen by

[223] Beth Kaiserman, "Dairy Industry Struggles in a Sea of Plant-Based Milks," *Forbes* (2019), https://www.forbes.com/sites/bethkaiserman/2019/01/31/dairy-industry-plant-based-milks/#246a3eb11c9e.

[224] Carly Sitzer, "US Milk Sales Drop by More Than $1 Billion As Plant-Based Alternatives Take Off," World Economic Forum (2019), https://www.weforum.org/agenda/2019/04/milk-sales-drop-by-more-than-1-billion-as-plant-based-alternatives-take-off/.

MFA investigative footage. The little bodies of laying hens often give out after just a year or two; given the toll that constant laying has on their bodies and the conditions they are subjected to. They are then sent to slaughter to suffer the same fate as other chickens.[225]

Most people don't think about chickens as cute and curious creatures. I remember seeing a video of a chicken running around on a farm with a dog. They were playing hide-and-seek and chasing each other. I was initially surprised to see the chicken interacting so playfully with the dog, but after a few moments, there was no difference between these two species. This is another example of animal friends having a great time freely playing in the countryside.

Farm-animal sanctuaries are doing a great job at raising awareness on the plight of farm animals. They often share stories of their rescue chickens and other farm animals in a positive light. By doing so, they are helping to shine a spotlight and to elevate their status. The key for change is to show farm animals as unique individuals with personalities, which deserve better treatment. When we start to realize that farm animals are no different from other animals, including companion animals, in their ability to feel and express themselves, change can happen.

When I visited Coveted Canines Rescue and Sanctuary, I got to hold one of the rescue chickens named Albert Eggstein (no joke that is his real name). To my delight, he was easygoing and an agreeable friend. He was patient and kind with me, and he let me hold him as he gazed into my eyes. He was a gentle creature that was cuddly too. I was told that he would be easy to work with because he was a friendly and nice guy, which was exactly the way I found him to be. He was trusting and gentle. I read an interview with the *Toronto Star*'s founder, Carly Werle.

> "People can pick up turkeys and kiss chickens," Werle says. "Then they can hug the horse and rub the pig's belly. It

---

[225] "The Problem," Mercy for Animals (2022), https://mercyforanimals.org/the-problem/.

just becomes this incredible experience because all these animals are so full of love."[226]

Aquatic Animal Protection: Fish Have Feelings Too

Fish are fascinating creatures. I learned about fish from our oldest son, Andrew, who has been interested in fish and in particular, sharks, from a young age. I think he was only two years old when he displayed this fascination with fish. I read children's books and stories about fish to him especially sharks, and we both became educated about endangered fish species and the impact on our oceans and environment. From the time they are taken out of the water alive until the cutting table, fish are tormented without a second thought. They are suffocated, skinned, and dismembered, often while still conscious and able to feel pain.

The stark reality is that fish are living creatures and just like other animal species, they can feel pain. They undergo suffering on a scale far larger than any other animal on this planet. Scientists are exploring the depth of a fish's inner lives to show that fish have emotions, social needs, and even individual behaviors. They are smart, sentient beings too.[227]

Seaspiracy is a Netflix documentary that exposes the fishing industry's impact on the oceans. It has been popular, and a must-watch documentary. I was particularly interested in watching *Seaspiracy* with my son, Andrew. He had tons of shark books. He had been interested in learning more about saving sharks from extinction. The documentary is helpful, as it promotes a plant-based lifestyle and provides recipes and meal ideas on their website.[228]

---

[226] Steph Davidson, "For Carly Werle Running a Rescue Kennel and Sanctuary Is a True Labour of Love," *Toronto Star* (2021), https://www.thestar.com/life/together/pets/2021/10/03/for-carly-werle-running-a-rescue-kennel-and-sanctuary-is-a-true-labour-of-love.html.

[227] Rachel Nuwer, "Fish Have Feelings Too," NOVA (2018), https://www.pbs.org/wgbh/nova/article/fish-have-feelings-too/.

[228] Seaspiracy (2022), seaspiracy.org.

Terrific Turkeys

Turkeys are gentle birds. I met a rescue turkey named Lucy at Coveted Canines. I was impressed by her friendly personality and curious nature. Initially, I was intimidated, as she was bigger than I had imagined. She was sweet and playful. I had to chase her for a few minutes, but when I held her, she seemed genuinely interested in interacting with me. She was a big, beautiful bird. I took some photos for social media. I learned that she had been an owner-surrender. Someone kept her as a pet but no longer wanted her. I posted the photos for Thanksgiving, to show that turkeys are loving, gentle, smart, and sentient creatures like other animals. Turkeys are kept as pets due to their likeable and gentle personalities. A goal that came from my interaction with Lucy was to show that turkeys were lovable and to encourage people to consider plant-based for that holiday.

MAKING THE CONNECTION TO FARM ANIMALS THROUGH RESCUES AND SANCTUARIES

Farm Sanctuary

Sanctuaries are long-term homes for rescued animals. Farm Sanctuary, a renowned and reputable farm-animal organization with locations in both California and New York provides a safe haven and home for some of the most abused farm animals on the planet. They save calves that have suffered in tiny veal crates and pigs that were headed to a violent slaughter. These farm animals can experience love and trust. They have the chance to live peacefully in a safe environment.

I read about the real-life rescue of the first animal rescued at Farm Sanctuary—a sheep named Hilda. She was found almost dead. She had been discarded from a slaughterhouse transportation truck after being too weak to walk out of it and into the stockyard. The conditions in the transportation truck had been so inhumane that despite not having previously suffered from any injuries, she was almost lifeless by the end of the ride. When she was found at the side of the road, she was barely able to lift her head, but she was taken to a veterinary hospital where she began to recover, standing, eating, and drinking only twenty minutes after her arrival.[229]

The truck driver who had thrown her out of the transportation truck admitted that he had done it because she was what the industry typically called a "downer," and it was standard practice to discard animals that couldn't be slaughtered and leave them to die on their own. Despite the cruelty of this situation, what the truck driver had done was not illegal—Hilda the sheep had little legal protection, and the thing that had happened to her was a common occurrence. Luckily, Hilda quickly regained her health and spent over a decade in the peaceful Farm Sanctuary in New York. She grazed lush green pastures and enjoyed her days with new animal friends. Hilda knew nothing but love and compassion for the rest of her days. On Farm Sanctuaries website, it is wonderful to see that there is a tribute to the life of Hilda. On their website it says, "In honor of Hilda, and to recognize people who have made a major contribution to the ongoing work initiated by her, Farm Sanctuary has established the *Friends of Hilda Club*."[230]

The Save Movement

There are farm-animal organizations doing fantastic work to raise awareness and offer protection to farm animals. The Save Movement started in 2010, with Toronto Pig Save, and it has grown to over six hundred chapters worldwide. It is composed of farm-animal activists around the world who advocate on behalf of nonhuman animals that are farmed for food, clothing, and human entertainment and are used for research. The goal of the Save Movement is to promote a vegan lifestyle and to raise global social awareness regarding the suffering of these animals.

The Save Movement started as a grassroots movement. It is gaining momentum and has been forming more chapters, through protests, demonstrations, and vocal coverage on the news. Part of this was thanks to Anita Krajnc, the founder of Toronto Pig Save, who you may recall was arrested and was prosecuted for giving a thirsty pig a sip of water on route to slaughter.

---

[229] Gene Baur, "Hilda: The First Animal Rescued by Farm Sanctuary," Farm Sanctuary (25 September 2000), https://www.farmsanctuary.org/news-stories/hilda/.
[230] Ibid.

Farm Animals as Friends

We have seen from this chapter that farm animals are complex individuals that are intelligent, curious, and lovable creatures, which experience the world from their unique perspectives. They share similar emotions to other animals. They can experience joy, sadness, suffering, and loneliness. They can form connections with humans and other animals—even different species. I provided the example of the video that I watched with a chicken and dog playfully interacting. Although most of us don't have an opportunity to interact with farm animals, we can learn from farm rescues and sanctuaries more about their lives. By doing so, we can extend our compassion for farm animals and educate and raise the awareness of others, especially children and teenagers. We can teach children to be more empathetic to other creatures, including farm animals.

Although most of us don't realize that farm animals crave companionship and that they can form connections, this can help to inform us that they are more similar to other animals, such as dogs and cats, than we ever imagined. Farm sanctuaries are providing glimpses into their lives and educational opportunities to learn more about these creatures and to see them as fantastic farm-animal friends. When we begin to awaken to the reality that their lives are precious too, we start to show compassion for farm animals, and we will want to protect them from suffering. For the time being, we can learn from farm sanctuaries. For instance, farm animals respond to their names, and they can even develop bonds with other animals that are not of their species.

Here's a special, true rescue-farm animal story from Animal Place sanctuary. It's about a goat named Mr. G and a donkey named Jellybean, which had a special, unbreakable bond.

They were separated after welfare officers seized animals that were forced to live in atrocious conditions, and Mr. G and Jellybean were sent to live in different sanctuaries. After Mr. G refused to eat for six days, staff decided to track down Jellybean. On their reunion Mr. G immediately perked up and ate for the first time in almost a week![231]

This heartwarming story shows us that farm animals can form bonds,

---

[231] Abigail Geer, "8 Unexpected Farm Animal Best Friends," One Green Planet (2016), https://www.onegreenplanet.org/animalsandnature/unexpected-farm-animal-best-friends/.

have best friends, crave love, become attached to other animals, and develop friendships. They similarly crave companionship and connection with other species of animals.

These rescued farm animals are given a unique privilege that is not afforded to most, to live free from suffering and enjoy their lives in sanctuaries. Sadly, most farm animals don't have this privilege, as they live alone in crammed cages and have to endure unthinkable pain and suffering during their short lives. We can begin to change the future for farm animals as we see them as unique, friendly, fun, social, and loveable creatures, which are not food but are friends.

Farm Animal Advocacy

Spreading awareness about the dirty dairy industry and exposing the secrets of the horrific way factory farm animals are treated can inspire others to either consume less factory-farmed products or stop consuming them altogether. Farm Sanctuary has great educational resources on their website about the animals that are affected by factory farming, as well as offers to get involved. They teach about the negative effect that factory farming has on the environment. If you are an advocate or teacher, Farm Sanctuary even has a curriculum that can be used in classrooms to teach children about factory farming.[232]

Sadly, many people know that farm animals are treated poorly and are raised and killed for human consumption; however, they are not aware of or educated about the way that animals are abused during their short lives and before they are slaughtered. I love this famous quote by Sir Paul McCartney and his powerful documentary on the horrors of factory farming in *Glass Walls*. He said, "If slaughterhouses had glass walls, everyone would be a vegetarian."[233] Hearing famous people's stories on their journey into advocacy and while becoming vegans can inspire people. For instance, Sir Paul McCartney shared his personal experience about making the switch to

[232] Farm Sanctuary, https://www.farmsanctuary.org/learn/factory-farming.

[233] Jennie Richards, "Sir Paul McCartney Narrator of Documentary," Humane Decisions (October 2015), http://www.humanedecisions.com/paul-mccartney-narrator-of-documentary-if-slaughterhouses-had-glass-walls/.

vegetarianism almost forty years ago. One day, he was sitting at the window eating meat, and he looked outside on his Scotland farm at the lamb, sheep, and horses in the pasture. He made the connection with the individual lives of those animals and those killed for meat.[234]

You can become a farm-animal advocate and teach others to respect farm animals. For instance, many farmers know that mother cows call frantically for their babies for days after their calves have been taken from them. If the mother and calf are separated by a fence, the mother waits by the fence, through rain and extreme heat, forgoing meals and water while waiting for her baby. Some mothers even break through fences and wander for miles while searching for babies that have been sold at auctions.[235]

We have been taught from a young age that cow's milk is necessary for strong bones, especially in children. This is a myth. Show others the numerous studies that have shed light on the negative effects of dairy consumption on human health. Research has shown that regular dairy consumption can lead to higher rates of cancer, heart disease, and Alzheimer's disease.[236] But again, much of this information is shielded and largely not known by the public, so it's up to us to spread these studies and to prove it. Another myth is that individuals who consume a plant-based diet lack nutrients and are weaker than those who consume animal products. You can watch *The Game Changers*, which examines the health benefits of a plant-based diet on top athletes and details how this diet enables exceptional athletes to perform better.[237]

The negative effects of factory farms are an example of farm animals suffering under our societal normality. Animals on factory farms endure unthinkable pain and suffering during their shortened lives. They experience miserable, short lives, both before and after slaughter. Many people understand that their family dogs can suffer and realize that their dogs have complex emotions, but they don't understand that other animals, such as chickens, cows, pigs, turkeys, goats, sheep, and other farm animals, can

---

[234] Ibid.

[235] Global Action Network, http://web.archive.org/web/20140729150301/http://www.gan. ca:80/animals/cows.en.html.

[236] "Health Concerns about Dairy," Physicians Committee for Responsible Medicine, https://www.pcrm.org/good-nutrition/nutrition-information/health-concerns-about-dairy.

[237] Shannon Kornelsen, Mark Monroe, Joseph Pace, *The Game Changers*, Netflix (2018).

experience those same emotions. Society draws an arbitrary line between our beloved, furry family friends and the dead cow (steak) that is served for dinner. A farm animal has his or her own life story—where it came from, who it is, and the personality it has like every other type of animal does.

Farm animals are no different from other animals, in that they are special, individual, and sentient creatures. I know that each farm animal's life is precious. The turkey that I spoke of earlier named Lucy was a special creature with her own life story and personality. She displayed happiness when given attention, and she didn't seem to mind being held in my arms.

Unfortunately under our current social construct, most of society views her as a commodity and a consumer product. Most farm animals like Lucy experience a lifetime of pain, hurt, fear, and suffering, before they are slaughtered at too young of an age. This situation can improve if we take action to help farm animal's gain the attention of mainstream society and to be regarded as special, sentient beings.

Farm animals deserve better. They can sense fear. They have love and expression in their eyes, intelligence, curiosity, and an ability to connect with us far beyond what we have previously imagined. I have gained insight from my personal encounters with the lives of farm animals that they are lovely and loveable creatures. They are individuals that are full of love. They are worthy, not only because of the similarities they share with our family pets but also because they are alive—living, breathing, sentient creatures with real feelings and emotions—and they deserve to live and crave to be loved.

Action Plan: What Can Be Done to Help Farm Animals

There are many ways to get involved in improving the situation for farm animals for the better. Showing support for farm-animal rescues, sanctuaries, and organizations and participating in efforts against ag-gag laws can help. You can become a farm-animal advocate. Simply start by spreading awareness, sharing facts, research, and information, educating others on farm animals, or participating in vigils and farm-animal rights marches. You can make a difference personally when you make better food choices by switching to a vegan diet and ditching dairy. You can donate to farm sanctuaries or provide volunteer services. You can offer alternatives to others when they come over for dinner and swap animal products for vegan recipes, thereby encouraging others to switch to plant-based foods even by sharing recipes.

Most people don't want to harm farm animals, but they do not know what happens to them on farms, or they have to think about it, so they turn a blind eye to their plight. I have said our social conditioning since childhood is part of the problem. A culture that views animals as disposable condones disregard for animal lives. The other problem is that profitable businesses of consumerism treat farm animals as cheap commodities with no value or worth. Of course, this is far from the truth. Farm animals are worthy of love and should live free from suffering.

I encourage everyone to visit farm-animal sanctuaries and to meet individual farm animals. Bring a friend or family member. I promise that will be a worthwhile experience, which could change your life and transform other people's perceptions to witness farm animals in a new light. Sanctuaries are places to connect with farm animals, which humans do not have an opportunity to do in their daily lives. You might even wish to sponsor an animal that left an impression on you or be involved in rescuing an animal headed for slaughter.

Farm animal sanctuaries that save innocent animals from slaughter and provide safe havens for farm animals to live out the rest of their lives are wonderful places, but they need our help. Most, if not all, farm-animal sanctuaries are nonprofit organizations, which are run by volunteers. They get no financial support from the government, and they do not have paid staff. They rely on volunteers to care for the animals and on donations. Helping in some of these ways can enable them to continue to operate in the future and make a difference.

Those of us who have had the privilege of getting to know farm animals realize that they are wonderful creatures with personalities of their own and a desire to live free from suffering. By getting involved through farm advocacy or activism or by politically writing to congress and spearheading campaigns to raise awareness, you are making a difference for these animals. As well, go meat-free and ditch dairy and eggs by making compassionate food choices that do not use the flesh for animal products. By doing so, you are helping to keep this industry from continuing operations in the future and protecting precious farm animal lives.

Most importantly, please share stories and information with your friends, family, coworkers, community and neighbors about the plight of innocent farm animals. Encourage others, especially children, to get to know farm animals. Meeting individual farm animals and experiencing them personally can change people's views and transform their perceptions.

Seeing the animals' facial expressions when they are playful, hearing their voices, and realizing that they have personalities shows us that farm animals are special creatures with capacities to love. These encounters can help others to reconsider their views as they learn about the individual species and lives of farm animals, such as pigs, chickens, cows, goats, and others. It will open their hearts so that they empathize with their plights and expand their compassion for other species beyond their pets. Farm animals are here *with* us not for us.

CHAPTER 13

The Rise of Veganism from Fringe to Mainstream

When I see bacon, I see a pig, I see a little friend,
and that's why I can't eat it. Simple as that.
—SIR PAUL MCCARTNEY

I often say that going vegan just makes sense—for animals, the planet, and your health.

The Birth of Veganism

Veganism has evolved from a small fringe movement, which had punk rockers and hippies, to a well-known term, which is being embraced more widely by mainstream society. Its popularity has increased tremendously over the last few years. It is becoming a familiar word in popular culture, and it is even considered cool and trendy.

Most people have heard the word vegan. They are aware that there are many vegan food options to choose from, with the rise of meatless products, which are taking the fast-food industry by storm, and almond, soy and oat milk as healthy alternatives to drinking dairy. With headlines such as this one: "2019 will be the year Veganism goes Mainstream" plastered on major media outlets,[238] especially for teens and millennials who are growing up in a world full of options and surrounded by all these new vegan food choses, it is easier than ever to embrace veganism as an appealing lifestyle choice.

At least 25 percent of Americans between the ages of twenty-five and thirty-four say they are vegan or vegetarian.[239] There is no doubt that more people are becoming vegan. By increasingly becoming more aware that embracing a vegan lifestyle or plant-based diet is essential for reducing animal suffering, benefiting their health, protecting the environment, and combating climate change, it is easier to choose this lifestyle.

Join Veganuary

The year 2018 brought with it huge victories for the animal-rights movement through veganism. One of these victories was the rapid explosion of Veganuary, a robust public-awareness campaign for omnivores and vegetarians to sign up to try out veganism as a New Year's resolution for the month of January. There is no doubt that vegan influencers and well-known celebrities are helping to make veganism popular, especially amongst millennials and younger generations. Currently, there is a shift in popular culture, which is growing the vegan movement.

Some of the celebrities who have contributed to the growing popularity in pop culture to embrace vegetarianism or veganism include Sir Paul McCarthy, Richard Branson, Simon Cowell, Moby, Alicia Silverstone, Billie Eilish, Brad Pitt, Joaquin Phoenix, Casey Affleck, Ellen DeGeneres, Ellie Goulding, Olivia Wilde, Natalie Portman, Ariana Grande, Russell Brand, Thandie Newton, Woody Harrelson, Liam Hemsworth, Pamela Anderson, Jessica Chastain, and many more. Some celebrities have dabbled

---

[238] Maria Chiorando, "'2019 Will Be Year of the Vegan' According to the Economist," Plant Based News (28 September 2020), https://www.plantbasednews.org/post/2019-year-vegan-the-economist.

[239] "The Economist Says 2019 Is the 'Year of the Vegan,'" Animal Outlook (24 September 2021), http://cok.net/blog/2018/12/economist-says-2019-year-vegan.

in vegan cuisine such as the married superstar and singer couple Beyoncé and Jay-Z, who adopted a plant-based diet for almost a month.[240]

Veganism as a Creed

As mainstream society shifts to accept that veganism is a social movement with more and more people moving toward it, individually and collectively, the legal system is moving toward social acceptance of veganism as an integral part of people's lives and identities. I heard about a legal case in Canada to consider ethical veganism as a creed. It involved a vegan firefighter named Adam Knauff who was deployed to a base camp and was deprived of vegan food there. He ended up losing his job due to his strongly held beliefs. At this point, I have not read that a decision was reached in this case or that veganism was considered a creed. A creed must be sincerely, freely, and deeply held and integrally linked to a person's identity. There are other criteria like governing one's conduct and having a connection to a community with a shared system of belief.

In Adam's application, he explained that he embraced veganism because of concerns about animal welfare and the environment and not for dietary or health reasons. He says,

> "As part of my sincerely held belief system, I fully reject the commodity status of animals," he writes. "A commitment to ethical veganism is, at least for me, an essential element of my personal identity. It guides who I support politically, and what government policies I endorse, among other things. To me, veganism is not a 'preference' or a trendy fad; it is a commitment to a way of life and a strongly held belief system that impacts my decisions on a daily, if not hourly, basis."[241]

---

[240] Dan Hancox, "The Unstoppable Rise of Veganism: How a Fringe Movement Went Mainstream," *The Guardian*, Guardian News and Media (1 April 2018), https://www.theguardian.com/lifeandstyle/2018/apr/01/vegans-are-coming-millennials-health-climate-change-animal-welfare.

[241] Wade Poziomka, "Employee Cites Ethical Veganism as a Creed," *Law Times* (March 22, 2018), https://www.lawtimesnews.com/practice-areas/human-rights/employee-cites-ethical-veganism-as-a-creed.

Because ethical veganism manifests itself as an all-encompassing life-style, which governs the way people act and the things they purchase, it may fall into the definition of a creed and become protected as a human right under the Human Rights Code. This issue is being considered in other places, such as a tribunal in the UK, which is being faced with a similar question of whether it is illegal to discriminate against someone in the workplace based on that person's ethical veganism. In 2011, a British tribunal ruled in favor of Joe Hashman, a subcontract gardener who lost his job as a direct result of his belief in anti-fox hunting activism, which conflicted with his employers. He was an ethical vegan, committed to preventing cruelty to animals. Thankfully, the Tribunal recognized his deeply held belief that "people should live their lives with mindful respect for animals and [that] we all have a moral obligation to live in a way which is kind to each other, our environment and our fellow creatures."[242]

If veganism ends up being recognized as a human right in other countries, it can lead to widespread societal acceptance, and accommodations can be made for vegans, to protect those who stand by their morals and legitimize the cause as being more than just a dietary choice.

Before the twenty-first century, vegan was a term that was virtually nonexistent, and the concept of veganism was viewed by many people as radical, fringe, and extreme. Vegans were seen as out-there extreme activists, representatives of animal welfare organizations like PET, and protesting while holding their banners and wearing T-shirts spray-painted red for blood. For some, veganism recalls images of beautiful, scantily clad women lying on the streets of New York City to protest wearing fur and killing animals for human consumption.

The Birth of Veganism

The term *vegan* was coined in 1944 by a British woodworker and nutritionist, Donald Watson, who with his wife and a group of friends, created the Vegan Society. Almost a decade later, the Vegan Society defined *vegan*

[242] Veromi Arsiradam, "A Case for Recognizing Ethical Veganism as a Creed," Obiter (March 10, 2020), https://obiter-dicta.ca/2020/03/10/a-case-for-recognizing-ethical-veganism-as-creed/.

as "the doctrine that man should live without exploiting animals." This is when animal suffering that was caused by human exploitation started being considered. Watson's group published articles in a magazine called *Vegan News*, which gave insight into the early development of vegan philosophy and the way that the members remained aligned with their conscience, despite the social difficulties they then faced. More recently, the Vegan Society defined its mission and *veganism*.

> The object of the Society shall be to end the exploitation of animals by man.

> The word veganism shall mean the doctrine that man should live without exploiting animals.[243]

Although veganism might seem like a new idea, vegetarian and plant-based eating has been around for a long time. The world defines *vegetarianism* as those humans who do not eat meat and fish. It dates as far back as before the Common Era (BCE). The earliest record of vegetarianism comes from the seventh century BCE, as societies touted values like instilling tolerance toward all living beings. Even further back in history, vegetarian societies existed in places such as ancient Greece and India, and in religions like Hinduism, Buddhism, and Jainism, in which adherents practice nonviolent living and abstain from animal consumption altogether.

Veganism encompasses a variety of subcategories, from ethical veganism to environmental veganism. But regardless of the reasons for being an ethical vegan, they abstain from consuming all animal products, including meat, dairy, eggs, and honey and from wearing any animal products, such as leather, wool, or silk.

My Vegan Journey

My personal experience into veganism took a while. I started to dabble in vegetarian food when I was a child. Although at that time, I could not

---

[243] Leslie Cross, "The Word Veganism Defined (1951)," Gentle World, (August 7th 2023), online: https://gentleworld.org/veganism-defined-written-by-leslie-cross-1951/

possibly have considered myself a vegan or even a real vegetarian, I made the connection, early in life that animals matter. I was fortunate to be loved by furry friends from childhood, so I was able to develop bonds with them. As an only child, I coped with loneliness better because from an early age I made it a point to be surrounded by animals to play with. I brought home feral cats. I played with dogs, tried horseback riding, and adopted a bunny and a dog. I loved interacting with other animal species too. I enjoyed going to Toronto Island during the summer, where there were farm and livestock animals. I loved to interact with the lambs, pigs, goats, and other farm animals living there.

I did not know that billions of animals were killed for mass human consumption—that realization occurred years later. As a very young child, my first beautiful bunny was named Susie (I named her after me), and she was my first pet. She was a cuddly, cozy, docile, and gentle best fur friend. I took care of and loved her deeply. She was a big gray bunny rabbit, which was more like a teddy bear. One night when I was supposed to be sleeping, I overheard a conversation that the grownups were having in my living room. They brought up rabbit as the main course for dinner as they were talking about a restaurant. I was horrified that rabbit meat was a dinner option. I will never forget that moment, as I held Susie in my arms, when I heard that rabbits were eaten by people. In that moment, I made the connection that rabbits are similar to other species of animals that are eaten.

As a child, I visited rabbits in pet stores. Since pet stores were in shopping malls, it was an activity that I really enjoyed; however, I didn't know that some of these cuddly creatures were bred for the purpose of being consumed. Years later, I wondered what the difference was—a rabbit or a pig being raised for meat—when both animals could feel pain and wanted to live. The distinction between animal species goes to the root of speciesism and the reason that society condones this brutality. To think that some animals are here with us for loving while others are raised for food is perplexing. It is the main reason that animal lives are so often devalued. Companion animals, such as dogs and horses, continue to be killed for human consumption in some places or to be used for experiments and discarded when they are no longer viewed as desirable. It goes back to the root of the problem: disposability—devaluing an animals' life.

Contradictions to our Relationships with Animals

This list of commoditized animals is expanded when we start to think about other places around the world that treat animals differently than we do. For instance, beloved dogs and cats being taken from families, killed, and consumed as a delicacy during the Yulin Dog Meat Festival is incomprehensible to Western society, yet sadly, it is still happening in some parts of Asia.

I had a chance encounter with a sweet senior dog, which had been saved from the dog-meat trade, when I was at a pet store. From the corner of my eye, I noticed a beautiful, beige, midsize, friendly dog that approached me to say hello. This dog resembled the Japanese dog named Hachiko from earlier. She came over to greet me with her tail wagging happily. I started a friendly conversation with the dog's guardian, an elderly lady. She shared the dog's story with me. The dog's name was Angel. She was a rescue dog, which had been saved from the dog-meat trade by a prominent animal-welfare organization called Soi Dog Foundation. It helped save street dogs and cats in Thailand. This kind lady was eager to share that Angel was a blessing in her life, and she brought so much comfort and joy. She told me that Soi Dog Foundation does amazing work to save dogs and even trains them before they are ready for adoption.

The collective public outcry in western countries to this issue once again, points to our contradictory perceptions of animals—the ways that we make distinctions between different species. Choosing which animals are worthy of living and which are to be killed is a form of discrimination—an arbitrary distinction that classifies some animals as important and others as worthless. Choosing to be vegan is a way of avoiding this double standard, and it acknowledges that *all* animals deserve to live without harm. The dog-meat trade is an example of yet another horrific practice and cruelty, and for many like me, the slaughter of dogs is simply unthinkable. But the slaughter of so many other animal species on an even larger scale is no less tragic.

Choosing a Vegan Lifestyle Is Easier than You Think

Making the switch to a vegan lifestyle is easier when people consider the benefits of health and caring about the planet. They witness animal suffering or come face-to-face with the realities of animal farming. After re-alizing that the cost of eating meat is the killing of an innocent animal who did not want to die, the choice to live without consuming animal products becomes easier. Many vegans, if you ask them, can vividly remember the moment they made the switch from eating meat to becoming vegetarian or vegan. A strict vegan diet contains absolutely no animal products. In other words, vegans don't consume meat, seafood, poultry, dairy, eggs, and honey.

A plant-based diet consists of whole, unprocessed foods. It has been championed by leading doctors for some time. It is like a vegan diet; how-ever, it places emphasis on whole plant-based foods, such as vegetables, fruits, legumes, nuts, and grains. It can take a while for some people to make the transition. But it's actually easier to make the transition when you have the right attitude. There are many plant-based foods to buy.

I was eleven years old when I seriously started to dabble in vegetari-anism. I recall the moment that I made the connection that the meat on my plate was a dead animal. It happened when I was out for dinner at a fancy steakhouse with my parents. I ordered a Caesar salad for an appetizer, followed by a filet mignon steak with baked potatoes. I ordered the meat well-done, so I assumed the steak would be cooked well. When the server brought the steak to our table, it was rare. It was so rare that when I cut into the meat, it looked like a bloodbath on my plate. I was nauseated, and I felt like I could smell the suffering in the blood. Even when the waiter seemed apologetic and then offered to replace it with another steak that was well-done, I refused to eat it. I lost my appetite and immediately decided that steak would no longer be a food option for me.

At that moment, I became aware that I was about to eat an animal that had been killed. I do not recall if I knew that steak was the dead corpse of a cow, but I realized bacon was a pig. In any event, something deep shifted inside me that day, and it was brewing. This experience led me to become a vegetarian back when it was relatively unknown and definitely weird and unpopular. I did not care that much about being different, but there were pressures to conform.

For the rest of my childhood, into my later teen years, and until I could make my own decision to refrain from eating certain foods, I had a complicated and uneasy relationship with meat. My mother is of Eastern European descent, where meat is viewed as essential to health, and it is served at dinner. She considered meat a staple in almost every meal. It's "an essential nutrient," she would tell me, whenever food was prepared.

Looking back, I think it was difficult for her to understand my vegetarian lifestyle choice. Although she deeply cares about companion animals, she can disconnect from the meat that is placed on the dinner table and that she sees in the butcher shop. I can't blame her, given how prevalent it is for people around the world to care about their companion animals but disconnect from others killed for food—or at least it appears that way whenever I try to convince her or other family members to consider eating less meat.

It took years after my realization that eating animals was against my moral principles for my mother to agree not to include meat in my dinners. When I was a teen, I truly was inspired to become a vegetarian. I felt less like a weirdo when I heard this famous quote by singer Sir Paul McCarthy, which inspired me to go vegetarian. I share this powerful quote with you again: "If slaughterhouses had glass walls, everyone would be a vegetarian." I started my journey to veganism as a vegetarian, when it was still unpopular, but knowing that someone as famous and influential as a member of the Beatles was a vegetarian was enough. I started by refusing to eat beef, pork, lamb, or veal, and then eventually, I eliminated chicken from my menu. I did, however, eat fish for many years, without much thought or consideration that fish were living creatures. I now know that fish are remarkable sentient beings that can develop lifelong bonds, use tools, conduct courtship rituals, and live rich and complex lives.[244] Knowing what I know now, I would not reduce them to mere commodities that are slaughtered by the trillions for consumption. I remained a vegetarian for many years.

Years later when I turned to animal rights as an advocate and my passion into a profession as an animal-rights lawyer, I was hired to defend companion animals' interests. I worked mainly with pet parents and their pet disputes. I was strictly vegetarian. I didn't have to think about other animal rights issues. At that time, most of my staff was vegetarian too, so we did not turn our minds to the hypocrisy of eating dairy and eggs, as we were focused on advancing the legal rights for companion animals. I stopped eating fish during that time.

I hope that my story can inspire others. I encourage people to become

---

[244] "What a Fish Knows," Jonathan Balcombe (22 June 2021), http://jonathan-balcombe.com/what-a-fish-knows.

thoroughly informed about the food on their plates and to realize the horrors of the animal agriculture industry so that they can make an educated choice and transition to a plant-based lifestyle. I admit that I was ignorant for years about the horrific realities of the dairy and egg industries. That is the reason why opening people's eyes to the realities of farm animals are imperative.

Like other people, I did not have to think about farm animals used for dairy, and I could not relate to animals that were so out of reach for me. Like so many, I did not understand the suffering of farm and livestock animals to the extent that I do now. It was a slow awakening that happened over several years. However, there was the pivotal moment when I realized what was happening in the dairy industry. I made the switch to a vegan and mainly plant-based diet, and it was easier than I thought. The more I became aware of what was happening and the heartbreaking stories I was reading on social media, the easier it became. One day I decided that I would never consume milk, cheese, or egg products again. I never looked back, and I feel much better knowing that I am not contributing to animal suffering.

There are many inspiring stories about people converting to veganism for the animals, planet, and/or their health. For example, in a compelling article from *Plant Based News*, Dane Rios shared the details of her transition from meat eater to vegetarian and from vegetarian to vegan. She demonstrated how it was a win-win decision.

> I went vegan sixteen years ago … I first went veggie after watching the movie *Brother's Keeper*. There is a scene where they kill a pig, and he will not die. He doesn't want to die and keeps walking around, crying—it was horrific. I decided never to eat meat again."[245]

Sometimes it takes illumination of the animal's suffering to comprehend the brutality of that life to make the connection and switch to veganism. Other times it is easier to convert for lifestyle choices or climate issues. Either way, others share their stories.

---

[245] Diana Lupica, "10 Life-Changing Vegan Stories that Will Amaze You," Plant Based News (1 October 2021), https://www.plantbasednews.org/post/10-life-changing-vegan-stories-that-will-amaze-you-copy.

Meeting Vegan Activist James Aspey

A few years ago, I found out that animal-rights activist and social-media influencer was speaking at the University of Toronto on the topic of veganism. His name was James Aspey, and he was from Australia. He garnered worldwide attention when he took a vow of silence for one year to raise social awareness about animal-rights issues. His talk on that evening changed me forever. I woke me up from my sleep and learned about the horrors of the dairy and egg industries. His convincing talk cemented my decision to refrain from consuming animal products ever again.

I arrived at the talk late, so by the time I entered the auditorium, the room was packed with deeply engaged, bright-eyed university and college undergrad students, law students, professors, activists, advocates, and those who seemed interested in what this Aussie had to say about the vegan movement. James Aspey was mesmerizing. He was an outstanding speaker with a great presence. He was convincing, and strong in his convictions, yet he did not for one second, make his audience feel guilty or shame them. Rather, he was approachable, and relatable, regarding the way that he spoke about his own transformation and brought education about the brutal ways in which we use and abuse animals. It was an awakening in my life and animal-rights journey. Here's an excerpt from one of James Aspey's animal rights speeches:[246]

> On 1 January 2014 I went vegan. Prior to that, I had gone vegetarian as an experiment. I was surprised at how great I felt, and soon discovered we can be far healthier and are likely to live longer lives without eating animal products … I now look at an animal and see a person, a non-human person, who has their own life, desires, thoughts, and feelings, just like I do. It has enriched my view of life on this world.[247]

Veganism is essential to the bigger picture of advancing the animal-protection movement. Many say that it is the least that we can do to stop

---

[246] James Aspey, "A Voice for Animals," The Vegan Society (10 August 2018), https://www.vegansociety.com/whats-new/blog/james-aspey-voice-animals.
[247] Ibid.

causing harm to animals. It is viewed by some as more of a philosophy, lifestyle, and set of deeply held ethical and moral principles to adhere to. It is not only a food diet or trend but also an all-encompassing lifestyle choice.

Like other historical social-justice movements, veganism has mobilized millions of people. It is leaving a lasting mark on the world. I admire strict vegans and their commitment and discipline to adhere to this lifestyle.

Those who commit to a vegan lifestyle are greatly contributing to the rising social-justice movement for animal protection. Vegans act against the pain and suffering of farmed animals. Additionally, so many compassionate people in the world care about animals but are not vegan. Perhaps they have not yet made the connection between their food and animal suffering.

I have found that most people on this journey start off with vegetarianism or even a flexitarian diet, which allows people to explore the lifestyle while reducing their contribution to animal suffering. Starting off with a flexible diet and then moving toward veganism may appeal to those who care deeply about animals but are still educating themselves about veganism.[248]

GO VEGAN FOR ANIMALS, THE PLANET, AND YOUR HEALTH

Vegan Lifestyle

People have the right to select the diet and adopt the lifestyle that suits them best for their health, lifestyle, and core beliefs. I have met lovely, kind, and compassionate animal lovers (pet parents) who have not made the transition to becoming vegan. I do not try to persuade them. I try to convince them by engaging in conversations and leading by example that following a plant-based diet is not difficult and that I can align my beliefs with my actions and moral code.

There can be danger in certain doctrines that preach and make others feel inferior if they do not follow the philosophy. Rather than lecturing to others or making people feel guilty if they are not a vegan, I am opting for

---

[248] Emer Delaney, "What is a Flexitarian Diet?" BBC Good Food (11 March 2021), https://www.bbcgoodfood.com/howto/guide/what-flexitarian-diet.

an open forum of conversation with those who are interested and curious about veganism. Rather than making veganism intimidating, let's make the conversation uplifting, focus on positivity and education. While veganism is an all-encompassing lifestyle, it may seem far less daunting when incremental changes are made.

Veganish Lifestyle

A veganish lifestyle is another way to transition to vegan, commit to eating mostly plant-based foods, and purchasing mainly animal-friendly products. It allows for flexibility, so it is probably most similar to flexitarians, as it is not a total commitment. For example, some people may want to commit to certain days of the week. It doesn't have to be drastic or sudden.

It is important to realize that humans have been socially conditioned to eat meat and dairy for so long that it can take time for some people to switch. There are many attractive options, such as committing to eat plant-based once per week as a start. For instance, Meatless Mondays is a great way to get started, or you can eat plant-based at home and enjoy other options when you go out to restaurants. It can be a gradual process and lifestyle choice as well. Some people can choose veganism as a diet and adapt to a cruelty-free lifestyle in their consumer choices. For mainstream society to adopt this lifestyle there must be room for tolerance, and flexibility.

Breeding Animals

Aside from animal agriculture, another issue that falls under veganism is the breeding of domesticated companion animals like dogs, cats, rabbits, and horses. It includes breeding wildlife, such as minks and foxes, on farms for human clothing and fur use. Further, the concept of animal ownership, in which animals are regarded as people's property, is reinforced when people *own* their pets because the human purchased the animal. As such, they can be sold, given away, or even abandoned. To perpetuate the cycle of disposability and animal breeding for human use it goes against the philosophy of doing as little harm to animals as possible.

The Power of Plant-Based Foods:
There Are Many Health Benefits

There are many health benefits to implementing a whole-food, plant-based diet into your lifestyle. When it comes to raising and using animals for food, the reality is that there is no biological necessity for humans to eat meat and dairy. The human species cannot only survive but can also thrive on a plant-based diet.

Numerous medical doctors have written on the health benefits of plant-based diets and have published plant-based books, which have even made the New York Times Best Seller list. For instance, Dr. Joel Furhman, who wrote *Eat to Live,* Dr. Michael Greger, who wrote *How Not to Die,* and Dr. Dean Ornish who wrote Undo It, discuss the health benefits of plant-based diets. Recently, another well-known medical doctor, Dr. William Li, appeared on television programs to talk about the health benefits of mainly plant-based foods for immunity. He is the author of *Eat to Beat Disease.* Whole-food, plant-based diets are shown to provide health benefits. According to the *American Journal of Clinical Nutrition,* vegan diets are higher in dietary fiber and various vitamins, and vegans often have lower cholesterol and blood pressure.[249]

There are many health benefits of eating plant-based foods. There is more widespread popularity, and it is gaining momentum in society when received from the medical profession. For instance, a news story featured on *Good Morning America* (GMA) caught my attention and captured my interest. It was on the health benefits of eating plant-based protein. The GMA television headline was "A New Study on Plant Protein Benefits" published in a medical journal. A study of 100,000 postmenopausal women over eighteen years found that women who ate more protein from plant-based sources had lowered risks from dementia, heart disease, and all-cause mortality (meaning death from all causes) in comparison with people that ate more meat, dairy, eggs, and other animal protein.[250]

---

[249] Winston J. Craig, "Health Effects of Vegan Diets," *The American Journal of Clinical Nutrition* (2009), 89.

[250] Katie Kindelan, "Plant Based Diets Reduce the Risk of Heart Disease and Dementia, Study Finds," *GMA* (21 February 2021), **https://www.goodmorningamerica.com/ wellness/story/plant-based-diets-reduce-risk-heart-disease-dementia-76108931**.

There is significant scientific research from the medical community with staggering data that demonstrates that meat consumption is linked to many diseases. The consumption of high amounts of animal products including dairy has been linked to cancer, heart disease, stroke, obesity, osteoporosis, arthritis, diabetes, foodborne illnesses, and more. Because a plant-based diet tends to be higher in fiber and lower in cholesterol, it provides many health benefits.

If that is not enough to make us rethink our dependence on animal products, most meat in the United States is not tested for drugs or chemical deposits. This is alarming given that animals are injected with large amounts of antibiotics for them to stay alive despite the overcrowded and stressful conditions they experience. Sulfamethazine is an antibiotic known for its carcinogens, which is routinely given to pigs. These antibiotics not only end up in our bodies but in our water.

Plant-Based for the Planet

Animal agriculture has had devastating impacts on the environment on both a local and global scale, which is another factor in people's decisions to live a vegan lifestyle. Studies have uncovered environmental effects felt by those living around factory farms, which impact their health and livelihood. There are high levels of particulate matter and ozone levels emanating from animal farms and slaughterhouses. These have been linked to the neurological development of children, who are vulnerable to suffering adverse effects from high levels of pollution, given that they consume more air per unit of body size and spend large amounts of time outdoors.[251] These pollutants are also damaging to the lungs. They have been shown to lead to asthma and other respiratory tract diseases.[252]

---

[251] Sam Brockmeyer and Amedeo D'Angiulli, "How Air Pollution Alters Brain Development: The Role of Neuroinflammation," *Translational Neuroscience*, vol. 7 (2016), 24–30, https://doi.org/10.1515/tnsci-2016-0005.

[252] Sara May, et al., "Respiratory Health Effects of Large Animal Farming Environments," *Journal of Toxicology and Environmental Health*," (2012), 524–41, https://www.ncbi.nlm.nih.gov/pmc/articles/PMC4001716/>.

On a global scale, animal agriculture is one of the leading causes of environmental issues, including climate change. A United Nations report released by the Food and Agriculture Organization states that this sector is one of the most significant contributors to air and water pollution, land degradation, loss of biodiversity, and climate change. Animal agriculture is responsible for more greenhouse gas emissions than exhaust from the entire transportation sector combined.[253] It is also estimated that livestock and livestock feed occupy one-third of the earth's ice-free land, as they need vast amounts of land to graze, and farmers must grow large amounts of feed needed for the billions of animals on factory farms.

It is the leading cause of species extinction and habitat destruction, given the loss of biodiversity when land is used for grazing and crops. It is also the leading cause of ocean dead zones, due to the eutrophication that occurs when the entire chemical nutrients from factory farming goes into our bodies of water, causing algae blooms.[254] This industry is wreaking havoc on our global environment, and it is becoming clear that animal agriculture is an unsustainable way to feed our growing population, causing many to explore a vegan lifestyle.

As more people become aware of the hidden truth behind of the cruel animal-agriculture industry and realize that farm animals undergo extreme suffering, the vegan population continues to grow each year. Many people choose to be vegan for the animals, others for the planet, and for their health. Several documentaries shine a light on the benefits of a plant-based diet. It is helpful to watch these Netflix documentaries with friends and family, such as *Earthlings, Forks over Knives, and Cowspiracy*, as they shed light on industry practices and their implications. These documentaries can help convince people that eating animals is cruel, unnecessary, and harmful to our health and the future of our planet. Veganism continues to gain popularity, making it easier than ever to live a plant-based life.

The Game Changers is another popular Netflix documentary, which highlights world-renowned athletes who follow a plant-based diet. They address the misconception that animal protein is necessary for muscle

---

[253] "Livestock's Long Shadow," Food and Agriculture Organization of the United Nations (2006), http://www.fao.org/3/a0701e/a0701e00.htm.

[254] "The Facts," Cowspiracy (2014), http://www.cowspiracy.com/facts.

growth or peak athletic performance. The documentary counters the stereotypes that are sometimes associated with a plant-based diet, including the notion that meat eating is inherent to masculinity or that real men must eat meat.

Strict vegans might make it difficult for some to uphold the regime and refrain from an animal product; at least, that is what friends have shared with me over the years. But these are excuses, and the truth is that people can make the switch if they want to. It might be easier to convince others to switch more gradually to plant-based eating and highlight the many health benefits that are discussed in film documentaries like *The Game Changers*.

Vegan Lifestyle

There is more to living an ethical vegan lifestyle than simply not eating animal products. Veganism is a social movement of non-exploitation and nonviolence toward animals. It encompasses more than just the food that we eat. At first, it is hard to think of all the items we use that are made from animal parts, are tested on animals, or are a product of their suffering. But one look into the average closet shows no shortage of fur, leather, wool, and other materials made from animals.

Next, a look into our bathroom drawers exposes all the makeup, haircare, and skincare products developed through cruel and painful experiments on innocent animals. We have laundry detergents, toothpastes, and cleaners that come about from so much suffering. I recognize that it can be overwhelming for people who are just starting on this journey. Realizing how much their lifestyles impact animals takes some time and research, given how pervasive these consumer products are in our everyday lives.

While making the switch to vegan products may seem daunting at first, there is so much helpful information. It is encouraging to know that there is a growing movement on our side. It is helping us to make the switch easier with fashionable vegan clothing, cruelty-free vegan cosmetics, and other products with increasing regularity.

I meet people from all walks of life who care deeply about animals. I am honored to get to know them better, as our mutual interest and passion for animals unites us. When I share with people that I am an animal advocate, often, a friendly conversation ensues. The other person shares heartfelt stories about beloved pets and sometimes about his or her journey or interest in veganism. Have you ever noticed that whenever people talk about their own beloved companion animals, their faces light up? A conversation about fur friends puts people at ease and smiles on their faces. It is palpable to feel how much people care for their furry animals. I am inspired whenever I meet people equally or more committed to animal rights and making a difference.

The Truth is that Wearing Fur Hurts Animals

Those days when wearing fur was socially acceptable and in vogue are long gone, as we are starting to see a major shift in what consumers are looking for. This may be because the cruel and unnecessary practices used to create these products are finally coming to light.

> Over one hundred million animals worldwide are killed for fur every year. Many animals are trapped in the wild for their fur and when caught spend their remaining days living in tiny wire battery cages. These animals include foxes, bobcats, coyotes, wolves, raccoons, lynx, and others primarily throughout North America and Russia. Traps are incredibly violent and painful, inflicting great suffering on those wild animals unfortunate enough to be caught. It is unnatural and simply cruel.[255]

Animals have been known to chew off their limbs to escape, and they often die of blood loss, hypothermia, or sheer shock. Many times, they are trapped for days, scared, and defenseless against predators. These cruel practices do not only affect animals used for fur but also trap any animal

---

[255] "Investigation Reveals Animals Brutally Beaten and Skinned Alive on Fur Farms for the Sake of Fashion," The Humane Society of the United States (July 7, 2020), https://www.humanesociety.org/news/investigation-reveals-animals-brutally-beaten-and-skinned-alive-fur-farms-asia-sake-fashion.

that steps on it, including dogs, cats, and deer.[256] Most of the fur comes from fur farms, where animals like foxes, minks, and chinchillas are bred, confined in cages, and killed for their fur. Wild animals that have not gone through any process of domestication are meant to be free, to run, and to hunt. Putting them in small cages for so long causes immense stress, many health problems, and infected wounds. Studies also show that hazardous chemicals, including chromium and formaldehyde, are used in the process of treating fur to prevent it from rotting, which is both dangerous to our health and to the well-being of the environment.[257]

Fur Is *Not* in Fashion

Thankfully, the cruelty found in fur farms is helping to eradicate fur industries, and fur is no longer fashionable. Recently, California became the first state to ban the sale of fur. San Francisco became the first major city to ban the sale of fur in January of 2020. With San Francisco's victory on abandoning the cruel and outdated industry of the fur trade, society is entering a modern era—a time when people do not cause pain and suffering to innocent animals for barbaric and obsolete luxuries of the past. Luckily, many other countries are beginning to realize the horrors of the fur-farming industry, and they are enacting legislation to phase out these cruel practices. The United Kingdom, Austria, Bosnia, Herzegovina, Belgium, Croatia, the Czech Republic, Luxembourg, the Netherlands, and many more countries have introduced fur bans. Other countries like New Zealand are prohibiting the importing of mink, which stops them from being farmed. Most recently, Italy and Ireland introduced legislation to ban fur.

In 2018, Norway, which was the largest producer of fox pelts in the world, enacted legislation that prohibited fur farming. Belgium is planning to end fur farming in 2023.[258] All of these bans mean that fur-free

---

[256] "Trapping—Animal Welfare Problems," Fur Free Alliance (23 September 2019), https://www.furfreealliance.com/trapping.

[257] "The Environmental Costs and Health Risks of Fur," Fur Free Alliance (14 July 2020), https://www.furfreealliance.com/environment-and-health.

[258] "Fur Bans," Fur Free Alliance (3 February 2022), https://www.furfreealliance.com/fur-bans.

alternatives are being developed and that they will be made far more accessible, which great news for those is looking to accessorize in a cruel-ty-free way.

Major fashion houses have committed to banning the use of fur products from their runways. An increasing number of fashion designers and retailers have ditched fur, including Prada, Gucci, Armani, Versace, Michael Kors, Macy's, Bloomingdale's, Jimmy Choo, Calvin Klein, Stella McCartney, DKNY, Burberry, Chanel, H & M, Tom Ford, and Tommy Hilfiger. Other high-profile brands have announced fur-free policies. In addition, online fashion retail platforms Net-A-Porter and Farfetch have introduced no-fur policies. Other fashion houses such as Oscar de la Renta announced that it will stop using fur products after years of pressure from animal-rights activists.

Many of these noted fashion houses refuse to be part of this cruel in-dustry, and they have joined the fur-free fashion momentum. Thankfully, in this modern age, fashion is leading the way by abandoning the cruel fur-trade industry.

Animals Are Not Accessories

As cruel and violent as the fur industry is, their products are nowhere near as abundantly available as leather, which comes from an industry that is just as horrifying. Leather is used for belts, bags, shoes, jackets, and countless other clothing items that we use every day. Because it has undergone such a rigorous process to change it from the animal skin it once was into a clothing item that we purchase, it is hard to connect the product to animal cruelty. However, it is important to know that leather comes from animals that have endured tremendous violence.

The leather tanning industry involves the use of toxic chemicals, including highly carcinogenic heavy metals to turn the raw flesh of an animal into the finished products that we see in stores. While some com-panies like Chanel are shunning exotic animal skins, not much thought is going into ending the cruel practice that is the leather industry. By refusing to purchase leather and speaking out against it, we can help ani-mals. Nowadays, it is easier to purchase animal-friendly products that are fashionable, affordable, and trendy, as celebrities are endorsing faux leather brands. Leather made from pineapple leaves, mangoes, and mushrooms, for example, are great alternatives.

Choose Compassion over Cruelty and Cruelty-Free Products

Shunning products that were tested on animals is also an important part of the vegan movement. Despite much backlash from cosmetic companies that test on animals, animal testing is declining. In 2011, almost eleven and a half million animals were experimented on across Europe, including tens of thousands of experiments on dogs and monkeys.

Despite the number of animals being tested on, it has been shown that 95 percent of drugs that are found to be safe and effective in animals do not pass human clinical trials, showing that there must be a more effective and humane way to ensure the safety of the products that we use.[259] Organizations like the Center for Alternatives to Animal Testing (CAAT) and the Canadian Centre for Alternatives to Animal Methods (CCAAM) are working to put an end to cruel animal-testing practices. In fact, CCAAM is Canada's first and only research center that is primarily dedicated to creating superior alternatives to animal testing.

While these organizations are doing important work, you can do your part individually as a consumer by refusing to purchase products that have been tested on animals. Other international organizations include Cruelty Free International (CFI), which works internationally to put an end to cruel animal experiments. CFI has gained notoriety with publicity campaigns and celebrities joining forces as spokespeople and for its impressive work in exposing the cruelty of cosmetic companies that test on animals. To date, CFI has obtained over a million signatures, including mine, with the goal of finally ending cosmetic testing on animals worldwide.[260]

---

[259] "Welcome to CCAAM/ Cacvam," *Canadian Centre for Alternatives to Animal Methods*, University of Windsor, http://www.uwindsor.ca/ccaam.

[260] "About Cruelty-free International," Cruelty Free International (2021), https://cruelty-freeinternational.org/.

Move to a Kinder, Gentler, and More Compassionate World

The world would be a kinder place for animals if people chose cruelty free. The inhumane treatment of animals would be reduced, and animal suffering would be a far less normalized part of our society. As the demand for eating meat and animal products reduces, the number of animals bred into existence for food decreases. This means that the amount of feed needed to sustain these animals can be greatly reduced. We are producing huge amounts of feed and using vast areas of land to nourish the animals that are then slaughtered. It is an inefficient use of industrial resources, so a reduction in the number of farm animals raised will divert resources to people who most need them. One study found that replacing all US animal-based foods with plant-based foods would free up enough resources to feed 350 million additional people.[261]

Given the rise in plant-based eating and veganism, there are many helpful resources for those interested in moving toward a plant-based lifestyle. Challenge 22 is an online program that guides people toward veganism in an accessible, informative, and judgment-free way. It provides free online support for twenty-two days and pairs participants with mentors, dietitians, and a community for guidance. Another one is Veganuary, which was mentioned earlier. It is an excellent online resource, which gives motivation about how to transition to veganism. I am delighted to share that a few of my friends and supporters on my social media platforms were inspired by my posts on Veganuary and have signed on.

Along with these resources, there are endless vegan recipes, videos, and tools for those looking for more information. The most important part of adopting this lifestyle is keeping an open mind and commitment. The decision of whether to consume animal products is, a personal one, albeit one with far-reaching impacts. You can surround yourself with like-minded individuals who are vegans. For instance, you can eat out at vegan restaurants, attend vegan festivals, and even travel to vegan friendly destinations for vacations and make new friends.

---

[261] Alon Shepon, Gidon Eshel, Elad Noor, and Ron Milo, "The Opportunity Cost of Animal Based Diets Exceeds All Food Losses," PNAS (26 March 2018), https://www.pnas.org/content/115/15/3804.

As an animal advocate, you might have expected me to take a definitive stance on this topic, with moral implications of that decision and an offering of my reasons. Rather than do that, the idea that I wanted to put forward is that the decision to consume and purchase animal products should be an educated and conscious personal choice.

It might seem that that progress is slow, but if we consider how far veganism has come, it is growing, and it will be the norm in the future. Taking the time to learn about the processes by which foods get to your plate and the consumer products that you use might allow you to think twice. Whether or not you follow a vegan lifestyle or plant-based diet, your dietary choices have the power to mitigate the harmful effects that animal agriculture has on both the animals and our environment. Choosing to consume fewer animal products, purchasing cruelty free products, or replacing a few meals a week with plant-based alternatives helps the animal-rights movement. It can also be a fun way to get inspired in the kitchen and to cook in a healthy way and that aligns with your moral and ethical values. Making conscious consumer choices can leave a positive impact on the environment and your health and help our planet to heal.

CHAPTER 14

Why Wildlife Matters: Respect Wild Animals and Nature

If we can teach people about wildlife, they will be touched. Share my wildlife with me. Because humans want to save things that they love.
—STEVE IRWIN

As I often say, wild animals are majestic, precious, mysterious and rare. We can learn so much from them. They live in the forest which is their home, and they have every right to dwell there.

My affection for wildlife and wild animals started early in life when I was gifted a children's book called *Bambi*. Reading that book changed my life and cemented my love for wild animals. I learned as a young child that wild animals could form bonds and friendships with other species—as Thumper and Bambi became best friends. This touching story has stayed with me. It helped me feel more connected to wild animals throughout my childhood. I read it many times before bedtime, and although it's a fictitious book, its message resonated. I still have this particular book and keep it as a fond memory. I read it to my children and look forward to reading it to my grandchildren in the future as well. Similar to other animal causes, it helps to make a positive difference for wild-animal species, including education.

Australia on Fire

Wild animals suffering are connected with natural disasters. Heartbreaking news' stories of bushfires that swept over Australia popped up on my news feed daily in 2019. There were horrific and disturbing images of burned koalas and charred kangaroos, which grabbed global attention and led to millions of dollars in donations for recovery efforts. However, it is the species with smaller habitats and fewer numbers that are more vulnerable to being wiped out. It is estimated that over one billion wildlife species have perished in these fires to date, which is a catastrophe for the natural habitat and future of some of these native species in our world.

Koala bears are under threat of becoming extinct, as they are utterly defenseless against the bushfires. Koalas are native to Australia and are one of the country's most beloved animals. They are gentle, caring creatures, which are known to be loyal to their families. They were endangered even before these wildfires. Many tear-jerking images of koalas being saved from the wildfires are etched in my mind forever. In particular, I was captured by a heartwarming video of a crying koala bear. This koala was rescued from the burning wildfires and was crying like a helpless baby. In the video, there was a woman who took off her shirt and offered a bottle of water as another man appeared with a blanket. She then covered the whimpering koala with the shirt and blanket and poured water on him. He was so badly burned that the couple rushed him to an Australian hospital. They later named him Lewis.[262]

Not only koala bears were affected by these bushfires but also entire native populations were affected. These burning bush fires have taken an enormous toll on other wildlife animal species, including kangaroos, birds, reptiles, and insects. Through this heartbreak and devastation, there were many uplifting stories of hope and inspiration from people that cared: veterinarians, animal rescuers, and other compassionate humans joining forces for recovery. Communities came together to rescue and save these innocent wild animals.

Veterinarian Dr. Scott Miller filmed his journey to Kangaroo Island. More than half of its koalas were believed to have perished. He was trying to save the remaining koalas from Australia's continuing bushfire crisis. Dr. Miller helped rescue a mother and her baby and a joey (later named Little

---

[262] Mark Pygas, "Woman Saves Burned and Screaming Koala Using the Shirt off Her Back," Distractify (November 20, 2019), **https://www.distractify.com/p/koala-bushfire-rescue**.

Scottie). He called them Auzzie icons. They were taken from a tree, but the rescue was not simple, as the mother was very protective of her baby. This video accurately demonstrates the difficulties of dealing with distressed and traumatized animals that are trapped in the burned landscape. Dr. Miller came to the rescue and took them both to an emergency wildlife hospital where they eventually recovered with a lot of effort and care.[263]

The Australian bushfires were a global catastrophe causing so much damage. There is even consensus from the scientific community that they were caused by climate change. Although there is no going back and fixing this devastation, it is a real wake-up call. It can be an amazing opportunity to create solutions for humanity and to improve the situation—to do better both individually and collectively. Although the prime minister of Australia has denied climate change as the cause of the wildfires, climatologists are convinced, and the scientific research is overwhelming. Scientific studies have concluded that global warming is leading to an increase in hot, dry weather around the world, which creates the conditions for wildfires.[264]

Despite this disaster for Australia and its inhabitants, the glimmer of hope was the thousands of animals that were saved from living in captivity. It is said that in every tragic situation, it is possible to find hope and to focus on the positive side. After all, hope is what keeps humanity going and moving forward. There have been many captivating stories of hope to inspire humans to learn and act. Somehow, we know that Australia can recover from this loss.

Climate Change Is a Real Threat

Climate change is having the most prominent impact on wildlife species around the world. This human-induced environmental change is causing warmer global temperatures, shorter winters, and rising sea levels, to name only a few of its grave impacts. Clear examples of wildlife species impacted

[263] Abigail Gillibrand, "Koala Screams for Baby in Heartbreaking Scenes from Australian Fires and This Morning Viewers Are Inconsolable," Metro 50 (January 15, 2020), https://metro.co.uk/2020/01/15/koala-screams-baby-heartbreaking-scenes-austra-lian-fires-morning-viewers-inconsolable-12061951/.
[264] Alejandra Borunda, "The Science Connecting Wildfires to Climate Change," *National Geographic* (September 17, 2020), https://www.nationalgeographic.com/science/article/climate-change-increases-risk-fires-western-us.

by climate change include polar bears, which are losing their habitats due to melting ice, and marine life, losing theirs to coral bleaching because of rising global temperatures.

The Amazon Rainforest Is Under Threat

Another example of climate change is in the Amazon Rainforest. As an ecosystem, the Amazon is one of the most biodiverse places on the planet. Over three million animal species live in the rainforest, and over 2,500 tree species sustain this vibrant ecosystem. The Amazon contains our planets largest tropical rainforest, which helps regulate our earth's climate. The Amazon rainforest holds 90 to 140 billion tons of carbon, which would significantly increase the rate of global warming, even if a small fraction of it were released.[265]

Global warming due to climate change threatens the Amazon in a variety of ways. Increased temperatures are leading to more drought-like symptoms throughout the region. For instance, the high-altitude regions of the Amazon, which thrive among the clouds, are where the flow of water down the mountains start and join the Amazon's major network of rivers.[266] As drought-like conditions start to take over the Amazon, this flow of water is susceptible to interruption because of unstable soils and decreased rainfall.[267] This, in turn, impacts the wildlife in the regions, which either have to adapt to less water or move to a new habitat to access water.

I watch wildlife documentaries on National Geographic. I was mesmerized when I saw a documentary with the wild animals that live in the Amazon Rainforest, such as sloths, macaws, jaguars, black spider monkeys, and more. The balance between all the parts of this system helps sustain this diverse ecosystem and keeps its inhabitants thriving. Every animal living there is important, and the loss of one species could throw the entire ecosystem out of balance. There is also a strong link between the health of

---

[265] "The Extraordinary Amazon," World Wildlife Fund, wwf.panda.org/knowledge_hub/where_we_work/amazon.

[266] "Climate Change in the Amazon," World Wildlife Fund, www.worldwildlife.org/pages/climate-change-in-the-amazon.

[267] Ibid.

the Amazon and the well-being of our planet. Deforestation is a threat, as it releases significant amounts of carbon, which is having negative consequences around the world.

Another Amazon species, which is among the many affected by the changing rainforest, is the yellow-banded poison dart frog. Due to increased temperatures and loss of habitat, the poison dart frogs' current habitat is becoming unsuitable, and the population is declining.[268] It has been projected that the poison dart frog will have to move hundreds of kilometers to find a new suitable habitat.[269] The yellow-banded poison dart frog is only one of many species of wild animals that are affected by habitat loss and changes in climate, due to human-induced global warming. We need to follow through on our commitments and reconsider our relationship to these creatures and to Mother Nature.

The World Wildlife Fund (WWF) is the largest wildlife conservation organization that protects endangered wildlife species. Thankfully, WWF is acting for a variety of animal species impacted by climate change in the Amazon, including the yellow-banded poison dart frog. The conservationists at the WWF are working with both indigenous groups and farmers, teaching farmers how to raise their crops sustainably in drought-like conditions to reduce the risk of forest fires. Furthermore, WWF has established protected areas within the Amazon to shield it from human activity, such as deforestation.[270]

Hunted Animals

In addition to human-induced climate change, certain human actions have led to the demise of animal populations. These include trophy hunting—hunting animals for their tusks, horns, or bones or breeding animals for specific body parts. Two species and their sad stories emphasize the need for humans to change their actions and behaviors to save wildlife animal populations from extinction.

---

[268] "Poison Dart Frog," World Wildlife Fund, www.worldwildlife.org/species/poison-dart-frog.
[269] "Climate's Impact Will Move from Artic to Tropics," University of Washington (16 October 2015), www.futurity.org/climate-change-amazon-basin-1027382-2/.
[270] Amazon, *Supra,* note 193.

The first is the northern white rhino. At the time I am writing this chapter, there are only two female northern white rhinos left in the world and protected from poachers. This wildlife species used to thrive in Africa, but due to mass hunting for their horns, they quickly became at risk of extinction.[271] The two remaining female northern white rhinos currently reside in a conservation park in Kenya, where they have guards protecting them day and night.

Scientists and conservationists tried desperately to breed the remaining male with the females before he died, but age and other complications led to an inability to breed. With the death of the last male northern white rhino, the species is now basically extinct. In the hopes of reversing the wildlife specie's path to extinction, scientists were able to harvest sex cells from the last remaining male before he died and from the remaining female. Scientists and wildlife conservationists hope that they will be able to use in vitro fertilization (IVF) to impregnate a southern white rhino as a surrogate, to save the species from extinction.[272] With further technological advancements, scientists hope that they will be able to bring the breed back from extinction successfully.

Another animal species affected by changes to their environment by human actions are lions. Humans are breeding lions for their bones, which are in high demand for use in traditional medicine.[273] There are over three hundred breeding centers in South Africa, with around ten thousand lions being held captive in horrible conditions.[274] The reason this trade is so prolific in South Africa is because it is legal. There are no consequences for breeding and killing lions for their bones, and the South African government is encouraging it.[275] Moreover, trophy hunters can go to these breeding centers, where the lions are released into a fenced yard for the hunters to shoot.[276] This provides hunters with the delusional belief that they got

---

[271] "Can We Save the Northern White Rhino?" Save the Rhino (1 March 2017), www.savetherhino.org/thorny-issues/can-we-save-the-northern-white-rhino/.

[272] Ibid.

[273] Jane Wharton, "Shocking Lion Bone Trade Is Putting Species 'At Risk of Extinction,'" *Metro News* (18 August 2018), metro.co.uk/2019/08/18/lion-bone-trade-puts-species-at-risk-of-extinction-10588132/.

[274] Ibid.

[275] Ibid.

[276] Ibid.

prized trophies while the breeders can sell the lions' bones. The lions, as a result, live in cramped quarters, rarely get to roam outside, and eventually are put into an enclosure to be shot.

Tribute to Cecil the Lion

Most of you have probably heard Cecil the lion's story, as he has captivated the hearts of millions of animal lovers around the globe. A dentist from Minneapolis killed the well-known lion in a Zimbabwe trophy hunt with a bow and arrow. Cecil had been something of a star. He attracted tourists because his black mane made him identifiable and because he allowed safari sightseeing vehicles to come close to him. He was also part of an Oxford University wildlife study, and he wore a GPS tracking collar.

Cecil's killing provoked outrage, and the media storm made the dentist an international pariah.[277] News of Cecil's death was received with profound heartbreak and sadness around the world. This majestic creature was killed for human entertainment. Since Cecil's tragic and senseless killing, France has banned the importation of lion trophies, and other countries are starting to take a stand. For instance, American and British airlines banned the transport of hunting trophies, and the US Fish and Wildlife Service added lions to its endangered species list, making it more difficult for Americans to hunt them under American law.[278]

Every year, hundreds of thousands of wild animals around the world are killed by trophy hunters. Many of these hunters acquire animals' body parts for bragging rights.[279] Approximately 80 percent of trophy hunters worldwide are Americans, who travel to exotic destinations to kill animals. This devastation speaks to the consumer-oriented economic commodification of animals and disrespect for living, breathing, wild creatures. Wild animals are regarded as no more valuable than other species, including

---

[277] John Campbell, "Wildlife Conservation in Africa, Outrage in the West, and Cecil the Lion," Council on Foreign Relations (9 July 2019), https://www.cfr.org/blog/wildlife-conservation-africa-outrage-west-and-cecil-lion.

[278] Ibid.

[279] "Banning Trophy Hunting," Humane Society of the United States, https://www.humanesociety.org/all-our-fights/banning-trophy-hunting.

domesticated animals, such as farm animals and companion animals. The root of the problem of wild animal commodification that leads to animal species extinction stems from a society that values consumerism and economic profit over preservation for the natural world and respect for animals.

Public anger at the deaths of majestic wildlife creatures and lions like Cecil prompted a push for the American government to do something. For instance, Arizona's governor introduced the Conserving Ecosystems by Ceasing Importation of Large Animal Species Act (the CECIL Act). The bill prohibits all importation and exportation of animal species listed under the Endangered Species Act. This bill would impose a total ban on importing hunting trophies of elephants or lions taken from certain African places.[280]

To end wildlife exploitation and the commodification of wild animals and to save them from extinction, it is important to let your voice be heard. You can contact wildlife and conservation organizations such as WWF or wild animal sanctuaries involved in protecting wildlife animals to see how you can become involved in advocating for these vulnerable animals. Finally, you can share and sign petitions to show your support for ending lion farming[281] or to save another wildlife species, such as the northern white rhino, from extinction. You can also educate yourself. Learn more about wildlife extinction and how to become involved politically so that you can write to your local politicians and lobby new laws.

Mia's White Lion, Charlie

I watched a captivating movie on the horrific trade of lions in Africa called *Mia the White Lion*. It was based on a true story about a lion-breeding farm in South Africa. It captured my heart. It also has left a deep imprint on me and those whom I have talked to about the movie. The film was based on a

---

[280] Taylor Mooney, "Congress Considers Crackdown on Trophy Hunting," *CBS News* (19 July 2019), https://www.cbsnews.com/news/trophy-hunting-import-ban-cecil-act-hearing-in-congress.

[281] "End the Great Betrayal," Born Free, https://www.bornfree.org.uk/great-betrayal and Care2 Petitions, "Save the Northern White Rhino from Extinction," The Petition Site, https://www.thepetitionsite.com/774/715/623/save-the-northern-white-rhino-from-extinction/.

family from London, England, which moved to South Africa. Their teenage daughter named Mia, whose father owned a lion-breeding farm, was given a lion cub as a present, and she named him Charlie.

Finding out about the making of this movie was the coolest part. It was made by documentary filmmaker Gilles de Maistre, who came up with the idea of a child who bonds with a lion. He collaborated with conservationist and known lion whisperer Kevin Richardson, who told him the only way to do it without green screens or special effects would be to let a kid and a cub grow up together over a period of several years. So the story follows the fearless girl from the age of twelve to fifteen, with the lion cub, a rare white lion named Charlie in the movie (who is named Thor in real life), which grew into a majestic lion.[282]

Mia forms a special human-animal bond with the lion cub, and there is a deep connection and friendship between them. The film shows the depth of unconditional love that forms between this girl and the lion cub, but as he grows, he gets too large to handle. Eventually, Mia's father decides to sell Charlie to the lion trade, and this is when Mia discovers the truth about lion farms and the horrific trophy hunting industry. She doesn't sit idly by, but instead, she takes action to help save her lion best friend from an unthinkable fate and finds a safe resting place and sanctuary for her beloved friend. When people get to know wildlife animals, they love and respect them and realize that they deserve their freedom and not to be exploited by humans.

The Truth about Zoos and Circuses

Zoos are another way that humans have exploited wildlife animals and forced them to live in unnatural environments. Exotic animals are often taken from their native habitats or a falsely advertised animal sanctuary. They are placed in zoos far from their country of origin. The truth is that zoos operate mainly for profit and human entertainment. They can have devastating effects on animals when the animals do not adapt to their new environments.

---

[282] Chris Knight, "Far-fetched It May Be, Mia and the White Lion Is the Real Deal," National Post (April 10, 2019), **https://nationalpost.com/entertainment/movies/far-fetched-it-may-be-mia-and-the-white-lion-is-the-real-deal**.

In one noteworthy animal-rights case, an Asian elephant named Lucy did not adapt well to her new environment at a zoo in Edmonton, Canada. Lucy the elephant came from Sri Lanka when she was just two years old. The Edmonton Valley Zoo was the most northern location that an Asian elephant had ever resided. As a result, this extreme change of environment had a negative impact on Lucy's physical health and emotional well-being.[283]

Elephants are fascinating creatures. They are social, empathetic, intelligent, caring, compassionate, and bonded with their families. They love to wander and play with others, but this lonely elephant did not have the privilege of exploring her natural instincts. Instead, Lucy is confined. For the past forty years, she has lived in isolation at the Edmonton Zoo in cold Canada. While Lucy does have ample space to wander the zoo's grounds, she is usually confined to a small enclosure for much of the year, due to Edmonton's cold climate. In the summer months, which are short, you can see Lucy outside, interacting with her human zookeepers. In the winter months, which can start as early as November and last until April, Lucy has the option of wandering outdoors and braving subzero temperatures or staying in her small indoor enclosure. It goes against an elephant's natural instincts to play and interact with other elephants.

As a result of being the most northern elephant in the world, Lucy has spawned public outcry and media attention among animal activists, and other concerned public citizens. The main debate is centered on Lucy's need to be moved to a warmer climate where she can interact with other elephants. Her zookeepers argue that this is all she has known her whole life and that moving her after forty years would cause her extreme stress. They have explained that Lucy is well-socialized with the zookeepers and that she gets lots of mental stimulation each day through various games and activities. They maintain that she is too sick to move, although they refuse to allow an unbiased, external veterinarian to confirm this. Activists are fighting for an independent expert to evaluate Lucy's health and determine if it would be possible to move her.[284]

[283] "The World's Coldest Elephant? Activists Demand Lucy's Removal from Canadian Zoo," *The Guardian*, https://www.theguardian.com/world/2017/mar/01/lucy-the-elephant-canada-edmonton-valley-zoo.
[284] Ibid.

Lucy's Legacy

They brought this issue to court on behalf of Lucy. Well-known animal-welfare organizations such as PETA and Zoocheck Canada brought a lawsuit against the City of Edmonton. The lawsuit alleges that the City of Edmonton, the zoo's owner, is not properly caring for Lucy and is therefore breaking the law.[285] The hope is to ensure that the zoo will not be able to renew its license. This is a different tactic than an earlier court attempt to have Lucy relocated.[286]

The Alberta Court of Appeal dismissed this argument, concluding that they did not have the legal ability to ask the court to review the zoo's license renewal.[287] One important takeaway from this case is the dissent, where one judge stated that animals must be afforded some form of legal standing if they are to be protected in any way.[288] Further, the judge stated that this decision sets a dangerous precedent for anyone who brings forward an animal or environmental issue, if there is no personal interest involved in the matter.[289] This dissent highlights the activists' key point—if they cannot get recourse for Lucy through the courts, how will her interests be protected at all?

AQUATIC SENTIENCE

Friendly Fish: The Story of Sonny the Sweetie Pie

I will always fondly remember the sweet story of Sonny the sweetie-pie rainbow fish and a diver's bond. My husband shared this unforgettable video with me from the Dodo. The headline read, "Fish Loves to Greet His Favorite Diver and Bring Her Gifts." It was a remarkable, real-life

---

[285] Paige Parsons, "Activists Take Lucy the Elephant Fight to Appeal Court," *Edmonton Journal* (8 March 2018), edmontonjournal.com/news/local-news/activists-take-lucy-the-elephant-fight-to-appeal-court.

[286] Ibid.

[287] Tyler Dawson, "Advocates for Lucy the Elephant Fail to Convince Courts to Review her Confinement Conditions at Edmonton Zoo," *National Post* (28 May 2019), nationalpost.com/news/canada/lucy-the-elephant.

[288] Ibid.

[289] Ibid.

story about friendship between a diver named Rachel and a friendly yellow butterfly fish, which she named Sonny.[290] You have to view this video to truly grasp the connection and to see Rachel sharing this human-fish bond with her viewers. You can actually see Sonny recognize Rachel and come to greet her. For two years and during sixty dives, Sony has been greeting Rachel. You can see him excited, actually showing her creatures, and leading her. As Rachel describes in the video, the fish behaves more like an excited puppy than a fish. You can see his body wiggling from excitement. Her husband was skeptical at first, but after sixty dives, the same fish greeted his wife. As well, Sonny has unique markings, and he is slightly larger than the other butterfly fish. It has changed my perception of a fish's ability to have feelings for others. We are limited in our understanding of aquatic sentience. These personal encounters can teach us that fish are sentient creatures that love too.

Whale and Dolphin Captivity

I am truly amazed by the remarkable work of animal activists and advocates as they fought to free a captive orca named Kiska, which is the last captive orca to be held in a Canadian facility at Marine Land. A former employee at Marine Land turned into the activist leading this campaign. It is tragic to see images of this beautiful sea creature confined to a tank. The cruel practice of keeping marine life in solitude for human entertainment is barbaric.

The promising news is that more people are becoming aware of the truth for aquatic animals such as Kiska and the devastating effect on them. Activists are leading the way for necessary changes. An online petition is circulating to free Kiska, and it has nearly four hundred thousand signatures. The goal is to get to five hundred thousand signatures, which can happen.

> She was captured almost forty years ago off the coast of Iceland and is currently living alone in Marine Land. The negative developmental effects of orcas in capacity have led

---

[290] Molly Hawkins, "Little Yellow Fish Gets So Excited whenever He Sees This Diver—Watch Him Surprise Her with a Gift," The Dodo (17 December 2021), https://www.thedodo.com/videos/fish-loves-to-greet-his-favorite-diver-and-bring-her-gifts.

to deterioration in their mental and physical well-being. Captivity has left these animals without the skills they need to survive in the open ocean. By taking action and placing Kiska into an appropriate facility, such as a whale sanctuary, she can begin to acclimate to the wild and live a more natural and healthy life.[291]

On a promising note, whale and dolphin captivity was banned in Canada thanks to the efforts of advocates and activists. The federal government passed Bill S-203, which grandfathers cetaceans' that are already in aquariums, but makes it a criminal offence to capture wild cetaceans and breed them in captivity. It allows for cetaceans to be rescued and rehabilitated.

The success of this bill had a lot to do with public opinion and animal-rights activists and advocates working to expose the plight of dolphins and whales in captivity. Canadians voiced their public opinion by signing this petition in favor of the bill and sending letters to the federal government, indicating their support. I remain hopeful that Kiska will be freed from her cruel fate as this petition circulates and garners more signatures and pressure mounts on politicians. I am thankful to animal-rights activists that make these wins possible by working tirelessly to speak on behalf of sea animals and to convince the public that it is cruel to keep marine life in captivity. As well, promising news comes from the UK, which passed legislation to recognize animals, including orcas and octopuses, as sentient beings that deserve legal protection.

Wild Animals Need Protection: Take Action for Wildlife

You can do something to help Kiska, Lucy, and other wild animals that are kept in captivity by signing petitions or writing to your local members of parliament.[292] You can speak up and be part of this movement. Also, write to zoos at issue and highlight your concerns regarding a specific animal's treatment.

---

[291] Molly McKinny, "Free Kiska: The Last Orca Held in Captivity in Canada," Change. Org, https://www.change.org/p/free-kiska-the-last-orca-held-in-captivity-in-canada.
[292] "Take Action for Lucy," Save Lucy, www.savelucy.ca/take-action-for-lucy.

Another important way to voice your concern for captive wildlife animals is to educate yourself and others by sharing information. You can let others know your concerns about zoos, outline the problems with keeping wild animals in captivity, and discourage them from visiting these institutions.

Social media provides an amazing opportunity to spread the broader message about zoos keeping wild animals in captivity and encouraging people not to support them. If visitors stop going to zoos, these places can turn from profit for human entertainment to wildlife sanctuaries focused on preserving species. As well, signing and circulating petitions can be an effective and powerful tool for real change to occur.

In another wild-animal captivity case, an Asian elephant named Ramba was held captive for years and was abused by her owners. She was used and was exploited most of her life for profit and human entertainment. After fifty years of loneliness and working for the circus, Ramba was finally rescued, and she found sanctuary at a resting home in Brazil.[293]

These wild-animal stories show us that the tides are turning and there is public outcry for wild animals being held captive and exploited by humans for profit and entertainment. There is a concern around the globe to protect wild-animal species. As an example, the United Kingdom has phased out circuses that have performing wild animals. Other countries like Greece, Israel, Austria, Mexico, Peru, and Singapore have similarly announced circus bans. Some South American countries have passed national bans to prohibit the use of performing elephants.[294]

Beautiful Birds

During an animal-law presentation, I learned about issues affecting migrating birds. I was surprised and shocked to find out about the devastating impact of bird collisions. It was reported that each year an estimated

---

[293] Sharon Vega, "Chile's Last Circus Elephant Is Retired to a Sanctuary," One Green Planet (2020), https://www.onegreenplanet.org/animalsandnature/chiles-last-circus-elephant-retired-sanctuary.

[294] "Last Performing Circus Elephant of Chile Is Rescued and Moved to New Sanctuary to Live out Her Golden Years," Good News Network (18 October 2019), https://www.goodnewsnetwork.org/last-performing-circus-elephant-of-chile-is-rescued.

twenty-five million birds are involved in fatal building collisions in Canada. These fatal incidents tend to be the highest in the spring or fall when the birds are migrating. Light pollution is a big contributing factor, according to this presenter. When birds are flying at night, they rely on the moon and stars to see, and city lights from buildings can be disorienting. Birds are attracted to the bright lights inside skyscrapers, mistaking them for safe places to land. [295] As I write this chapter, I listen to beautiful birds singing outside my window. I heard that bird's singing have a positive effect on a human's mood and mental health benefits. I cannot imagine these innocent creatures having to endure such tragedy, so we must act to help.

Here are ways you can help reduce light pollution and keep migrating birds safe. Turn off exterior, decorative lighting at night. Turn off exterior lights on higher stories. Use blinds to cover windows at night. On a larger scale, North American cities started Lights Out, where buildings turn their lights off to raise public awareness of the dangers that the urban environment poses to migratory birds. It also encourages people to help reduce light pollution, by asking them to turn out unnecessary lights at work and home. The Lights Out initiative is working to save birds so that they don't get confused and collide as they fly through urban landscapes at night.

Taking proactive steps to decrease the amount of light minimizes bird deaths, and it can save money by reducing energy consumption. You can find out if your city or municipality is participating in Lights Out, and if they are not, you can contact your local politician.

On another note, I would like to take this opportunity to talk briefly about keeping birds as pets. Birds are wildlife creatures, which are meant to fly and soar in the sky. Taking them from their natural habitats and keeping them in cages is unnatural. That view is held by some animal activists. Personally, I feel that people should make their own choices. There are many bird lovers that have adopted birds from rescues and from sanctuaries. As well, I met a lovely couple that rescued a pet Parrot named Duke and that clearly love him and he cares for them too.

Although humans are not presented with opportunities to interact personally with wild animals such as birds, thankfully, research is showing us that they have complex abilities and that they are far more intelligent than

---

[295] Nature Canada (March 8, 2022), https://naturecanada.ca/news/blog/pollution-from-lights/.

it seems. For instance, I was fascinated to learn that crows are known to be intelligent problem solvers. They might be as smart as a seven-year-old.[296]

Close Encounter with a Coyote

I had come across news stories regarding the wild cull of coyotes in the province of British Columbia. The story went on to describe a frightening situation for the public, which was attacked by wild coyotes. The government is taking action by killing them.[297] This showed that the situation was the direct fault of humans who were feeding them in Stanley Park, but it didn't describe the horrific manner in which these creatures were killed. They are placed in cruel, painful, horrible, and inhumane traps and then killed. By the way, catching wild animals in traps is excruciatingly painful for those creatures. Coyotes are wild animals that need to be left alone, if they are found wondering in a public park. Perhaps humans can allow coyotes the freedom to roam in their natural habitat instead of feeding and allowing them to lose their lives. There are petitions circulating that call for an end to culling coyotes to end this situation for them.

Humans are invading this wildlife specie's natural habitat and place to live. In a petition to save coyotes, it says,

Culling is an ineffective method of dealing with the aggressive interactions at Stanley Park. Studies have shown that there is a correlation between aggressive behavior in coyotes and the occurrence of wildlife-feeding by humans. To solve the issue of the aggressive attacks, we need to maintain a healthy fear of humans in coyotes and ensure they do not get habituated to our presence.[298] Coyotes are a wild species, so we need to respect that creature's innate nature and natural desire to be left alone. We can peacefully cohabit with them.

---

[296] Candice Gaukel Andrews, "Crows Are as Intelligent as a Seven-Year-Old Child," *Natural Habits Adventures* (October 23, 2018), **https://www.nathab.com/blog/crows-are-as-intelligent-as-a-seven-year-old-child/**.

[297] **Chad Pawson**, "B.C. to Cull up to 35 Coyotes from Vancouver's Stanley Park Following Attacks," ***CBC News*** **(3 September 2021)**, https://www.cbc.ca/news/canada/british-columbia/stanley-park-coyote-cull-1.6164627.

[298] Leilani Pulsifer, "Save Vancouver's Coyotes," Change.Org, https://www.change.org/p/save-vancouver-s-coyotes?signed=true.

Wildlife Sanctuaries

There are wonderful wildlife sanctuaries around the world that care for orphaned, injured, captive, and neglected wildlife-animal species. You can find wildlife sanctuaries in the resources list at the end of the book or research them in your area if you would like to get involved. These wildlife sanctuaries are similar to other types of sanctuaries, in that they care for wild animals. They do not breed the animals in their care, and most of these animals remain at the sanctuaries for the rest of their lives. Similar to other types of animal wildlife organizations they are mainly are run by volunteers and rely on donations and caring humans to continue to exist.

Wildlife Education Is the Key to Spreading Awareness

The more we can educate the public about wildlife animal's plights, and issues affecting them, the greater the chance that more people will become interested in the cause. As Steve Irwin's quotation stated, we need to teach others about wildlife, as people want to protect those they love. This is true when we consider the younger generations who are glued to their cell phones and technology. It is important to provide them with opportunities to learn about wild animals and ways that they can contribute to their preservation and continuation through exploration.

Since it's not easy to get in contact and make a personal connection with wild animals, it's essential to provide children, teens, and even adults with visits to wildlife sanctuaries and outings to interact and learn. We can teach them to be more respectful and understand why wildlife matters. As Angus Hamilton, founder of Life Gone Wild, said,

> For me it's the words of Steve Irwin, the late, great Crocodile Hunter, that best summarize why I started Life Gone Wild. People like him that truly show how much of a difference wildlife education can make. For Steve, it seemed that the key was to teach as many people as possible about "his" wildlife, about our wildlife; to make people

love it as much as he did. I want to be able to do for you, what Steve did for me. I want to show you why our wildlife is worth falling in love with; why it's worth saving.[299]

Each Wild Animal Is Special and Unique

Although humans rarely ever get a chance to interact and get to know wild-animal species, they can learn they are unique sentient creatures with personalities. Each wild animal is special and offers uniqueness. For instance, garden snakes are known to be shy and reserved while dolphins are known to be smart and very friendly. Scientists that have interacted and even formed human-animal bonds with wild animals can attest to this. There are amazing true stories of humans who have connected deeply with rescued wild animals. Even beyond these distinctions between the species, each wildlife animal in the wildlife kingdom is special, worthy and it deserves to live.

In a chance encounter with a wild rabbit the other day as I walked in our neighborhood, we spotted a gray cottontail wild rabbit that resembled Zoey. That wild rabbit stood still, looked frightened, and quickly ran away. That wild rabbit clings to its life like every other animal, and it is a unique individual and sentient creature. Like our family pet rabbit, it has an interest in not only surviving but quality of life. Every wildlife creature is an individual with an interest in its own life. Survival is a natural instinct. Humans that are protecting wild animals by respecting their natural habitats and keeping our planet from climate change are supporting them.

We have seen that human-induced environmental change and activities have devastating impacts on our natural world, particularly for wildlife. One example is the negative impact of the changing climate on many species' habitats: Australia's bushfires pushing koala bears to the verge of extinction, polar bears in the arctic and poison dart frogs in the Amazon. Climate change is impacting species in all regions of the globe. It will likely result in the extinction of many wild-animal species if it cannot be prevented or slowed. Similarly, human activities, such as trophy hunting, lion-breeding farms, poaching wildlife animals for their tusks or horns, and

---

[299] *Supra,* footnote 261.

urban development have impacted animal populations, in some cases, to the brink of extinction.

This is a call to action for more humans to voice their opinions and concerns to force governments to implement laws banning these practices and protecting vulnerable wildlife. Other important issues, such as changing a wild animal's native environment by taking that animal overseas to a foreign zoo, are detrimental to animals' well-beings and species. Sharing real-life stories, such as Lucy the elephant's plight, provides an example of seeing wild animals as individual sentient beings, which have an interest in their own lives. You can voice your disapproval for wild animals such as Lucy being held in captivity and educate others so that these institutions will stop receiving profit and business for their exploitation of wild animals. Hopefully in the future with enough public outcry support, institutions such as zoos will be a thing of the past and will be banned, unless they are rehabilitation centers or sanctuaries.

The plight of wildlife animal species is under severe threat. We must take action. The commodification of wild-animal species for human entertainment and profit is at the root of the problem. Sadly like other animals, wildlife is viewed as disposable. We must do something to protect these innocent creatures from extinction.

Poaching and the illegal animal trade are also major problems for wildlife. Numerous species of wild animals have been hunted to extinction or to the brink of extinction. Wildlife crime is a huge and dangerous business, which is akin to the drug trade. Because of this, it is almost impossible to obtain an accurate representation of the illegal wildlife trade's value, but it's estimated to be in the billions of dollars. The WWF has an entire page on their website where you can find resources to help wildlife. You can help by fundraising, going green, and becoming a wildlife animal ambassador by speaking up for wildlife species.

You can take action for wildlife by making it clear to local politicians that you do not support current practices in your city or country. You can speak up and encourage politicians to pass wildlife-protection laws for these vulnerable wild animal species and to improve current laws. You can do this by contacting your local members of government or signing petitions that call for legislative change. You can even become a politician and push for laws to be changed. You can create your own petition and circulate it on social media and to your friends and family.

Become a Wildlife Advocate and Friend to Wildlife

You can inspire others in your community to get involved to help wildlife species. There are meaningful ways to advocate on behalf of wildlife issues. Admittedly, it can be daunting to try to advocate for international wildlife issues, but you can choose to participate in local efforts in your community. You can create a wildlife sanctuary in your backyard by choosing animal-friendly plants that help certain wildlife species, such as bees, birds, wild rabbits, and even insects, to survive and by leaving out water for them. In other words, by treating wildlife with kindness and not as intruders, you are helping these wild animals survive in their natural habitats. After all, wild animals coexist on this planet, and they should have a right to their space. They belong there as much as we do. Many species lived on the earth before humans did.

One of my students loved wildlife animals. She rescued injured baby squirrels and raccoons. She talked about ways to get involved in wildlife rescue. I suggested that she contact the local wildlife center. I knew that it did good work on behalf of wildlife rescue and education in the community. They rely on volunteers, donations, and community support. She became a volunteer there.

You can do the same. Search for a wildlife center in your community and become a volunteer. It might lead you to a future career path. You may not be aware of the impact that humans have had on wild animals in your city. The simple act of doing something, speaking up for these creatures, educating others, and sharing information can make a difference in changing attitudes toward wildlife in society. You can attend wildlife conferences which are held annually.

It is important to remember the small, everyday things to reduce your carbon footprint, help slow climate change, and support for wildlife. This can start by using less electricity and plastic, increasing you're recycling and composting, or taking public transportation to work.

One of the most helpful things that you can do to protect the natural environment and wildlife habitats, and reduce your carbon footprint, is reducing or eliminating your meat consumption. Greenhouse gas emissions from the agriculture industry contribute to climate change. Reducing your meat consumption even by one day a week can make a difference. There is growing concern for the environment. People are becoming more informed and larger wildlife animal organizations help to raise awareness. As this chapter has shown, there are many individual ways to help wildlife creatures and to preserve the natural environment.

One of the best ways to preserve wildlife is to become involved with ethical tourism and not support industries that exploit wild animals for profit. For instance, visit wildlife sanctuaries that are focused on preserving wild animals especially those that are under threat of extinction.

You can remind others that wild animals sharing the earth with us are trying to survive. What were once green pastures and vast forests are condominiums, subdivisions, skyscrapers, and shopping centers. More wild species are seen in cities because we have taken over their habitats. They are trying to live, search for food, and find places to nest and take care for their babies and families. Teach others to respect wildlife animals. If you take a walk in the woods, you can sense that there is harmony and balance among the wildlife species. You can hear the singing birds, smell the fresh air, we are all part of this ecosystem. We must learn to respect it.

Kindness and compassion for wildlife will result in future generations that will respect and live cooperatively with animals in the forest and on the land. The future generations are the ones that can make a difference. There are wildlife conservation efforts including programs to conserve wild species such as turtles and elephants around the globe. With education and awareness, we teach them to understand that these vulnerable, wild creatures are survivors. They share the land with us and have every right to be there. Every wild animal's life is mysterious, precious, and worthy. Every wild animal has its own unique experience of existence on Earth.

Wild animals have intrinsic value and worth. They can teach us to respect the environment and live in peace and harmony with humans and the natural world. Wildlife matters because respect for wild animals and the natural world—plants, trees, wildlife species, and balance in our ecosystem—creates a better future for our planet. Humans depend on wildlife to maintain balance with nature, and similarly, wildlife depends on humans to preserve and protect them so that they can survive in their natural habitats. Therefore, mutual respect between humans and wildlife species is needed, where they can coexist on this sacred shared planet.

Wild animals are here *with* us and not for us.

CHAPTER 15

Call to Action: Participate in the Animal Rights Movement

Animals have no voice. They can't ask for help.
They can't ask for freedom. They can't ask for
protection. Humanity must be their voice.
—A.D. WILLIAMS

We have learned throughout the chapters of this book that all animals, regardless of their species, are sentient creatures with personalities, and feelings. They have every right to live on this earth as humans do. Unfortunately, animals have historically been treated in the laws as objects or things, and viewed as owned possessions and personal property. In many places around the world, they are still treated like inanimate objects rather than living, breathing beings.[300]

Many times, Western society reinforces this notion that we are above and better than all other species on this earth. This phenomenon is called speciesism.[301] Whether conscious or not, humans have been instilled with

---

[300] "Animals' Legal Status," Animal Legal Defense Fund, https://aldf.org/issue/animals-legal-status.

[301] "What Is Speciesism?" PETA, https://www.peta.org/about-peta/faq/what-is-speciesism.

the belief that we are entitled to use and exploit animals as we wish, despite the negative impacts this has on animals and the natural world.

Animal Rights Is the Next Frontier

Thankfully, these views are changing. There is increased awareness about the devastating effects of exploiting and hurting animals. The rise and momentum of the animal-rights movement is a strong indication that we are shifting to a more compassionate, and empathetic humanity. The view that humans are better than all other species solely because they were born human is no longer socially acceptable. The tides are beginning to change for a better future, where our animal friend's best interests are considered as growing public awareness toward the daily injustices and lack of accountability for those who abuse animals continues to grow.

During the last century, the status of animals in the law has seen great advancements. These advancements have led to some improvements in standards, which have been set in place to prevent animal abuse and to impose harsher penalties and accountability toward those who neglect or abuse animals. While these advancements are promising, there is still a long road ahead of us as we help the billions of animals that continue to suffer in our consumer-driven world. The Animal Legal Defense Fund (ALDF) said it well by stating,

> The core purpose of our system of laws is to protect the vulnerable from exploitation and to ensure fairness. Animals deserve a legal status that reflects the kinds of beings they are—individuals with their own desires and lives, who have the capacity for pain and pleasure, joy and sorrow, fear and contentment.[302]

The ultimate goal is to have animals' legal statuses recognized with more stringent guidelines, to ensure people are held accountable for animal maltreatment. However, because we have a way to go before society

---

[302] The Animal Legal Defense Fund, *Supra,* note 221.

fully acknowledges this sentient classification for all species, humanity's individual efforts can now help the animal-rights movement advance into the future.

You can help through educating yourself and your community about the issues that animals face in our world and by advocating for the cause— be it for companion animals, farm animals, wildlife, veganism, advocacy/ activism, conscientious habits, ethical lifestyle choices, or financial contributions. By doing so, you are participating in the movement. Attend and educate yourself by signing up for animal rights conferences. Thankfully, there are so many conferences with concerned citizens and advocates, activists, law students, organizations, etc. You can meet other people with an interest in animal rights and expand your social network.

Animal activism is the policy of using vigorous campaigning to bring about political or social change. Animal advocacy is the public support or recommendation of a particular cause or policy. Although activism and advocacy are somewhat different, both are vital to strengthening the animal rights movement. They involve education, outreach, legislative, and policy changes. There is momentum to advocate for the legal protection of animals when we speak up for them. The second part of this strategy is information sharing, gathering, and political pressure.

Humans are hardwired for social connection with like-minded individuals. There's ripe opportunity to stay connected to others on social media, meet people at galas and conferences and even to start political campaigns. Signing and sharing petitions is an example. We can gather support on social networks to spread the word and encourage wider participation in the animal-rights movement. By gathering in our communities in person at events or going online, we can spearhead campaigns for strong community support. We can put pressure on our politicians to implement these changes and to strengthen and codify animal protection laws.

Call to Action: Become an Animal Activist

It is easy to become more involved through direct action and active participation. You can become an animal activist. You can look up animal-rights marches in your area or attend events that you can travel to. Demonstrating support at rallies, protests, and marches, which spread awareness about animals suffering under our current societal constructs, shows the public that there are large numbers of people who deeply care about animal rights.

At first, activism in the form of attending marches or participating in public protests might feel uncomfortable. However, I can reassure you, from personal experience, that it gets easier and that all forms of participation help to bring about change, which can make a difference for animals. Even if you are not comfortable at first participating in public displays of activism at demonstrations as a speaker, showing your support by attending events or rallies is beneficial for the movement. Who knows? One day, you may find yourself being the individual who grabs the megaphone and leads the chants at marches!

I recall first public protest that I was invited to speak at a few years ago. On a cold afternoon in the middle of winter, I stood in front of my parliament building in the city of Toronto on a crowded downtown street. The protest was organized by local animal activists to educate people on the horrors of the dog sledding industry and the chaining of dogs in Canada. I spoke up against it and brought public awareness to the inhumane conditions that these dogs are forced to work under.

I talked to the public from my heart on the virtually nonexistent laws of chaining dogs and encouraged them to sign the petition. Initially, I was nervous to speak at a public protest that was so large. I was concerned that I could not be heard well, as the microphone did not work. I quickly forgot about the technical challenges and overcame my fear of disappointing others when I noticed one of the rally's organizers holding her husky dog by the leash. He was a rescued former sled dog. I watched documentary films of sled dogs' plight. They uncovered the horrors and secrets of the sled-dog industry and showed the terrible treatment of husky dogs through consumer-oriented businesses, which neglect dogs and leaves them alone and chained.

I met a lot of interesting like-minded individuals too. This experience taught me that knowledge about and participation in public protests and rallies are useful, as the news media and a politician were there. For those who cannot attend or prefer to be anonymous, online social activism is a great way to become involved. Through sharing articles and blogs or writing articles, a large audience can easily be reached. Throughout this book,

I have shared the views that education and awareness are keys to affect change. Social media is another great platform for active participation. You can use the various platforms to educate others on important issues for animal rights. There are over a billion users. I have met many wonderful, kind animal lovers, activists, and advocates, vegans, pet parents, and other animal people from all over the world.

It is understandable that when looking at the various, widespread, and unique instances of abuse and neglect that animals face, the problem can become overwhelming. It's easy to turn a blind eye and fall into the mistaken mindset that the problems facing animals are too large and that one person cannot make a difference. However, taking steps to raise awareness can create a ripple effect and impact society. One individual's efforts can make a difference.

Become an Animal Advocate

If you believe in speaking up for animal issues, you can get involved through your efforts as an animal advocate. Animal advocates believe in the rights of animals to exist without pain and suffering and to live their natural life spans. We work hard to rally and lobby our governments, to push for more people to become educated and involved in animal-rights issues, and to speak up on those topics that are close to our hearts. As an animal advocate, you can be an individual, join an advocacy group, and work or volunteer with an animal welfare organization. There are many ways to speak for animals that need our voices as an advocate.

The journey toward advocacy starts with educating yourself and becoming familiar with animal issues. You can learn as much as possible by researching online. Many helpful resources are available, and many animal causes need help. You can join animal-welfare organizations, shelters, rescues, and advocacy groups. You can also participate in public campaigns, outreach programs, attend animal advocacy conferences, and do your part by spreading the word to others.

My path toward animal advocacy started as a volunteer at an animal shelter years ago. I personally found the plight of shelter animals was a cause that deeply touched my heart. It became an issue that I deeply cared about.

From there, I learned more about issues affecting shelter animals, and grew knowledgeable about other important animal issues over the years.

Choose Your Animal Cause: What Is Your Passion?

You can research online about becoming an advocate for a particular cause. The term *no kill* has been popularized throughout North America, so check if your local animal shelters have embraced these policies and if their progress has been effective. You can be the one to introduce no kill if they have not. You can find out if your jurisdiction has laws against chaining dogs or bans certain breeds. Some communities prohibit pit-bull terrier breeds, and you can advocate against breed discrimination. If you are a cat lover, you can help with trap-neuter-return (TNR) programs in your community, foster a homeless cat, or adopt a cat in need of a loving home.

Education through Advocacy and Activism Is a Key for Positive Change

Animals of all species face unique and substantial hardships in our complex society. If we can educate ourselves about their plights and realize their sentience, we can recognize each one of them as a complex individual with preferences, a personality, feelings, and emotions. Then we can awaken others and mainstream society to the huge, adverse impact of industries that exploit animals for profit. I believe that we can do better as a society, to call for immediate, lasting, and sustainable changes. This is especially true when knowledge of the negative effects on animals is coupled with concerns on human health and the natural environment.

Knowledge is power, so when the public is armed with the reality of facts and truths with data that are facing animals, human health, and the climate, change can be effectuated faster. Besides the resources listed in this chapter, there are documentaries, online resources, books, films, and podcasts, where individuals can learn about the ways that animals are mistreated in our society and how to help change that. I have listed some of these throughout the book.

Many animal-welfare organizations, rescues, and sanctuaries have so-cial-media platforms. You can show your support by following them, cre-ating your own social-media pages, and spreading public awareness. I like to share uplifting animal stories from animal rescues, sanctuaries, shelters, and organizations about their work. I show them the unique individuality of each animal and bring to light the sad realities that many of them were forced to endure before they were rescued and saved. I find that people re-spond well to positive, heartfelt animal rescue stories, so I try to keep them informed in a light and uplifting manner.

You can get involved in animal activism and/or advocacy and even dedicate your life to it as I have. The promising news is that animal rights and animal law is prevailing, with more law schools and colleges offering animal-law courses in their curriculums. There are many more opportuni-ties to earn a living in this field. I envision a bright future, where there will be more animal-rights advocates, activists, attorneys, lawyers, veterinarians, and practitioners in the field. Whether it is a vocation, an interest, a hobby or passion, part-time, full-time, or a volunteer position, there are many ways to participate directly in the rising animal-rights movement.

Gen X, Gen Z, Millennials and Animal Rights Rising

It is an exciting time for animal rights. The younger generations are playing an important part in pushing the animal-rights movement forward and to the next level. Social media is paving the way, and it allows for opportuni-ties to have meaningful conversations, as well as great exchanges of ideas. The millennials are not tolerating social injustices. They are speaking up and standing up for social-justice causes, which are a large part of the rise in this movement.

As highlighted throughout the book, social media is an excellent plat-form, and it provides a valuable tool for advocacy and activism. It is an op-portunity to be heard and to teach others. Animal images and heartwarming rescue stories are shared. These younger members of the population are more vocal and open to conversation. They question the status quo, and they can help to bring positive, lasting change. It is an important time to participate in the animal-rights movement, which can improve the situation for animals.

For instance, these younger generations can teach others that animals deserve to live out their natural life spans and that killing a shelter animal is morally and ethically wrong. Perhaps this knowledge can encourage them to adopt from shelters rather than purchase their pets from breeders or online. As well, we can inform them that hunting wildlife for sport is extremely cruel. Keeping farmed animals confined in cages without mobility so that humans can consume them is horrific, cruel, and unnecessary. Thankfully, I am seeing that younger generations are speaking up against and questioning what the norm has been for far too long. They are not tolerating cruelty to animals without any accountability. I believe the youth can bring much-needed law reform and policy change so that these practices are completely banned.

Individual acts can make a difference. Even before the laws and policies are changed, social acceptance of certain practices must be engrained in the minds of the public. As such, individual lifestyle choices make a difference. They can start the wave toward compassionate choices and informed consumers, who care about animals and the environment and question where their products come from. That conscious choice leads to better decisions.

Walk the Walk: Choose Cruelty-Free

Many people talk about helping animals. What are they doing to help the cause? During your morning routine, you may not be aware of the amount of pain and suffering that animals have endured for you to use some of your favorite consumer products. Those few sprays of perfume and that application of your lipstick could come from a long history of barbaric experiments and inflicted pain from cruel animal testing on innocent helpless animals in the name of beauty.

It is crucial to be a conscious consumer, to look at product labels, and to inspect the ingredients that you use. You might be surprised to learn that your eyeliner was tested on animals. Look for the cruelty-free logo with the leaping bunny symbol to ensure that animal testing was not conducted on the cosmetic products that you purchase. Leaping Bunny is a coalition of animal protection groups, which created an internationally recognized standard for animal-friendly products.

There are many options for cruelty-free, non-toxic, alternative consumer choices these days, making it easier to remain a conscious consumer. For instance, many cosmetic companies are joining the bandwagon of banning animal testing on their products. There is much hope and promise of a better future for animals including purchasing cruelty-free consumer products. You can do your part individually by making conscious consumer choices.

Make Small Lifestyle Changes for Animals and the Planet

When shopping for consumer food products it's easy to say to yourself that the pig has already been killed and that one person refraining from buying pork isn't going to stop farmers from raising pigs for slaughter. Or when looking for a companion animal to add to the family, you might think that the cute puppy in the pet store, from a puppy mill, was born, so it needs a loving home and that buying one puppy isn't going to change the world. In fact, these everyday decisions are making a difference for animal lives and animal rights, and becoming a conscious consumer can make a lasting impact on the movement.

Your everyday decisions can bring about positive change in a real way. For instance, every time you buy a product, you are keeping that company in business and validating that company's core values. It is a personal choice to decide the way you are going to spend your money. If you are not willing to become vegan and choose to continue to consume meat, research where your meat is coming from. Try integrating more plant-based foods into your diet. Start with meatless Mondays and be more conscientious and ethical about the food you're spending money on, bringing into your house, feeding your family, and putting on your table.

Adoption from animal shelters and rescues literally saves lives. It reduces animal overpopulation and makes room for other homeless pets. When one animal is taken out of the system, it opens the door for another animal to be saved. Your decision to not support puppy mills and to bring home an animal from a shelter or rescue is one of the best ways to help the cause. You can save that animal's life by giving it a loving home, making it part of your family, and caring for its life. By doing so, more animals can thrive and leave animal shelters alive. You can help end puppy mills in your community and promote adoption to family and friends. Often, people are open to listening. Lastly, you can help by spaying/neutering your companion animal.

Become an Informed Consumer: Making Conscious Choices

To become a conscious consumer, you can purchase products that have not been tested on animals or that use animal by-products. I discussed this topic in the vegan chapter briefly, but you can personally do your part and educate others. I try my best to encourage people to check consumer labels when they are buying everyday products. On social media, specifically look for the hashtag #crueltyfree or the Leaping Bunny symbol. I also provided a list of brands that are cruelty free to social media. You can do the same thing to educate your friends and family. I find that most people want to help the cause, love animals, and they don't know that animals are harmed, but they need accurate information to make informed consumer choices.

Taking small steps and making small lifestyle changes can make a huge impact. For example, you can order the veggie burger at dinner and feel better knowing that your meal selection helps keep vegetarian options available. You may find that you can inspire someone to add more plant-based foods and less meat into their diets. With the internet and today's technology, so many vegan and plant-based recipes are easily accessible. Many people are surprised at how delicious and easy vegan recipes are. I love to invite my friends and family to vegan restaurants or order plant based meals. Whenever I can I cook vegan and share recipes.

I am thrilled and motivated when someone confides in me that I've made a difference and convinced them to incorporate more plant-based foods into his or her diet or when social-media followers reach out to share their stories on going vegan. I find it very gratifying to connect with others as they love to share their personal journeys and feel better when they know that they are making a difference for animals, the planet, and their health.

Sometimes though, I am caught by surprise when I attend a dinner party and realize that there are no vegan options, and I go home hungry. I don't make a fuss. I've learned over the years, to inform others that I am vegan, and I refuse meat and dairy *politely*. Most of the time, people are kind and apologetic. I don't waste time trying to convince them to go vegan, unless they are open to conversations. An effective way to persuade others to incorporate humane, ethical, responsible, and cruelty-free lifestyle choices is to set a good example. Think about how to be a positive role model in your community and lead by example. Be gentle and patient with others as they are on their own journeys and convince them in a kind manner.

Ban Zoos, Circuses and Businesses that Exploit Animals

Another way to be a conscious consumer is not to support businesses that profit from animal exploitation. There is no such thing as a zoo, aquarium, or company where animals are used and are not imprisoned in an unnatural environment. They are *all* cruel and no place for wild animals.

Many businesses and companies exploit animals for money and treat animals horribly. These vulnerable animals are taken out of their natural habitats to be used for entertainment. Animals are forced to do tricks that they would never do in the wild and often beaten. Fear- and terror-based methods are used to force them to perform. What do you think happens to that animal's value and worth when it can no longer perform in that circus?

If industries that treat animals badly lose funding and consumers no longer support the unethical treatment of animals, these industries will no longer be sustainable and will go out of business. You can also help the animal-rights movement by donating to animal organizations that rescue and fight on behalf of animals to be saved from circuses. You can plans trips and visits to sanctuaries that have saved these innocent zoo animals and are focused on preserving animals.

Support Sustainability

Sustainable consumer choices that consider an animal's well-being and the environment are another great way to make an impact. Well-known fashion designer and animal-rights activist Stella McCartney made a bold statement at Paris Fashion Week in 2020. McCartney made it clear that she stands against fur and sent models dressed in animal costumes down the runway.[303] Later, she posted a series of cartoon animals alongside thought bubbles on social media. Other major fashion houses have jumped on the bandwagon of sustainability and have supported animal rights on their runways (as noted earlier).

You can support local sustainable clothing brands and fashion houses that care about animals and our environment. These days, it is easier to find these brands and learn about their values through social media or online. Also, there are many celebrities who love animals and use their platforms and influence to educate the public and stand up for animal organizations.

The world will not change from a few people living a vegan or cruelty-free lifestyle or celebrities that have influence and power. However, the world will change when millions of people are making a few ethical changes in their lives. For every person who cares about animals, there is a way to make a meaningful difference. Whether your passion is for companion animals, farm animals, wildlife, or the environment, you can get involved. I promise you can make a difference and be a voice for the voiceless. Make sure that your voice is heard.

Take Action and Get Involved

The first step to becoming more involved as an animal lover, an advocate, an activist, or simply a concerned citizen is to become educated by doing your research and gathering information. This important step empowers you and provides the opportunity to choose the causes that you want to join and personally support.

The second step involves doing something—actualization or active participation. You can join an animal welfare organization that speaks to you and touches your heart or speak individually on behalf of your chosen animal-rights cause. You can post updates on your social-media pages or create a dedicated social-media account or blog on these topics.

---

[303] Alyssa Kelly, "Stella McCartney Stages Anti-Fur Protest with Animal Models at Paris Fashion Week Show," People.com (March 2, 2020), **https://people.com/style/stella-mccartney-stages-anti-fur-protest-with-animal-models-at-paris-fashion-week-show/**.

Popular culture via social-media platforms is a great forum to vocalize animal rights. As animal lovers, advocates and activists, we are sending out powerful messages to push for change. People listen when topics touch their hearts and when they can relate to them personally. You can encourage friends to adopt animals from shelters. You might want to apply to law school and start an animal-rights practice. You can start your own rescue, sanctuary, or animal organization.

It's time to recognize animals as unique individuals, which deserve dignity and respect, and for positive changes in the legal system to reflect these sentiments. We have learned throughout the chapters that passing new animal-rights laws doesn't come easily. It takes community efforts through activism, advocacy, and political pressure for change.

In addition to advocacy and activism, your individual lifestyle and food choices can prevent unnecessary animal suffering when you choose to eat plant-based foods and buy cruelty free. By doing so, you are making a healthy choice, saving lives, and helping the planet. Your individual contribution to animal rights in your everyday life is making a huge difference.

CHAPTER 16

The Future Looks Bright for Animal Rights and the Next Frontier

All great movements, it is written, go through three stages:
ridicule, discussion, adoption. It is the realization of this third
stage, adoption that requires our passion and our discipline, our
hearts, and our heads. The fate of animals is in our hands.

—TOM REGAN

As I often say, the time will come when all animals are treated with kindness
and compassion, but they need our voices to get there. If you love animals,
please do something to help them!

How the Animal-Rights Movement Is Making Progress

Throughout the beginning of the book, we examined the many ways that
companion animals contribute to our well-being and make our lives better. We have bridged the gap between caring for fur babies that we share
our lives with and helpless, homeless animals in shelters. This book offers
much hope for shelter animals to have a brighter future, with sustainable

solutions to end the tragedy of the shelter debacle and throwaway pets. We have learned that it is society's responsibility to take better care of animals and that it takes a village for positive lasting change. Although individual efforts help, it's even better when communities work together. This book has demonstrated that animal cruelty is a serious crime, and that there is a direct correlation between violence toward animals and to humans.

In addition to dealing with companion animals, including dogs, cats, horses, rabbits, turtles, parrots, and other common and uncommon species that people share their lives with, the book has highlighted other issues that affect the plight of other animal species, including farm and wildlife animals that need our voices to speak up for them too. This book has shown that each animal's life is special, precious, and unique and that it deserves to be protected.

It has demonstrated that there can be a better future for animals. Readers are provided with tools to participate in the animal rights movement and offered many ways to help animals. For instance, choosing to adopt an animal, becoming a cruelty-free conscious consumer, wear fur free fashion, and do not to support industries that harm animals. Also, choosing to go vegan and eat more plant-based foods that do not contribute to animal suffering can contribute to the movement and helps to make the world a better place for our animal friends.

Many opportunities to take action and get directly involved in animal rights have been highlighted in the previous chapter. That chapter explores what we can do to advance animal rights and convince people to want to change the status quo. Animal rights is important because billions of animals are suffering around the world—animals in shelters, animals used for research, human entertainment in zoos and circuses and food, clothing, and scientific experiments, and animals kept as exotic pets.

We can lead by example and by showing others that using animals as inanimate objects is both unethical and immoral. It takes away from our moral obligation to show others compassion and humanity. When humans allow the exploitation of animals, even unintentionally, they contribute to animal suffering. Instead, humans can live in peace, harmony, and balance with Mother Nature and nonhuman animals for a healthier planet. Every animal deserves to be here, and it is a unique individual that can have an enjoyable life free from pain and suffering.

Be a Positive Role Model in Your Community

An effective way to convince others to want to change the system is to be a positive role model in society, to show others how, and to adopt a more humane lifestyle. You can be a change maker in your community and the change you wish to see in the world, whether it's adopting your next furry family member from a rescue or shelter or helping it find a loving home.

Choose to purchase products that are not tested on animals, go vegan, vegetarian, flexitarian, or even Meatless Mondays as a start. You can volunteer at an animal shelter, rescue, or sanctuary, start petitions, create websites, write blogs or letters to politicians, or participate in efforts that affect animals. I have outlined many ways to be a positive role model for others.

When I was a volunteer dog walker at an animal shelter, one day, I took my mom to meet the shelter dog that I walked regularly and grew to love (Gucci). She had no intention of adopting a dog that day, and it was a stretch for me to consider that she would take him home. The moment that I walked out of the shelter with him and she saw this dog running happily because he was set free from his lonely cage, she came out of her car. Once they met, it was love. It has been twelve years of companionship, and he has been a loyal canine friend and fur baby. Sadly, Gucci was diagnosed with terminal cancer, so he is in palliative care. He's had a good life! He was saved from the shelter and an unthinkable fate. He went on to live a happy life with love and care. In return, Gucci has given back unconditional love and has enriched our lives. He is fourteen years old. He will enjoy the rest of his days in comfort and showered with love.

You might want to encourage a friend or family member to visit an animal shelter, rescue, or sanctuary. You might be surprised by their reactions when they meet animals close up. It's a memorable experience for most people. You might go home with a new best fur friend.

Teach Children Compassion for Animals

Teach children and others in your community to care for animals. Bringing home a companion animal is an excellent way to show your child how to be an animal lover. As well, caring for rescued companions, farm animals, wildlife, and horses or taking kids to wildlife centers or sanctuaries teaches children to love and care for other creatures. Education and awareness are keys for progressive social change. When kids start to see animals in a positive light, they become caring teens and adults. It will become a ripple effect for generations to come.

I am always delighted when we take our boys to visit local animal rescues and sanctuaries and to see them interacting with animals they meet fills my heart with joy. I am proud they were taught to be kind, compassionate and gentle to animals and other humans. Andrew has expressed in interest in volunteering at an animal rescue or shelter for his high school volunteer hours. Both boys take care of our rabbit and walk and feed Freddie and Lily even when they are not asked to.

I read there are shelters that have programs for children to read to shelter animals such as cats. This experience is enriching for the children as they improve their reading skills and help an animal in need and the cats are comforted by the companionship of the children. There are other programs that are offered through schools for even excursions to visit rescues and sanctuaries. In the summertime, children and teens can enroll in summer camps to learn more about animals.

You can teach compassion to children. I read the story of *Berkley the Guru Saves the Day* to my children when they were younger. It is an inspiring, real-life story of a yellow lab that was born and trained to be a guide dog for the blind. It was decided that instead of being a guide dog that he should be adopted into a loving family. He went on to find a loving family and become an ambassador for all animals and a vegan lifestyle. It's a way to teach children kindness to animals. The message of compassion for animals comes from a gentle dog, as our teacher and friend[304]. In the author's note, I was moved by these words at the end of the book:

> For so many of us it is sometimes hard to find what we are good at or what our special talents are. Some go their whole lives and not find it but I have learned a lot from my dog Berkley. In this story, Berkley shows us all that just

---

[304] Tamer Kiykioglu, "The Story Berkley the Guru Saves the Day" (2019), printed in the United States of America.

being kind and motivated to act is one of the most special talents you can have in life.[305]

We can teach compassion to kids so they will learn to treat animals well with respect and kindness. Another way to teach children to be kind is to be a good role model. If you share your life with companion animals, you can motivate children to care for their pets—feeding, cuddling, or taking them to veterinarian visits—so that they can experience animals as individual sentient beings with feelings that need nurture and care, similar to humans. If we are kind to animals, our children will likely follow suit and emulate. We can advocate for enrichment and educational programs in our children's schools that focus on compassionate animal care.

Teach Don't Preach about Animal Rights

We can teach others to be kind to animals and remain open-minded to other people's opinions. For instance, even if we disagree with their opinions on veganism, we should not be dictatorial in our efforts to persuade people to adopt a vegan lifestyle. People are more likely to listen when we are open to conversations and respect their opinions. Even if we do not accept their views, we can be respectful and use the art of diplomacy to persuade them to want to do better for animals.

Focus on positive news. Share the big wins for animals. Showcase the many victories and show others what can be done. Many recent developments are pointing to a new era for animal rights. It is amazing to witness these changes in my lifetime; Zoos are being banned all over the world. Circuses, such as Ringling Brothers, are closing their doors. Animals that were used for human entertainment are sent to live in wildlife sanctuaries. More shelters are committed to saving shelter animals' lives. Judges are considering pets' best interests in divorce cases. Countries around the world are recognizing animals as sentient creatures and moving away from animals as property. Fashion houses are banning fur from their runways. Italy has declared animal protection in their constitution. Celebrities and more people are choosing cruelty-free products and embracing a vegan and

---

[305] Ibid.

a cruelty-free lifestyle. Countries have banned animal testing for cosmetics. The FDA passed a law in the US that it no longer needs to require animal tests before human drug trials. It is truly a remarkable time in the history of animal rights.

We can celebrate these monumental victories for animals, appreciate the efforts of those who have come before us and who got us here, and realize that animal rights are considered. It might not seem fast enough, and it can be frustrating that animals all around the world continue to suffer to this day; however, remember that progress is being made slowly but surely. Animal rights are on the agenda worldwide. We must remain determined, positive, and vigilant that we are moving in the right direction and that real, effective, and lasting change is happening, but it takes time. We have come a long way, and we can continue to make real progress for animals.

We are entering a new era for animal rights, and there is no turning back. These are monumental achievements, and amazing work is being done around the world. I applaud animal advocates and activists for their determination. We can thank the generations before us that took a stand for animals' rights. This momentum will continue, and there is more to come in the rising animal-rights movement. It will have more victories and positive changes with our continued efforts and voices. We can continue to be tactful and respectful and that includes participation through advocacy, activism, and speaking up individually for animals whenever we can, to educate others on the many ways to make the world a better place for human and nonhuman animals. We can appreciate those activists who are bold and who take a stand publicly, with public protests in our communities and speaking out against animal abuse, exploitation, and any harmful thing in the public. We can also appreciate that neighbor or friend who chose to adopt a dog or cat from a shelter and takes good care of it.

Stay Committed to an Animal Cause Closest to Your Heart

You can showcase your passion and commitment to animal rights by sharing those issues that are close to your heart. You can personally have a positive impact by connecting with others who are dedicated or with those who are not aware of the issues that are dear to your heart. You might be surprised when you share your passion for a meaningful conversation with your family, friends and colleagues who can become interested in what you have to say about animal issues.

Speak up for animals in your community. If you are not comfortable vocalizing your opinion in public, that is OK. You can share your views with family and friends about places that force animals to suffer and behave in unnatural ways. For instance, by not supporting institutions such as rodeos, racetracks, dog sledding competitions, animal fights, aquariums, zoos, circuses, and amusement parks that house animals for entertainment, you are setting a good example.

You can take up a cause in your community and contact politicians, for instance, against traps for wildlife, which are cruel and inhumane. You can share with others that devices like wildlife traps are harmful, leave wild animals in excruciating pain and prolonged suffering, and companion animals (people's pets) can get caught in those traps. As an example, a former client's beloved dog lost his life when they were out for a walk on a trail. He got caught in a trap. She spoke up for her beloved friend and urged her municipality to pass legislation to ban traps.

There are many ways to advance animal rights, as have been set out in this book. It takes effort, determination, and persistence to push forward, but we are making significant progress. As an example, when we look back to the horrible treatment of shelter animals around the globe, it is a relief to now see that no-kill shelters are becoming the norm. In New South Wales, Australia, legislation has passed to ban the killing of shelter animals. Prior to this law coming into effect, I read about a campaign to urge the Australian government to stop killing shelter animals and a plea that every companion animal should live, even if they don't have a home.

It is our responsibility to put pressure on local governments to protect companion animals and all animals need our voices to speak up for them. Sadly, this Australian law comes as a result of a heartbreaking situation, when fifteen puppies and dogs were legally shot dead during the corona pandemic in 2021 even after rescues were unwilling to take the dogs. There was public outcry at this horrific ordeal. People spoke up in New South Wales, and they were outraged. This is another instance, and there are many other ways to contribute positively to animal rights and a political leader whose efforts succeeded in passing legislation to protect shelter animals.

A career path in politics can be powerful for advancing animal rights. I met passionate politicians who were dedicated to change animal protection always. You can become a politician and use diplomacy, tact, determination, and your influence to change animal laws. As well, a career in animal law can be rewarding and can contribute to the field. You can help to pass laws to create a better world for animals. Making positive and lasting change for animals requires politicians, lawyers, advocates and other people in different roles for lasting progress. Or you can advocate for animals simply as a concerned citizen and provide information to politicians.

You can be a change maker and urge others to follow your commitment to animals. All animal species need legal protection. You can help them and choose the animal issues and cause that remains close to your heart. It does not matter as long as you are speaking up for them.

Encourage others to make better animal-friendly choices in their everyday lives, in the best way that you can. For instance, educate your friends, colleagues, and family about the importance of adopting animals rather than purchasing from breeders or puppy mills. Try not to criticize them if they don't initially understand or if they challenge your points. Also, if they insist on breeders due to a preference for a breed, encourage them to research the breeder to ensure that they are at least ethical and care about the well-being of the animals that they breed.

Although at times, it can seem like a lonely journey, it is not! So many of us are around, and there are more opportunities than ever to join groups on social media and meet like-minded individuals, who care for animals as much as we do. Stay committed and focused. Don't let those naysayers get you down if you are vegan and other people are not. Remember, you are not alone in this journey. You are part of the movement and shift that is taking place and will improve the situation for animals in the future and for generations to come. Don't let people who don't understand or who choose to turn a blind eye criticize you or make you feel like an outsider. I can empathize. I've experienced firsthand, situations that made me feel uncomfortable. I have many friends from different walks of life, and unfortunately, many are not vegans. Some of my friends continue to choose to purchase their pets from breeders, and that is their choice. I don't preach to or lecture them. Instead, I adopt my fur babies from shelters and rescues. I try to educate them and make them aware of puppy mills and to stay away from backyard breeders.

The Art of Diplomacy

These advancements show us that we are winning. We want this momentum to keep going, so remain motivated and triple your efforts, as much as possible. I know that sometimes it's hard to listen to the critics or witness innocent animals suffering. I considered the word *persuasion*, but I felt that we can't really convince people who don't want to listen. The reason I chose the word *diplomacy* to advance animal rights is because the word suggests that dealing with people in a sensitive manner is more effective than trying to persuade them to change or by being hostile.

I was a volunteer at the municipal politician's office because he cared for animal issues. We were in the midst of presenting to the city council, a municipal animal-protection legislation that included new provisions. I remained cool and diplomatic. I had to stay focused on the issues during difficult negotiations. I learned so much during that time, and this volunteer opportunity led to a career in animal law. Even though I knew that we could not convince every politician to agree with our views, I knew that if we could convince the majority of them, the legislation would get passed during the voting, and it did. At that time, these changes seemed small. I was younger and naïve. I did not know as much as I do now. Looking back, I am proud of the hard work and progress that we made for shelter animals. I realize that our efforts did help the cause.

When we speak up for animals, we are their voices, and we are winning for voiceless animals. The animal-rights movement gets stronger each year as more participants join the cause, and we are on the rise. The good news is that more people are joining the cause—celebrities that we know and love to everyday citizens across the world. This book has highlighted some of the wins. There are more victories for animals every single day around the world than ever before. I have no doubt that there will be even more in the future. The animal-rights movement is continuing to grow, and there is no sign that it will slow down. As an animal advocate, I can understand how difficult it may seem, at times, to try to convince people to change their views on animals, but with enough determination, we will succeed. We are winning the good fight for animals' rights, so we must keep up this momentum.

Celebrate the Victories with Others

The momentum for animal rights is happening, and it is here to stay. I am thrilled to share the many victories. We can celebrate triumphs and look forward to more positive news in the future. For instance, I am excited to share that the state of California is considering a bill of rights for dogs and cats, as a lawmaker has introduced a legislation called Dog and Cat Bill of Rights, to give the following rights to dogs and cats in California:

- The right to freedom from exploitation, cruelty, neglect, and abuse
- The right to a life of comfort and free of fear and anxiety
- The right to daily mental stimulation and appropriate exercise
- The right to nutritious food, sanitary water, and shelter in an appropriate and safe environment
- The right to preventive and therapeutic health care
- The right to proper identification through tags, microchips, or other humane means
- The right to spay and neuter to prevent unwanted litters

When this bill passes, which I believe will pass; California animal control agencies, shelters, and humane societies are required to post a copy of the Dog and Cat Bill of Rights in a prominent place on their property. Those agencies that do not do so would face a $250 fine.[306] Although these rights seem basic, and they should be granted to every animal, this bill offers promise for animals to enjoy rights that are enshrined in the laws for future

[306] Alex Hider, "California lawmaker proposes 'Dog and Cat Bill of Rights,'" The Denver Channel (23 February 2022), https://www.thedenverchannel.com/news/national-politics/california-lawmaker-proposes-dog-and-cat-bill-of-rights.

generations. It is an example of the momentum for animal rights, which has arrived, to view companion animals as sentient creatures that deserve to be protected and treated with kindness and compassion.

The future looks bright for our animal friends and animal rights. There have been many victories to celebrate and positive animal news stories surfacing every day. Most people want to hear heartwarming and uplifting animal stories, and want to do well for animals. Unfortunately, there are still stories of abuse and neglect, and more needs to be done, as too much animal suffering is happening. Understandably, it can be challenging at times. But remember to stay focused and committed to the cause you care about. Find your passion and pursue it.

Teach but Don't Preach

It is important to share your opinions and views on animal issues. I have learned the hard way that some people may not want to listen, or they are not ready. Thankfully, I have found that most people are willing to at least have a conversation about animal rights. More and more people do care about animal issues.

Join like-minded individuals and subscribe to the animal-rights organizations that are listed below. You can get involved in this rising movement and see the relentless efforts of fellow advocates and activists, as both smaller and larger organizations continue to push forward for animals. You can participate and celebrate the victories achieved to date for animals and be part of this exciting and growing movement, which will shift the situation for animals in the future and for generations to come. You can get inspired, spread messages of hope; teach others that humanity needs to be kinder to animals, as animal rights are part of social justice.

We can awaken others to take action for animal issues. There is no difference in animal species with respect to sentience or their desire to live freely and from suffering. In society, hunting condones violence to wild animals and similarly, the slaughter of farm animals and shelter killing of homeless companions. We can teach others to be kind to animals as doing otherwise goes to the root cause of disposability of animal life. The way we treat animals—companion, farm, and wildlife—is a reflection of our human moral progress and evolution as a species. This book has shown that you can take a stand, and by doing so, you are participating in animal rights and this social-justice movement. All life is precious and deserves protection. Take a stand for animals and be part of this important movement to make lasting changes. Companion animals, farm animals, and wild animals are here *with* us and not for us.

CONCLUSION

The Human-Animal Bond:
A Mutually Beneficial Relationship

In conclusion, the message throughout this book is that all animals; including companions, farm animals, and wildlife are special and worthy creatures. They are not disposable items; they are sentient beings. Humans share this planet with animals, and animals have every right to live on this earth. All animals (no matter the species or size) are unique and complex creatures.

Although historically, humans have treated animals as objects in the laws and have used them for their own interests that view is changing. Lawmakers are starting to align with society's views on animal sentience and stronger animal protection laws are being passed. For example, we have seen progressive changes such as restricting animal testing, shutting down puppy mills, circuses, fur sales are down, and much more. Animals are sentient creatures. They have an interest in their lives. We have seen in this book that it is possible for animals' best interests and needs to be considered so that they can live peacefully with nature and other humans.

Documented research has proven that companion animals can form special bonds. We also learned that other animal species such as farm animals and wild animals can form bonds with humans and other animals and can experience a wide range of emotions: joy, sadness, sorrow, and pain. They can suffer like we do. Animals deserve to be treated better;

with kindness, compassion, respect, love, and greater understanding. They should be granted legal protection to live happily, freely, and from suffering.

I have shared heartwarming animal stories to show that animals are amazing, intelligent, loving, and precious creatures. Although some of the stories were sad, I felt that they needed to be shared. Animals have an interest in their lives and want to enjoy their lives. They crave love and affection like we do. They have families of their own. They can serve as teachers to humans. Animals should have as much right to inhabit this planet as humans do. We share this planet with them. Although animals have every right to live, they rely on us to speak up for them. My hope is that this book has awoken something inside you so that you will want to do better for animals and that it has offered helpful information and practical tools to take positive action.

I am grateful that I was able to share my experience to show you it was not a straight line (as yours may not be). What started as a book intended for companion-animal issues became much more as I learned more about other issues. The book is intended to speak up for *all* animals: companion animals, farm animals, and wildlife. Throughout this journey, I transformed my views alongside this movement. I became a vegan and a conscious consumer, adopted animals from shelters and rescues. I am a spokesperson for an animal shelter, EHS, and other animal rescues. I check consumer labels (the leaping bunny) while shopping, keeping in mind that I don't want to contribute to animal suffering. I consider the health of our planet and purchase animal-friendly products that do not harm animals or pollute the environment, to reduce my carbon footprint. I support local rescues and shelters in my community and most importantly, I teach my own family especially my teenagers to be kind to animals and respect our planet.

I hope that sharing my journey helps you want to do better for animals!

Thank You

I am grateful to the animals that I have met along this journey, which are part of my heart and etched in my memory. Every animal has taught me something. They have soothed and comforted me with their ability to give unconditional love and ask for little in return. They are unique individuals with feelings and personalities, and they have their own life stories.

To give animals in shelters, rescues, sanctuaries, research facilities and those used in cruel experiments, as well as to the billions of farm animals and vulnerable wildlife a voice through the words of this book has been a privilege. I am grateful to be a voice for our animal friends.

I am also grateful to *you*, for caring enough about animals to read this book. You can make a difference and be a change maker. We can do well for animals and work together to make the world better. Let's join hands in this rising animal rights social-justice movement. I hope that you feel motivated to do well for animals. As Rai Aren said, "Know that the same spark of life that is within you is within all of our animal friends …The desire to live is the same within all of us."[307] Every creature wants to live. I witnessed that spark of life with every animal I met, no matter what size, species, or age they were. Every animal has a unique signature, life story, and spark of life. When we learn to respect animals, we spread compassion and empathy to others. Let's make this world a better place for humans and animal as a cooperative, peaceful, and loving human-animal family. Imagine a better world where all animals are here *with* us.

---

[307] Rai Aren, *"Know that the same spark of life that is within you is within all of our animal friends …The desire to live is the same within all of us,"* Vegan Posters (2022), https://vegan-posters.com/know-same-spark-life.

LIST OF RESOURCES

Animal Charities, Organizations, Rescues, and Sanctuaries

There are many ways to participate in the animal-rights movement. If you want to adopt an animal, check your local animal shelters and rescues, as they are the best places. Here is a list of numerous online resources and animal organizations with information and guides. These various resources can help you learn more about the many causes and can encourage you to become directly involved in animal advocacy or activism through your own individual efforts.

- African Wildlife Foundation at awf.org protects the wildlife and wild lands of Africa and ensures a more sustainable future for Africa's people.
- Alley Cat Allies at alleycat.org helps protect and improve the lives of cats.
- American Anti-Vivisection Society at aavs.org ends the use of animals in science through education, advocacy, and the development of alternative methods.
- American Humane at americanhumane.org is committed to ensuring the safety, welfare, and well-being of animals.
- American Society for the Prevention of Cruelty to Animals (ASPCA) at aspca.org provides the effective means for the prevention of cruelty to animals throughout the United States.
- American Vegan Society at americanvegan.org works toward a compassionate world by promoting veganism to a growing public audience.
- Animal Alliance of Canada at animalalliance.ca is committed to promoting harmonious animal-human and animal-environment relationships.
- Animal Equality at animalequality.org wants to end cruelty to farmed animals.
- Animal Ethics in Action at animal-ethics.org promotes respect for nonhuman animals.

- Animal Ethics Activist is at Instagram page @animalethicsactivist.
- Animal Haven at animalhaven.org finds homes for abandoned cats and dogs throughout the Tri-State area and provides behavior intervention … to improve chances of adoption.
- Animal Justice Canada at animaljustice.ca advocates for the humane treatment of animals.
- Animal Law Advocacy at Instagram page @animallawadvocacy, for education and awareness on animal-law updates, new laws and other issues.
- Animal Liberation Front at animalliberationfrontline.com promotes nonviolent direct action in protest against incidents of animal cruelty.
- Animal Love Rescue Center No Kill Shelter in Costa Rica at animallove.cr is a no-kill shelter that provides a home, proper medical attention, and care for animals.
- Animal Outlook at animaloutlook.org advocates against factory farming and promotes vegan eating.
- Animal Rebellion at animalrebellion.org compels government action toward a plant-based food system.
- Animal Rescue Foundation at arfontario.com rescues dogs and cats from public shelters, where they would otherwise be euthanized, and adopts them into new homes.
- The Animal Rescue Site at theanimalrescuesite.greatergood.com helps animals in need and the rescues that care for them.
- The Animal Save Movement at thesavemovement.org spreads the idea that we all have a moral duty to bear witness, end animal agriculture, and reforest the earth.
- Animal League Defense Fund (ALDF) at aldf.org protects the lives and advances the interest of animals through the legal system.
- Animal Liberation at al.org.au permanently improves the lives of all animals through legislation, consumer advocacy, action, and education.
  - Animals 24-7 at www.animals24-7.org is a U.S. based nonprofit independent online investigative newspaper and information service reporting about humane work worldwide.

- Animal Welfare Institute at awionline.org reduces suffering that is inflicted on animals by humans.
- Anonymous for the Voiceless at anonymousforthevoiceless.org uses conversation and standard practice footage to edify the public about animal exploitation.
- Anti-Cruelty Society at anticruelty.org is a comprehensive animal welfare organization that builds a community of caring, by helping pets and educating people.
- Best Friends Animal Society at bestfriends.org promotes pet adoption, no-kill animal rescue, and spay-and-neuter practices.
- Brother Wolf Animal Rescue at bwar.org is saving the greatest number of lives possible through strategic, creative, and impactful programming.
- Canadian Federation of Humane Societies at humanecanada.ca promotes respect and humane treatment toward all animals.
- Canadian Horse Defence Coalition at canadianhorsedefencecoalition.org bans the slaughter of equines for human consumption in Canada, as well as the export of live horses to other countries for the same purpose.
- Challenge 22 at challenge22.com is a supportive, online framework for trying veganism and promoting animal protection and cruelty-free living.
- Compassion in World Farming at ciwf.com campaigns against the live export of animals, certain methods of livestock slaughter, and all systems of factory farming.
- Cruelty Free International at crueltyfreeinternational.org creates a world where no animals suffer in a laboratory.
- David Sheldrick Wildlife Trust at sheldrickwildlifetrust.org protects wildlife and preserves habitats in East Africa.
- Defenders of Wildlife: at defenders.org is Defenders of Wildlife at defenders.org are on the ground, in the courts, and on Capitol Hill to protect and restore imperiled wildlife and habitats across North America.
- Direct Action Everywhere at directactioneverywhere.com brings revolutionary social political change for animals in one generation.

- The Dodo at thedodo.com has emotionally and visually compelling and highly sharable animal-related stories and videos to help make caring about animals a viral cause.
- The Elephant Sanctuary in Tennessee: elephants.com provides captive elephants a safe haven dedicated to their well-being.
  - Equine Advocates at equineadvocates.org promotes the humane and responsible treatment of horses.
- Esther the Wonder Pig at estherthewonderpig.com teaches leading a cruelty-free and compassionate lifestyle for you and for all the Esthers out there in the world.
- Etobicoke Humane Society at etobicokehumanesociety.com is a non-profit, no-kill private animal shelter run entirely by volunteers.
- Farm Animal Rights Movement (FARM) at farmusa.org promotes vegan lifestyles and animal rights through public education.
- Farm Sanctuary at farmsanctuary.org promotes laws and policies that support animal welfare, animal protection, and veganism, through rescue, education, and advocacy.
- A friend of Animals at friendsofanimals.org frees animals around the world from cruelty and institutionalized exploitation.
- Gentle World at gentleworld.org is a vegan nonprofit that provides online and in-person education on the vegan way of life and shares vegan recipes on the website.
- GLO Farm Sanctuary at glofarm.org is a safe and loving forever home to rescued farm animals, ensuring that their physical, social, and emotional needs are not just met but exceeded.
- Greenpeace at greenpeace.org creates peaceful protests to work toward a greener, more peaceful world and to confront the systems that threaten our environment.
- Happily Ever Esther at happilyeveresther.ca inspires kindness and compassion for farm animals everywhere.
- Happy Cow at happycow.net offers reviews of vegan restaurants across North America, healthy vegetarian food, natural food stores, vegan-friendly options nearby, recipes, and travel.
- Happy Tales Animal Sanctuary at happytalesanimalsanctuary.ca educates the community on the humane treatment of animals, the

impacts of animal agriculture on the environment, and the benefits of compassionate living.

- Horses in our Hands at horsesinourhands.org are a non-profit dedicated to ending horse slaughter through awareness, education, and lobbying.
- House Rabbit Society: rabbit.org rescues and adopts rabbits and educates the community with its curriculum on rabbit care.
- The Humane League at thehumaneleague.org informs the organization's evidence-driven approach to farm animal advocacy and communication through scientific research.
- Humane Society International at hsi.org leads the force for animal protection, with active programs in companion animals, wildlife and habitat protection, marine mammal preservation, farm animal welfare, and animals in research.
- Humane Society of the United States at humanesociety.org works to end all forms of animal cruelty and achieves the vision behind its name: a humane society.
- In Defense of Animals (IDA) at idausa.org makes a difference for animals all over the world through its hard-hitting campaigns, direct rescue, and sanctuary care.
- International Animal Rescue at internationalanimalrescue.org rescues and protects animals and their homes.
- The International Fund for Animal Welfare at ifaw.org rescues, rehabilitates, and releases animals and restores and protects their natural habitats.
- International Vegetarian Union's (IVU) at ivu.org purpose is to promote vegetarianism.
- Jane Goodall Institute at janegoodall.org protects chimpanzees and inspires people to conserve the natural world we share. It improves the lives of people, animals, and the environment.
- Kitten Lady at kittenlady.org is a kitten rescuer and humane educator, who find innovative ways to protect animals.
- Last Chance for Animals at lcanimal.org eliminates animal exploitation through education, investigations, legislation, and media attention.

- Life Gone Wild at lifegonewild.org—why our wildlife is worth falling in love with and worth saving.
- Lily Moss Animal Sanctuary NZ at instagram.com/lilly.moss.animal.sanctuary provides a safe and lifelong home to unwanted, abused, and neglected animals.
- Live Kindly: livekindly.co has the latest in vegan news and plant-based recipes and nutrition–worldwide.
- Local Humane Society (Almost every province in Canada and U.S. state has one).
- Loving Farm Animal Sanctuary at lovingfarm.org guarantees love, shelter, food, and medical care for all of our farmed family members for life.
- Maddie's Fund at maddiesfund.org funds innovative solutions and community-centric programs and projects for animal welfare.
- The Fur Bearers at thefurbearers.com is a nonprofit society dedicated to stopping trapping cruelty and protecting fur-bearing animals in British Columbia, Canada.
- The Marine Mammal Center at marinemammalcenter.org advances global ocean conservation through rescue and rehabilitation, scientific research, and education.
- Mercy for Animals at mercyforanimals.org wants to end the exploitation of animals for food.
  - The Movement for Compassionate Living at mclveganway.org.uk spreads awareness about the true nature of animal exploitation, to promote alternative methods of plant-based food production and to share knowledge about how a happy, healthy, and sustainable vegan lifestyle can be achieved.
- Nation Rising at nationrising.ca lobbies to shift multi-billion-dollar government subsidies away from animal agriculture and toward a plant-based food system.
- National Mill Dog Rescue at nmdr.org rescues, rehabilitates, and rehomes previously discarded breeding dogs and educates the general public about the cruel realities of the commercial dog-breeding industry.

- National Wildlife Conservation Society at wcs.org saves wildlife and wild places worldwide, through science, conservation action, education, and inspiring people to value nature.
- No Kill Advocacy Center at nokilladvocacycenter.org reforms shelters through litigation, legislation, education, consultation, training, and other direct assistance.
- No Paw Left Behind Rescue at nopawleftbehind.org is and all-volunteer, foster-home-based, emergency pet rescue network.
- Non-Human Rights Project at nonhumanrights.org changes the legal status of at least some nonhuman animals from that of property to that of persons.
- North Shore Animal League America at animalleague.org is the largest no-kill animal rescue and adoption organization in the world, saving the lives of pets through adoption, rescue, spay/neuter, and advocacy initiatives.
- Oceana at oceana.org preserves and restores the world's oceans.
- People for the Ethical Treatment of Animals (PETA) at peta.org expose animals suffering in laboratories, in the food industry, in clothing trade, and in the entertainment industry.
- Pet Smart Charities at petsmartcharities.ca is saving the lives of homeless pets.
  - Phoenix Zones Initiative at phoenixzonesinitiative.org is advancing the rights, health, and wellbeing of people, animals, and the Planet.
    - Friends PittieLove Rescue at pittieloverescue.org is a rescue dedicated to care, adoption, and understanding of the American Pit Bull Terrier.

- Primate Freedom Project at primatefreedom.com is a resource for education, advocacy, and support, regarding primates in laboratories.
- Regan's Refuge at instagram.com/regansrefuge tries to abolish animal exploitation.
- Royal Society for the Prevention of Cruelty to Animals at rspca.org.uk works to end cruelty, care for animals, educate a kinder generation, and more.

- Save the Elephants at savetheelephants.org secures a future for elephants and sustains the beauty and ecological integrity of the places they live in.
- Second Chance Animal Rescue Society at scarscare.ca adopts out dogs and cats, keeping the animals in a foster setting rather than an animal shelter.
- Soi Dog Foundation at soidog.org is for the welfare of stray dogs and cats.
- Toronto Pig Save at torontopigsave.org is a love-based community that is committed to holding vigils and bearing witness to farmed animals transported to slaughter.
- Vanderpump Dogs Pet Adoption at vanderpumpdogs.org creates a better world for dogs.
- The Vegan Awareness Foundation at vegan.org inspires people to be vegan to save the world.
- Vegan Outreach at veganoutreach.org tries to end violence toward animals. It seeks a future when sentient animals will no longer be exploited as commodities.
- The Vegan Society at vegansociety.com provides information and guidance on various aspects of veganism.
- The Vegan Women Summit at veganwomensummit.com inspires, educates, and empowers future and rising female leaders on how to bring compassion to their career and industry.
  - Voters for Animal Rights at vfar.org work to elect political candidates who support animal protection and lobby for stronger laws to stop animal cruelty.
- The Wild Animal Sanctuary at wildanimalsanctuary.org prevents and alleviates cruelty to animals, which are abandoned, and rescues and provides lifelong homes for large, exotic, endangered, and captive wild animals.
- Woodstock Farm Sanctuary at woodstocksanctuary.org rescues farm animals that are often victims of cruelty and neglect.
- World Animal Protection at worldanimalprotection.ca wants a world where animal rights matter and animal cruelty has ended.
- World Organization for Animal Health (OIE) at oie.int fights animal diseases at a global level.

- World Vegan Travel at worldvegantravel.com offers inclusive travel.
- World Wildlife Fund (WWF) at worldwildlife.org is there for wilderness preservation and the reduction of human impact on the environment.

BIBLIOGRAPHY

"7 Therapy Dog Stories that Will Melt Your Heart." Waggit. April 11, 2018. https://waggit.dog/blogs/news/7-therapy-dog-stories-that-will-melt-your-heart.

Aaron, Brad. "NYC Was Supposed to Be a 'No Kill' Animal Shelter City by 2015.

What Happened?" Gothamist. June 17, 2019. gothamist.com/2019/06/17/no_kill_shelter_nyc_pets.php.

"Adorable Chimpanzee Rescued from Poachers, Helps Pilot Fly to New Home." NBC. March 2, 2018. https://www.nbc26.com/news/national/adorable-chimpanzee-rescued-from-poachers-helps-pilot-fly-helicopter-to-new-home.

"Animals' Legal Status." Animal Legal Defense Fund. October, 20th, 2021. https://aldf.org/issue/animals-legal-status/> (ALDF).

Animal Welfare Amendment Bill, (NZ), 3A. 2021. https://legislation.govt.nz/bill/government/2021/0067/latest/whole.html

Art 898.1 CCQ.

ASPCA. "Pet Statistics." American Society for the Prevention of Cruelty to Animals. (2019). www.aspca.org/animal-homelessness/shelter-intake-and-surrender/pet-statistics.

ASPCA. "Pet Statistics," American Society for the Prevention of Cruelty to Animals (2022), https://www.aspca.org/helping-people-pets/shelter-intake-and-surrender/pet-statistics.

Austl, Murrumbidgee. Legislative Assembly, Parliamentary Debates. May16, 2019. 1806. (Mr. Steel, Minister for City Services). https://canliiconnects.org/en/commentaries/55018

Baker verses Harmina. NLCA 15. March 29th, 2018.

Bekoff, Marc. *The Emotional Lives of Animals,* California: New World Library, 2007.

BFAS. "2025 Goal." *Best Friends Animal Society.* May 28, 2019. bestfriends.org/2025-goal.

American Heart Association. "New Survey Finds 95 Percent of Pet Parents Rely on Their Pet for Stress Relief," Newsroom (June 2022), https://newsroom.heart.org/news/new-survey-95-of-pet-parents-rely-on-their-pet-for-stress-relief.

Balcombe, Jonathan. "What a Fish Knows," Jonathan Balcombe (22 June 2021), http://jonathan-balcombe.com/what-a-fish-knows.

BFAS. "No-Kill Timeline." *Best Friends Animal Society.* April 10, 2019. bestfriends.org/about/our-story/no-kill-timeline.

Brestrup, Craig. *Disposable Animals.* Camino Bay Book: Kendalia, Texas, March 1998.

Butler, Gavin, "New Laws in the ACT Aim to Acknowledge that Animals Have Feelings." Vice. May 14, 2019. https://www.vice.com/en_au/article/bj9vxa/new-laws-the-act-canberra-australia-acknowledge-animals-have-feelings-sentient-beings.

Carlton, Amber. "6 Things to Remember When You Have a Fearful Dog." Dogster. April 30, 2019. www.dogster.com/lifestyle/dog-behavior-training-tips-fearful-dogs.

Castle, Julie. "The Future of Animal Shelters|The Best Friends Blog." Best Friends Animal Society. December 6, 2018. bestfriends.org/blogs/2018/11/21/the-future-of-animal-shelters.

Chernak, Susan, *Animals as Teachers and Healers: True Stories* (Thorndike Press, 1997).

Choplin, Lauren. "New York Elephant Rights Case Moves Forward with World's First Habeas Corpus Order Issued on Behalf of An Elephant." Nonhuman Rights. November 19, 2018. https://www.nonhuman-rights.org/blog/first-habeas-corpus-order-happy/.

Clifton, Merritt, et al. "Who Invented No-Kill? (It Wasn't Nathan Winograd)." February 28, 2019. www.animals24-7.org/2015/10/25/who-invented-no-kill/.

Clifton, Merritt. "'No-Kill' Debacle: Will Pueblo Bring 'Responsible Sheltering' into Vogue?" April 22, 2019. www.animals24-7.org/2019/04/16/no-kill-debacle-will-pueblo-bring-responsible-sheltering-into-vogue/.

Cotroneo, Christian. "If Everyone Read This, The Shelters Would Be Empty." The Dodo. December 2015. www.thedodo.com/dog-shelter-guide-adoptions-1532460278.html.

Craig, Winston J., "Health Effects of Vegan Diets," *The American Journal of Clinical Nutrition* (2009).

Davis, Susan E. and Margo Demello, *Stories Rabbits Tell: A Natural and Cultural History of a Misunderstood Creature* (Lantern Books: New York, 2003).

D'Arpino, Sheila Segurson. "Behavioral Assessment in Animal Shelters." Maddie's Fund. 2007. www.maddiesfund.org/behavioral-assessment-in-animal-shelters.htm.

DeNoon, Daniel. "A Dog Could Be Your Heart's Best Friend" Harvard Health (29 Oct. 2015), https://www.health.harvard.edu/blog/a-dog-could-be-your-hearts-best-friend-201305226291.

Dunne, Daisey. "What Happens When You Leave Your Dog at Home Alone: Scientists Reveal the Stress Pets Go through When Isolated," Daily Mail Online: Associated Newspapers, (21 Apr. 2017), http://www.dailymail.co.uk/sciencetech/article-4432134/What-happens-dog-leave-alone.html.

Durwand, Bastian, "Heartwarming Animal Stories that will Cheer Anyone Up." Nest&Glow. May 6, 2018. https://www.nestandglow.com/life/heartwarming-animal-stories-cheer-anyone.

"What We Do." Etobicoke Humane Society. 2022. https://etobicokehumanesociety.com/about-us/.

"The Future of Animal Shelters." Cocheco Valley Humane Society. 2018. cvhsonline.org/the-future-of-animal-shelters/.

"2017 Animal Shelter Statistics." Humane Canada. 2018. d3n8a8pro7vhmx.cloudfront.net/cfhs/pages/427/attachments/original/1542135547/Humane _Canada_-_2017_Shelter_Statistics_-_FINAL.pdf?1542135547.

Garone, Sarah. "Perspective: Never Liked Animals. Then I Got a Pandemic Pet Bunny," *The Washington Post* (2 Apr. 2021), https://www.washingtonpost.com/lifestyle/2021/04/02/pet-bunny-pandemic.

Gartner, Suzana, "Who Gets the Dog or Cat in a Divorce?" Suzana Gartner-Vlaovic, Animal Lawyer and Advocate. November 30, 2018. https://www.suzanagartner.com/who-gets-the-dog-or-cat-in-a-divorce.

Gibbs, Nancy, *Animals and Your Health: The Power of Pets to Heal Our Pain, Help Us Cope, and Improve Our Well-Being* (New York: Time Inc. Books, 2016).

Good, Kate, "10 Important Life Lessons We Can Learnfrom Animals." One Green Planet. March 2019. https://www.onegreenplanet.org/ animalsandnature/important-life-lessons-we-can-learn-from-animals/.

Good News Network. "Dogs Became Perfect Human Companions Due to a Gene that Lowered Their Stress," Good News Network, (June 2022), https://www.goodnewsnetwork. org/dogs-became-human-companion-due-to-gene-that-lowered-stress/.

Harvard Medical School. "Get Healthy Get a Dog," Harvard Health (2015), https://www.health.harvard.edu/staying-healthy/get-healthy-get-a-dog.

Humane Canada, "Realities of Farming in Canada," Humane Canada, https://humanecanada.ca/our-work/focus-areas/farmed-animals/ realities-of-farming-in-canada/.

International Cat Care. "Thinking of Getting a Cat?" International Cat Care (7 Oct. 2019), https://icatcare.org/advice/thinking-of-getting-a-cat.

Jasmine, Aliya. "Clear the Shelters Dog Provides 'Emotional Support' for Veteran, Family." NBC Connecticut, July 2, 2019. www.nbcconnecti- cut.com/news/national-international/veteran-adopts-dog-clear-the- shelters-512067011.html?_osource=mobilesharebar.

Kethcart, Katie. "Colorado Veterinary Leaders Approve Statement Supporting the Socially Conscious Animal Communities and Opposing the No-Kill Movement in Animal Welfare." CVMA. 2019. colovma. org/2019/04/09/cvma-support-socially-conscious-animal-communities/.

Kail, Ellyn. "Soulful Photos of Animals Saved from Slaughter or Neglect," FeatureShoot (27 August 2018), https://www.featureshoot.com/2018/08/ soulful-photos-of-animals-saved-from-slaughter-or-neglect/.

McAdam, Sophie. "New Zealand Now Recognizes All Animals as Sentient Beings." Auxx. June 24, 2018. https://auxx.me/new-zealand-now-recognizes-all-animals-as-sentient-beings/.

Maslow, Abraham H. *Motivation and Personality* (Harper & Row Publishers Inc., 1954).

McAdam, Sophie. "New Zealand Now Recognizes All Animals as Sentient Beings," Auxx (24 June 2018), https://auxx.me/new-zealand-now-recognizes-all-animals-as-sentient-beings.

Mwenya, Mubanga, et al, *"Dog Ownership and the Risk of Cardiovascular Disease and Death—A Nationwide Cohort Study,"* Sci Rep 7, 15821 (17 Nov. 2017), https://doi.org/10.1038/s41598-017-16118-6.

Non-Human Rights Project. "Humans Are Not the Only Animals Entitled to Recognition and Protection of Their Fundamental Rights," Non-Human Rights Project (2022), https://www.nonhumanrights.org.

Odendaal and Lehmann, "The Role of Phenylethylamine during Positive Human-Dog Interaction," *Acta Vet.* (2000), 183-188, https://doi.org/10.2754/avb200069030183.

"Defining No Kill." PAWS Chicago. 2019. www.pawschicago.org/no-kill-mission/about-no-kill/defining-no-kill/.

"Petfix—Top 10 Reasons." Operation Petfix Northeast Ohio. 2007. www.aspcapro.org/sites/default/files/petfix-top-10-reasons_0.pdf.

"Quebec to Change Status of Animals from 'Property' to 'Sentient' Being." Canadians for Ethical Treatment of Farmed Animals. August 12, 2014. https://cetfa.org/quebec-to-change-status-of-animals-from-property-to-sentient-being/.

R V Krajnc. 2017. ONCJ 281.May 4th 2017. https://www.hlaw.ca/wp-content/uploads/2017/05/CanLII-2017-ONCJ-281-CanLII.pdf.

Schoberl et al., "Effects of Owner–Dog Relationship and Owner Personality on Cortisol Modulation in Human–Dog Dyads." *Research Gate.* June 2012. https://www.researchgate.net/publication/272138643_Effects_of_Owner-Dog_Relationship_and_Owner_Personality_on_Cortisol_Modulation_in_Human-Dog_Dyads

Segurson D'Arpino, Sheila. "Behavioral Assessment in Animal Shelters," Maddie's Fund (2007), www.maddiesfund.org/behavioral-assessment-in-animal-shelters.htm.

Scherer, Logan. "Why Ellen Went Vegan," PETA (November 9, 2009) https://www.peta.org/blog/ellen-went-vegan/.

Siebert, Charles. "Should a Chimp Be Able to Sue It's Owner?" The *New York Times Magazine.* April 23, 2014. https://www.nytimes.com/2014/04/27/magazine/the-rights-of-man-and-beast.html.

Siegel, Bernie, *101 Exercises for the Soul: Simple Practices for a Healthy Body, Mind and Spirit* (New World Library, 2010).

Singer, Peter. *Animal Liberation: The Definitive Classic of the Animal Movement.* (Harper Collins, 2009).

Smith, Melissa. "4 Service Dog Stories That Will Warm Your Heart." Petful. December 8, 2016. https://www.petful.com/service-animal/heartwarming-service-dog-stories/.

Sossamon, Jeff. "Senior Adults Can See Health Benefits from Dog Ownership," University of Missouri News Bureau (20 Apr. 2016), https://munews.missouri.edu/news-releases/2016/0420-senior-adults-can-see-health-benefits-from-dog-ownership.

Stewart, Portia. "DVM360 Investigative Report: For the Love of Dog: The future of animal sheltering." 2018. veterinarynews.dvm360.com/dvm360-investigative-report-love-dog-future-animal-sheltering/.

Takagi, Saho. "Cats Learn the Names of their Friend Cats in Their Daily Lives," *Scientific Reports,* volume 12, Article number: 6155 (2022).

"The Future of Animal Shelters—Best Friend—Pet Love." *Best Friend Pet Love.* April 16, 2019. bestfriend.site/the-future-of-animal-shelters/.

Tolle, Eckhart and Patrick McDonnell, *Guardians of Being* (California: New World Library, 2009)

"What Services do Dogs Provide?" Service Dogs Certifications. June 2, 2016. https://www.servicedogcertifications.org/services-service-dogs-provide/.

Winograd, Nathan. *Redemption: The Myth of Pet Overpopulation and the No Kill Revolution in America.* (Almaden, 2009).

Vega, Sharon. "Chile's Last Circus Elephant Is Retired to a Sanctuary," One Green Planet (2020). https://www.onegreenplanet.org/animalsandnature/chiles-last-circus-elephant-retired-sanctuary.

Yogananda, Paramhansa. *Autobiography of a Yogi* (Self-Realization Fellowship, 1971),

INDEX

G

W

Z

CPSIA information can be obtained
at www.ICGtesting.com
Printed in the USA
LVHW041401090523
746517LV00002B/66